The Open University

Archaeology: the science of investigation

Arlëne Hunter and Rob Janes

Science Short Course

SA188 Course Team

Chair	Arlëne Hunter
Authors	Arlëne Hunter, Rob Janes
Course Manager	Kat Hull
Course Team Assistant	Jenny Hudson
Academic Consultant	Irene Schrüfer-Kolb
British Museum Academic Consultants and Critical Readers	Jill Cook, Catherine Higgitt, Sue La Niece, Andrew Middleton, Sam Moorhead, Ken Uprichard and other staff
Critical Reader	Phil Perkins
Editors	Amanda Smith, Peter Twomey
Media Developers	Kate Bradshaw, Roger Courthold, Chris Hough, Sarah Hofton
Media Assistant	Emily Fuller
Rights Executives	Martin Keeling, Carol Houghton
Course Assessor	Professor I. Freestone, University of Cardiff

This course was produced in partnership with the British Museum and the York Archaeological Trust.

The Open University
Walton Hall, Milton Keynes MK7 6AA

First published 2008

Edited, designed and typeset by The Open University.

Printed in the United Kingdom by Cambrian Printers, Aberystwyth

ISBN 978 07492 2686 2

1.1

Contents

PART 1   INTRODUCTION

Chapter 1
Archaeology: the science of investigation

1.1   Preface

Welcome to SA188 *Archaeology: the science of investigation*, which has been produced in partnership with the British Museum (BM) and York Archaeological Trust (YAT).

During this course, you will examine various archaeological topics from a scientific perspective, before drawing on additional historical, social and cultural information to build up a complete picture. This will be done using information in this Study Book, the Study Guide, the Companion Text – *Archaeology: an introduction* by Kevin Greene, the course DVD and the course website. You should think of this Study Book as your main focus point, which will guide you through the other resources and develop your understanding of science (Box 1.1). It will also indicate when to read parts of the Companion Text (referred to as *Greene* and shown by ▨ in the margin), when to use the DVD (indicated by ◴ in the margin) and when to go to the course website (indicated by ◵).

Box 1.1 Understanding scientific terms

Throughout this Study Book, you will encounter unfamiliar scientific words. When you do, it is a good idea to underline or highlight this word before referring to the Glossary on the course website (in the 'Course Resources' section); you should then add your own brief definition of the word in the margin of this book to help you remember what it means. In *Greene*, the key archaeological terms are highlighted in **bold**, some of which are defined in his glossary (pp. 280–6). Unfamiliar terms which are not listed in either glossary can be checked in one of the online dictionaries in the 'Archaeology Links' section of the course website or in your own dictionary.

As you work through SA188, it is important to read *actively*. This means taking your time and thinking about what you are reading, and checking your understanding by completing the questions and activities in this course. In this Study Book, there are two styles of question; the first type (indicated by ■) is immediately followed by its answer (indicated by □) and can be thought of as a 'pause for thought' question, designed to encourage you to stop and think about an issue. Although you are not expected to make notes for this type of question (unless prompted), you will find it more beneficial to cover the answer and think about how you would approach the question, before reading on. The other type of question is numbered (e.g. Question 2.2) and is designed to allow you to test your understanding of different topics. With these questions, you should write down your answers in full before comparing them with those at the end of this book. There is more advice on good study skills in 'Developing your study skills' in the 'Learning with the OU' area of the course website.

1.2   Course structure

SA188 is divided into two parts: Part 1 consists of two chapters – this preface and an introduction looking at what 'archaeological science' means; Part 2 forms the bulk of your studies and consists of four chapters, linked to each of the four topics of investigation.

Topic 1 *Reading the archaeological landscape*

In this topic you will look at how archaeological sites are discovered, before examining some of the survey methods used before excavation. You will then investigate the excavation process in more detail, before considering some of the logistical problems involved in running an archaeological dig. The topic ends by considering some of the issues faced by the Field Site Officer in preserving and conserving objects from a dig, for safe storage and/or post-excavation research.

Topic 2 *From bog bodies, skeletons and mummies to forensic archaeology*

Under normal conditions dead bodies decompose, so in this topic you will investigate why the state of human remains can differ at burial environments. You will then investigate how human remains can be studied to determine the person's age, height, sex, state of health, cause of death and method of burial and, from this gain an insight into their living environment. You will end by considering some of the ethical debates on working with human remains, in relation to excavation, legislative requirements, cultural sensitivities and displaying remains.

Topic 3 *Making sense of materials*

Here you will examine the various analytical and investigative techniques used to identify different materials to establish where they came from, how they were used and how they were made. You also examine various carbon-based (organic) and mineral-based (inorganic) objects, and use chemical data and imaging techniques to determine their conservation and preservation needs associated with displaying and storing these objects for future reference.

Topic 4 *Our archaeological heritage: protecting finds for the future*

In this topic you will start by looking at some of the laws that protect archaeological sites and objects, as well as some of the key organisations involved in managing them, before hearing about the role of the Finds Liaison Officer. You will then assess some case studies, and apply the skills and knowledge you have developed in this course, to determine the archaeological significance and types of scientific investigation you need, to fully investigate each case study.

Topics 1–3 are written so you can study them in any order; however, you should end your studies with Topic 4. To complete each topic successfully, you must combine information from this book, specified sections in *Greene*, the DVD and course website. To help you work through each topic, you will encounter three major case studies, along with a series of smaller illustrative examples from around the world (Figure 1.1). The three major case studies are:

- the city mound of Tell es-Saʿidiyeh, Jordan
- the Hungate excavation, York, England
- the Wetwang Woman, East Yorkshire, England

MAIN CASE STUDIES

Wetwang grave, Wetwang, E. Yorkshire, England
Hungate Dig, York, N. Yorkshire, England
Tell es-Saʿidiyeh, Jordan

CASE STUDIES & EXAMPLES: Britain & Ireland

Carloway Dun, Isle of Lewis, Scotland
Vindolanda, near Hadrian's Wall, N. England
Lindow Man, Manchester, England
Grimes Grave, Norfolk, England
Stonehenge, Wiltshire, England
Boxgrove, Chichester, England
Swanscombe, Kent, England
Sutton Hoo, Suffolk, England
Tincomarus, Hampshire & Sussex, England
Hengistbury Head, Poole, Dorset, England
flint handaxe, London, England
Rillaton cup, Cornwall, England
Mold gold cape, Mold, N. Wales
Parys Mountain, Anglesey, N. Wales
Great Orme, Llandudno, N. Wales
chambered tomb, Guernsey, Channel Isles
World War II watchtower, Guernsey, Channel Isles
ancient rath, Hillsborough, Northern Ireland
Hills of Tara, County Meath, Ireland
Old Croghan man, County Meath, Ireland
Clonycavan man, County Cavan, Ireland

(a)

CASE STUDIES & EXAMPLES: Continental Europe

Krapina Neanderthal bones, near Zagreb, Croatia
Ötzi 'iceman', Italian–Austrian border
cave paintings, Altamira, N. Spain
Lapedo child, Lagar Velho, Portugal
Seianti Hanuia Tiesnasa tomb, Tuscany, N. Italy
Lycurgus cup, Rome, Italy
Portland vase, Rome, Italy
terracotta mask, Rome, Italy
Troy, NW Turkey
Ephesus, W. Turkey

CASE STUDIES & EXAMPLES: Egypt & Middle East

Egyptian pyramids, Giza, Egypt
Nesperennub, Luxor (Thebes), Egypt
Tutankhamun, Luxor (Thebes), Egypt
animal mummies, Luxor (Thebes), Egypt
Faience eye, Egypt
Jebekhetepi's coffin, Egypt
Nabonidus, (Babylonia), S. Iraq
City of Ur, S. Iraq
Ashurbanipal, (Mesopotamia), Iraq & Syria

CASE STUDIES & EXAMPLES: Rest of the world

Llullaillaco mountain children, NW Argentina
Juanita ' ice maiden ', S. Peru
gold ring, (Mixtec), Mexico
Aztec obsidian mirror, Mexico
Mayan cities, Belize
Nariokotome, (West Turkana), NW Kenya
porcelain bowl, Jiangxi Province, China
cave paintings, Australia

Figure 1.1 (a) Summary lists of the case studies and illustrative examples arranged by broad geographic groups that are used throughout this course. Part (b) of this diagram appears overleaf and shows the relative location of each of the main case studies (in bold) and illustrative examples.

China
Australia
Iraq
Kenya

Mexico
Belize
S.Peru
NW Argentina

Syria
Iraq
Jordan

Tell es-Sa 'idiyeh
(Jordan)

Turkey

Egypt

Austria

Croatia

Italy

Hungate
& Wetwang
(England)

Scotland

England
Wales

Guernsey

Ireland

Spain

Portugal

(b)

Now do the first activity (Part 1 Activity 1.1) in which you start to work with the learning resources that make up this course.

Part 1 Activity 1.1   Getting to know the course resources

(The estimated time needed to complete this activity is 40 minutes.)

Main learning outcomes developed: KS2 and KS4.

(a) Spend 5–10 minutes browsing through this Study Book and *Greene*, to get an overview of their content and structure. As you do this, do not read the text in detail – just look at the headings, photographs, diagrams and tables.

You will find a full list of learning outcomes and their abbreviations in this Study Book (p. 178) and in the Study Guide.

Some people find it useful to read the summaries at the end of the chapters *first*, as these flag important terms and concepts to look out for when reading the whole chapter. If you do this, remember to read the summary at the *end* of the section as well!

Furthermore, note that at the start of each of activity and in the end-of-section summaries (after Part 1 and Topics 1–4), you will encounter references to some learning outcomes referred to as: KU – Knowledge and understanding; CS – Cognitive skills; KS – Key skills; and PS – Practical and/or professional skills. (You should refer to the full list of learning outcomes at the end of this Study Book or in the Study Guide.) Although each activity and summary statement is associated with several course learning outcomes, only the main ones are listed to help emphasise which ones are being developed in particular. As the End of Course Assessment (ECA) is based on the course learning outcomes, you should pay particular attention to these references.

You will also find summary notes for some of the activities in this course in the 'Activities' section on the course website. These are *not* full answers but give additional guidance to the type of information or learning skills you should have developed when completing the activity.

(b) Now familiarise yourself with the structure, content and layout of the course website and DVD, spending no more than 10 minutes on each one, before taking one or two minutes to look through each of three main case studies (in the 'Case Studies' section on the DVD), noting:

- the geographic location of the case study
- the approximate size of the site
- the age of the site being excavated
- the different types of objects recovered from the site (so far).

Chapter 2
What is archaeological science?

2.1   Introduction

The title of this course – *Archaeology: the science of investigation* – is intriguing, but what does it mean, and how does 'archaeological science' differ from 'archaeology'?

◼ Pause and make some brief notes on what *you* think archaeology is (e.g. the topics or areas of study; how it is carried out; why you are interested in it.)

☐ Defining what is meant by the term 'archaeology' is not a straightforward task because it covers a wide range of topics including cultural, social, historical, technological and scientific issues, and can mean different things to different people. For example, if you compared your answer with those of other students on this course, a range of answers would probably emerge, representing each person's interests. Closer examination however, would reveal some similarities, such as: digging up, identifying and dating buildings and objects; investigating the past; understanding ancient cultures from around the world; stone circles and chambered tombs; Egyptian mummies; reconstructing the past to see how ancient cultures lived and worked (Figure 2.1). You might also have included a few more eclectic and culturally-specific examples including some fictional archaeologists from Hollywood and Bollywood (e.g. Indiana Jones, Lara Croft and Professor Kapil Acharya) or the term 'geophys', used in the UK's television programme *Time Team* – the list is endless!

So, what does archaeology *actually* mean?

The term 'archaeology' is derived from the ancient Greek, meaning 'ancient study' or the 'study of antiquities'. This goes only part of the way to help you understand what it means; more helpful is this commonly used definition, which describes archaeology as:

> '... the systematic study of past human life and culture by the recovery and examination of remaining material evidence, such as graves, buildings, tools and pottery.'
>
> *The American Heritage® Dictionary of the English Language*, 2004[1]

Two points to note from this definition are that it includes 'the systematic study' and 'the recovery and examination of ... evidence'. In other words, archaeology involves working with information from real objects in a logical manner, to gain an understanding of the human past. In essence, archaeology could involve

---

[1] *The American Heritage® Dictionary of the English Language* (2004), 4th edition, Houghton Mifflin Company. Dictionary.com. http://dictionary.reference.com/browse/Archaeology [accessed 9 November 2007].

Figure 2.1   Different aspects of archaeology: (a) standing inside a chambered tomb (ancient monument) in Guernsey; (b) archaeologists on a dig in Dungannon, Northern Ireland; (c) an excavated grave at Tell es-Sa'idiyeh, Jordan; (d) the end result – using a composite of original and replica finds to reconstruct the façade at Ephesus, Turkey.

(a) (b) (c) (d)

anything to do with past human developments around the whole world, making it an impossibly large subject to study. As a consequence, different aspects of human development are generally categorised into distinct fields of study as follows:

- **Anthropology**, which can be subdivided into *social anthropology*, which is concerned with the development of 'culture' (e.g. the non-biological aspects of human beings) and how different social and belief systems (e.g. laws, language, culture, morals, knowledge) have developed, along with the adoption and use of technologies within and between present-day societies, and *physical anthropology*, which is concerned with human evolution and the study of skeletal remains, investigating how communities mixed and migrated over time, as well as where they lived and what their state of health and the physical environment were like.

- **Archaeology** covers the development and study of *past* cultures and cultural artefacts within and among communities that were separated both geographically and over time. Archaeology can be subdivided into *prehistoric* and *historical archaeology*, with historical archaeology covering the time period in which written records exist. In relation to archaeological

'Artefact' is a general term used for any human-made object. You can look up terms like this in the glossary.

finds and information, investigating the cultural implications of artefacts allows them to be put into context in terms of why they were developed, how they were used and what they tell us about a society.

- **Archaeological science** (the main focus of this course), complements the other two areas. It allows sites and objects to be dated, as well as providing environmental and forensic information that enables a detailed picture of how artefacts or sites were used and developed in the past. Archaeological science is about the investigation and interpretation of 'physical evidence' (e.g. objects, materials and landforms) modified by human beings, and draws on a range of theories and concepts across science (Figure 2.2). It involves the careful visual examination of sites and objects, and the systematic collection and interpretation of data (e.g. size, shape, composition, location, age), to devise a hypothesis or theory to be tested, proved, adapted or rejected as more data is collected and tested against the original theories. Archaeological science differs from historical investigations in that scientific data on its own cannot indicate why an object or a site was made or used, or what their cultural role was. This requires an all-encompassing 'forensic approach' to investigation, in which scientific data is combined with historical and/or cultural information to make sense of the object or site in relation to its cultural origin (Box 2.1).

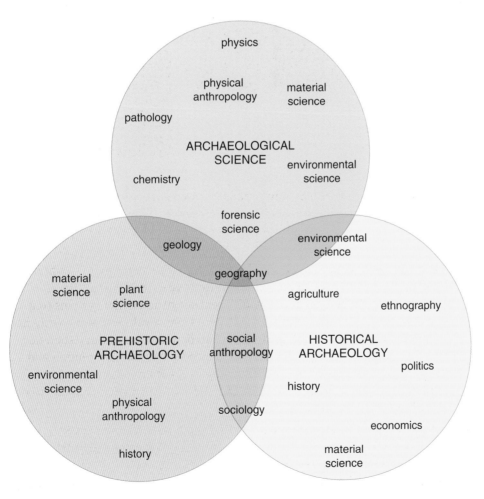

Figure 2.2 The different sides of archaeology, showing how prehistoric archaeology, historical archaeology and archaeological science are interconnected, drawing on information and skills from various subject areas in the sciences and humanities.

Box 2.1 How old is it? Resolving the problem of time

To understand how human civilisations and their artefacts have changed over time, it is important to be able to arrange everything in chronological (time) order. This requires a baseline (zero point) to be set so that an object or event, irrespective of its geographical location or actual age, can be compared with other things.

In the western world, the conventional baseline is the (assumed) birth of Christ, which is set at AD 1 (AD stands for *Anno Domini*, which is Latin for 'in the year of our Lord'), with each subsequent year increasing in value (e.g. AD 550 occurred 500 years *after* AD 50); while time before AD 1 is referred to as BC (before Christ), each earlier year counting backwards (e.g. 4050 BC was 4000 years *before* 50 BC) (Figure 2.3).

Note: this timescale goes from 1 BC to AD 1, with no year 0, as the premise is that Christ had either been born (AD 1) or not (1 BC). It can help to think of AD and BC dates as lying along a uniform timescale, where AD dates are 'positive' values (all greater than AD 1) and BC dates are 'negative' values (all less than AD 1) (Figure 2.3).

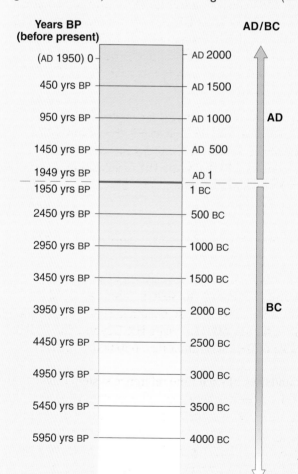

Figure 2.3 The relative timescale between AD and BC dates.

As a large proportion of the world does not follow the Christian calendar, this has caused problems when comparing the relative ages of archaeological finds around the globe. This has led some archaeologists to use BCE ('before the common era') and CE ('during the common era'), to allow a system that does not refer to a specific culture or belief system. The BCE/CE scale is most commonly used in the Middle East, South Asia and in North American museums, but is rarely used in Europe.

A further complication is that scientists working with large timescales (e.g. archaeologists, geologists, planetary scientists, palaeontologists) use a different system in which all measured (or absolute) dates are referenced to a fixed baseline that represents the 'present', with all other dates referred to as 'years before present', abbreviated to 'years BP' or 'yrs BP' (e.g. 1000 years BP) (Figure 2.3). When this system was set up, the 'present' was fixed at 1950, so 1000 years BP is equal to AD 950 (rather than AD 1008, at the time of writing in 2008). A date of 4500 years BP would therefore equal 2550 BC (1950 − 4500 = −2550 years or 2550 before the AD/BC baseline, which is 2550 BC).

Conversely, 1550 BC can be converted to 'years BP' by changing this into a 'negative' value (see above), and subtracting it from the scientific baseline of '1950', e.g. 1950 − (−1550) = 3500 years BP. In mathematics, subtracting a negative number is the same as adding this number, so 1950 − (−1550) is mathematically the same as 1950 + 1550, both of which equal 3500 years BP. *(For further advice on working with negative numbers, see the Maths Skills ebook on the course website.)*

As geologists, palaeontologists and some archaeologists deal with time periods of millions of years, such as 4500 000 years BP, this is simplified to 4.5 Ma, where 'Ma' is the abbreviation for 'millions of years'. A date of 0.25 Ma is therefore the same as 250 000 years BP, which could also be written as 250 ka BP or 250 ky BP (where both ka and ky mean 'kilo years' or thousand years)!

■   Which system should be used to refer to archaeological artefacts and events?

☐   The current convention in European archaeology is to use the AD/BC reference system for recent events back to 8000 BC. Beyond this date, the years BP convention is used (so 9050 BC becomes 1950 − (−9050) = 11 000 years BP), back as far as ~500 000 years BP. Beyond this, 'ka' or 'Ma' are used (e.g. 650 ka or 0.65 Ma rather than 650 000 years BP).

You will find that at the boundaries of each time reference system (AD/BC, years BP and ka/Ma), there are overlaps between which system is used, depending on who is doing the work: e.g. historians tend to use AD/BC, while geologists use years BP (for geologically young events less than 1 Ma) and Ma (for events over 1 Ma), while archaeologists bridge this divide and use all three! The important point is that all systems are equally valid and can be used in different circumstances. During your studies, you will therefore need to be flexible because no particular system is right or wrong, and as such you will use each system at different points in the course.

'Before present' (BP) and 'years ago' are used interchangeably, so any reference to 'years ago' should be read as meaning 'BP'.

Now try Question 2.1 to check that you can apply each dating system. You can refer back to Box 2.1 for examples of converting dates between systems and Figure 2.3 to check your answers.

Question 2.1

(a) Which of the following dates is the same as 752 years BP?

AD 752	752 BC	AD 1198	1198 BC	AD 1248

(b) Convert the following dates from the AD/BC system to years BP.

1245 BC	AD 234	AD 1950	5560 BC

(c) If a pottery bowl initially dated in 1950 was found to originate from 2025 years BP, what is its relative age in 2008 if the same dating method is used?

The symbol '~' means approximately.

In terms of timescales, archaeology typically begins with the manufacture of the first human artefacts dating to ~2.5–3 Ma (although some archaeologists investigating early human ancestors, work at older sites dating to ~5–7 Ma), and covers all of human time up to the present day. It is then subdivided into 'prehistory', relating to the time period before written documents (e.g. ~2.5 Ma to ~3000 BC) and 'history' (e.g. ~3000 BC to the present day) (Figure 2.4).

Part I Activity 2.1   Defining archaeological time

(The estimated time needed to complete this activity is 30 minutes.)

Main learning outcomes developed: KU3 and CS2.

(a) Read *Greene* Chapter 1, Section 1.1 (pp. 2–5), which examines the classification and problems of describing archaeological time as 'prehistory' or 'history' (Figure 2.4). As you read, make brief notes on:

- the key factor used to distinguish *prehistorical archaeologists* from *historical archaeologists* in terms of the people, places and time periods they study.

- the two frameworks (or basic outlines) used by prehistoric and historical archaeologists to put their findings into a chronological context.

Note: you do not need to remember the details in Table 1.1, but it is a useful reference showing how different European historical periods viewed past cultures and archaeological remains.

(b) Now read *Greene* Chapter 1, Section 1.2 (pp. 5–6), which examines some of the problems associated with the concept of time relative to when objects and monuments were created and used.

Question 2.2

What were the two developments in the mid 19th century that allowed archaeologists to start to arrange artefacts according to their date of origin?

By now, you have probably realised that archaeology not only uses information from various subject areas (multidisciplinary) but also combines approaches and evidence from different disciplines (interdisciplinary) in the humanities, social sciences and science, to understand the human past (Figure 2.2). Although the main focus of this course is archaeological science, it is still important to consider historical and interpretative information to understand the full cultural context.

2.2   The emergence of archaeology as a subject

Throughout history, there is evidence to show that each successive society was intrigued by the past and tried to make sense of how and why different cultures developed. An example of what might be interpreted as the earliest archaeological investigation can be traced to Nabonidus (Figure 2.5), the last king of Babylon who reigned from 555 to 539 BC, and who excavated the foundation stone of the temple of Shamash (laid ~2200 years earlier), in an attempt to understand who built it. It is speculated that his daughter, En-nigaldi-Nanna continued this interest in past cultures, and is credited with establishing the world's first museum in the ancient city of Ur (located in modern-day southern Iraq) (Figure 1.1).

Figure 2.4   Archaeological timescale from ~10 Ma to the present day, showing the division of time into geological, prehistory and history time periods.

Figure 2.5   Stela (a stone tablet) of Nabonidus, wearing the traditional dress of a Babylonian king.

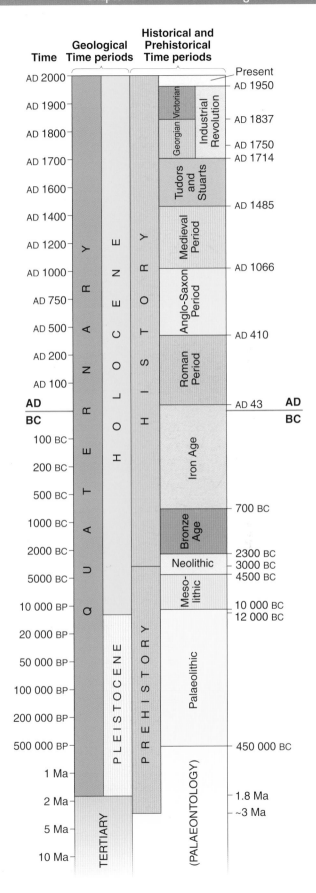

13

Part 1 Activity 2.2 Exploring the British Museum website

(The estimated time needed to complete this activity is 30 minutes.)

Main learning outcomes developed: KU1, KU3 and KS2.

Here you will explore part of the British Museum website and simultaneously investigate the Babylonians, their early archaeological role, and some of the artefacts retrieved from Ur during a series of excavations in 1922–1934 led by British archaeologist Leonard Woolley (1880–1960).

Now go to the 'Activities' section on the course website and complete Part 1 Activity 2.2.

Antiquarian is a historical term for someone who studies ancient sites and objects.

Throughout the 14th to 16th centuries (see the relevant entry in *Greene*, Table 1.1, p. 3), the collection of 'curios' and artefacts became a popular pastime although objects were displayed without regard for their origin or what they were. By the mid 16th century, attitudes were changing with field investigations producing more systematic approaches to describing and interpreting objects and field monuments, culminating in the first publication of an account of British antiquities in 1568. This style of investigation continued through to the 18th century, with antiquarians comparing and classifying objects, monuments and field sites according to new interests in human and natural history. This resulted in collections being arranged into some semblance of order, with geological specimens being grouped separately from human-manufactured objects. By the middle of the 18th century, some scholars and antiquarians started to keep methodical field-based records, accompanying their descriptions with carefully constructed plans and field sketches, marking the start of archaeology as a recognisable subject. This was quickly followed by early attempts at field excavations, although some workers effectively destroyed their sites by removing large sections from ancient mounds and earthworks to create a cross-section through the internal structure of the feature, while others used more discrete tunnelling methods to access the interior. It was not until the late 19th century, that methodical scientific methods of excavation were adopted, with excavation techniques gradually improving throughout the late 19th to 20th centuries.

This is a brief overview of how interests in ancient cultures and civilisations culminated in the rise of archaeology as a recognisable subject, drawing on scientific and historical methods of investigation. A more detailed account is provided in *Greene* Chapter 1, Sections 2.5 and 2.6 (pp. 12–16), 2.8 (p. 18) and 7 (pp. 43–48), which you will read in Part 1 Activity 2.3.

Part I Activity 2.3   Effective reading and note taking

(The estimated time needed to complete this activity is 30 minutes.)

Main learning outcomes developed: CS4 and KS4.

Most people do not think about how they read – they just do it! Active reading requires a more conscious effort to ensure you extract the important information and can find it for later use. Before you read a section of academic text, you should always stop and think about *why* you are about to read it and *what type* of information you want to extract.

(a) Start by reading *Greene* Chapter 1, Section 2.5 (pp. 12–13), up to the section on John Aubrey. Don't be tempted to take any notes; just read the text.

■   What can you remember?

☐   Possibly not that much!

Although you might remember some details, it is difficult to remember everything by simply reading the text, and the amount you remember will decrease over time (e.g. a day, week or month later); this is why notes are important. Good note taking provides a means to check something quickly without having to read the whole text again. You can make notes in two ways: brief notes and highlighting.

Brief notes

Brief notes are a summary of the information you are reading, so it is important not to make them too long. They can be made by: writing key words, phrases or comments in the book margin; producing a flow chart linking points or issues in a logical sequence; summarising information in a table; creating a mind map of branching key words or phrases, each link representing a connection in events, theories or concepts.

Highlighting

Some people prefer to highlight key words and phrases in the text, by drawing a line under the words or using a highlighter pen. When you do this, it is important to only highlight selected words, phrases or sentences. Do not highlight the whole page: you want to use this approach to *emphasise* key points.

Further advice on reading and note taking is available on the course website in 'Develop your study skills', which is in the section 'Learning with the OU'.

As the margins in *Greene* are rather narrow, you may prefer to highlight text and make brief notes in a separate notebook, which can be cross-referenced to *Greene* by writing the chapter, section and page numbers at the start of each note.

(b) Return to *Greene* Chapter 1, Section 2.5 (pp. 12–13) and read through the first section again this time making brief notes as you go, before comparing them with those in Figure 2.6.

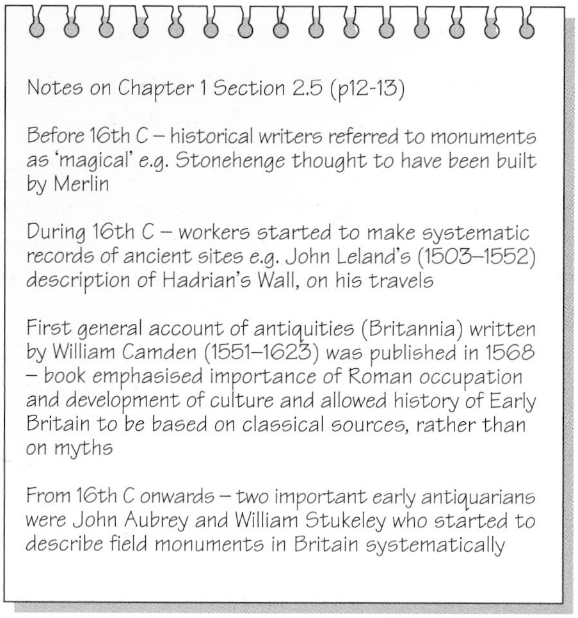

Figure 2.6 Extract from a student's notebook, showing how they have summarised part of *Greene* Chapter 1, Section 2.5 using short notes.

Notes on Chapter 1 Section 2.5 (p12-13)

Before 16th C – historical writers referred to monuments as 'magical' e.g. Stonehenge thought to have been built by Merlin

During 16th C – workers started to make systematic records of ancient sites e.g. John Leland's (1503–1552) description of Hadrian's Wall, on his travels

First general account of antiquities (Britannia) written by William Camden (1551–1623) was published in 1568 – book emphasised importance of Roman occupation and development of culture and allowed history of Early Britain to be based on classical sources, rather than on myths

From 16th C onwards – two important early antiquarians were John Aubrey and William Stukeley who started to describe field monuments in Britain systematically

Your notes may differ slightly from Figure 2.6, but this does not matter. The key points are that your notes will: (i) be easier to re-read than the full text; (ii) have a particular meaning to you; and (iii) will summarise the main points you identified in the text.

(c) Now make notes on the rest of *Greene* Chapter 1, Section 2.5 (pp. 13–15), using the subheadings to divide up your notes, before reading and summarising *Greene* Chapter 1, Section 2.6 (pp. 15–16), Section 2.8 (p. 18) and Section 7 (pp. 43–48).

If you would like to know more about the development of archaeology as a subject, the British Museum has a virtual tour called Enlightenment: the birth of archaeology; go to the 'Activities' section on the course website and click on Part 1 Activity 2.3.

2.2.1 Making sense of relative timescales

The one area that eluded early antiquarians and scholars was the ability to date artefacts and field monuments relative to each other and to determine whether they were used at the same or different times. In much of the Christian world and until the mid 17th century, historical time was referenced against the biblical estimation of the creation of the Earth, which was thought to be 4004 BC. As scientific understandings of physical, geological and biological processes developed throughout the mid 17th to 19th centuries, new methods of estimating the Earth's age (and the historical development of humans) started to emerge, and by the 1860s, the chronological system based on the Bible was finally dismissed in favour of more scientific methods.

Part I Activity 2.4   Putting artefacts and monuments in order

(The estimated time needed to complete this activity is 45 minutes.)

Main learning outcomes developed: KU1, KS3 and KS4.

(a) Read *Greene* Chapter 1, Sections 3–3.2 (pp. 19–25) and Chapter 4, Section 2.1 (pp. 145–7), making brief notes on the different methods by which early archaeologists assigned *relative* dates to artefacts and monuments (e.g. stratigraphy, typology, the presence of ancient coins and seriation).

(b) Now go to the DVD, click on 'Topics', find 'Part 1 Course Introduction' and complete Part 1 Activity 2.4, in which you will compare some of the different *absolute* dating techniques (e.g. radiocarbon, thermoluminescence, U–Th and K–Ar) with *relative* dating techniques (e.g. stratigraphy, typology, coins and seriation).

To summarise, before the discovery of radioactive decay (in the late 19th century), and the development of radiocarbon dating (in the 1950s) and other isotopic, physical and chemical techniques (e.g. thermoluminescence) that allowed *absolute ages* of artefacts to be determined, antiquarians and archaeologists used a series of techniques (e.g. stratigraphy, typology, coins and seriation) to establish the *relative age* of artefacts.

Question 2.3

Examine the three archaeological timescales for Britain, Jordan and the South American Andes in Figure 2.7 (on p. 18), which are all drawn to the same scale (e.g. 1 cm on each diagram represents the same amount of time). In one or two sentences, describe the main differences between these timescales. Why do these differences occur?

Figure 2.7   Comparing and contrasting three archaeological timescales, extending from the Middle Palaeolithic (10 000 years BCE) to the 16th century, for Europe (focusing on Britain), the Middle East (focusing on Jordan) and South America (focusing on Argentina and the Andes).

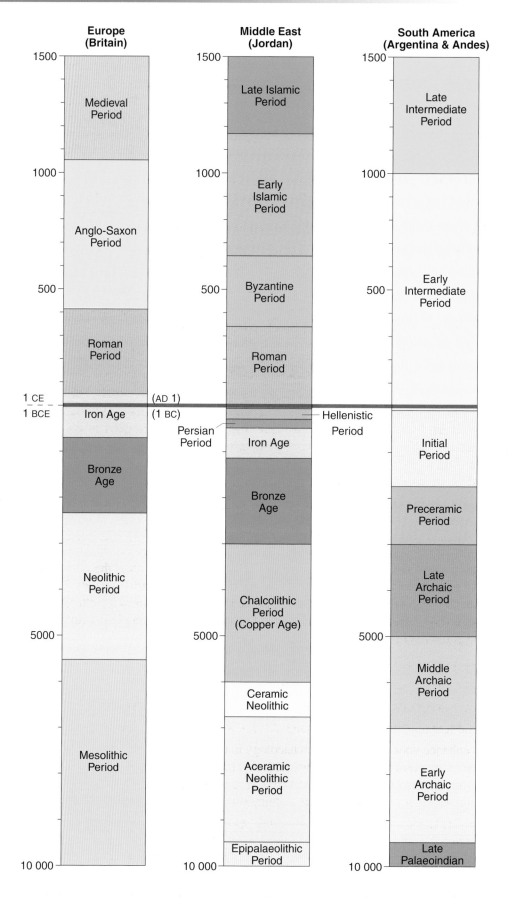

2.3 Why is archaeology of interest?

General interest in archaeology and heritage continues to grow, with the more popular archaeology television programmes in the UK attracting ~3–10 million regular viewers. Although much of this is driven by an interest in historical and cultural perspectives (e.g. who we are, where our ancestors came from, what they looked like), there has also been a growing interest in the role of archaeological science.

Now read *Greene* Chapter 6, Sections 6.1–6.3 (pp. 266–70), which describe some of the issues facing museums, heritage centres and the government, in relation to preserving archaeological sites and artefacts in response to commercial developments and growing public interest. Your notes from these sections will help you with Part 1 Activity 2.5, which examines the remits and roles of the British Museum, the Jorvik Viking Centre and York Archaeological Trust.

Part 1 Activity 2.5 Promoting archaeology in museums, interpretative centres and by charitable trusts

(The estimated time needed to complete this activity is 20 minutes.)

Main learning outcomes developed: KU4, CS2 and PS1.

In this activity, you will hear Neil MacGregor (Director of the British Museum), Sarah Maltby (Head of Attractions, Assistant Director of the Jorvik Viking Centre) and Richard Hall (Director of York Archaeological Trust) each describe the role and responsibilities of their respective organisations in archaeology, and the changing ways in which they balance scientific research with meeting the needs and interests of the amateur archaeologists, commerce and the general public.

Now go to the DVD, click on 'Topics', find 'Part 1 Course Introduction' and complete Part 1 Activity 2.5.

Read *Greene* Chapter 6, Section 6.6 (pp. 275–6), which examines the changing face of archaeology in the (British) media, before starting Part 1 Activity 2.6. Greene's final comment about the cultural conflicts and the need for ethical awareness of archaeological issues in the media is of increasing importance and one you will consider throughout this course.

Part 1 Activity 2.6 Archaeology and the media

(You will do this activity throughout the duration of the course.)

Main learning outcomes developed: KU2, CS1 and KS2.

To enhance your awareness of archaeology in the media, you should start to collect interesting news items, information leaflets and articles on archaeological issues, as well as bookmark online sites that relate to the topics of investigation. You could also make a note of any future television or radio programmes of interest.

Now go to the 'Activities' section on the course website and complete Part 1 Activity 2.6, in which you will examine ways of classifying, categorising and ranking the news stories and resources you find, in a way that is consistent and useful for future reference.

2.4 Archaeological science

So far, you have examined different social, cultural and historical influences on archaeology, looking at how it has developed over time, what interests people about it and the changing attitudes to how archaeological information is presented. The final section of this chapter focuses on archaeological science in terms of how information can be integrated across the sciences to gain a greater understanding of the archaeological landscape and the human materials it contains.

2.4.1 Archaeological investigations – a fourfold process

Archaeological science is a progressive process that involves the four stages of *discovery*, *investigation*, *analysis* and *interpretation*. With each successive step, new questions arise that need resolving. These in turn may result in other discoveries, investigations, analyses and interpretations being made, and so on. Using this approach allows archaeologists to progressively build up a more complete picture of past societies and environments, enabling them to devise, test, prove and disprove different theories. Like many other sciences, it is important to realise that in archaeology, there may not be a 'right' or a 'wrong' answer. All that can be stated is the most plausible explanation for a particular artefact or site based on the information available at that point in time (Box 2.2).

Box 2.2 The archaeological jigsaw?

One analogy is to think of archaeology as a puzzle in which the instructions and some of the pieces are missing. The only way to understand what you are looking at is to try piecing it together as logically as possible and to suggest what may fill any gaps. As more bits of the puzzle are found, a more complete picture may appear. Alternatively, this new 'evidence' may show that part or all of the puzzle actually fits together in a completely different way, altering your final interpretations.

This is why it is vital that all observations, descriptions and analyses are done as carefully and systematically as possible, to enable other scientists to reuse and reinterpret the data as new information or more accurate analytical techniques become available. Science is about proving and disproving different theories, based on interpretation of the evidence that is currently available.

2.4.2 Archaeology and the natural sciences

Read the grey box at the beginning of *Greene* Chapter 5 (pp. 182–3).

In this last section, you will start to investigate how human activities have altered the natural environment, geosphere and biosphere, and how past human activities have in turn been affected by the natural environment and global climate.

The natural environment

Part I Activity 2.7   Environmental archaeology

(The estimated time needed to complete this activity is 15 minutes.)

Main learning outcomes developed: KU3, CS2 and CS4.

Read *Greene* Chapter 5, Section 2 (pp. 184–5), and make brief lists on:

- the type of evidence used by environmental archaeologists
- the subject areas studied (e.g. zoology, plant science, human geography)
- how this information can be used to investigate the interactions and activities of humans, animals and plants, etc.

Question 2.4

Greene starts Chapter 5, Section 2 by saying 'Environmental archaeology is one of the clearest demonstrations of multidisciplinarity to be found in archaeological science'.

Describe one example in *Greene* that illustrates the multidisciplinary nature of environmental archaeology.

The geosphere

Part I Activity 2.8   Using geological information

(The estimated time needed to complete this activity is 20 minutes.)

Main learning outcomes developed: KU3, CS2 and KS2.

(a) Read *Greene* Chapter 5, Section 4 up to Section 4.1 (p. 188).

(b) Now go to the DVD, click on 'Topics', find 'Part 1 Course Introduction' and complete Part 1 Activity 2.8, in which you will investigate two very different Palaeolithic sites at Boxgrove and Swanscombe in England. As you read about the finds at these two sites, complete the blank version of Table 2.1 in the Study Guide to compare and contrast some of the key points about these illustrative examples. *(You can also download a blank version of this table from the 'Documents' section on the DVD.)*

Table 2.1 Comparison of the types and location of finds made at Boxgrove and Swanscombe, and how this impacted on the interpretations that could be made.

Use the version of Table 2.1 in the back of the Study Guide to complete your answer to Part 1 Activity 2.8.

	Boxgrove	**Swanscombe**
Type of finds		
Finds in situ or reworked?		
Date of sediments		
Date of finds		
Method used to date finds		
Interpretation of finds		

If you are unfamiliar with the technique of potassium–argon (K–Ar) dating, go to the 'Techniques' section on the DVD to find out more.

Question 2.5

In which time period is geological and geomorphological (landform) evidence most useful in archaeology?

Question 2.6

Why is the lower unit at Boxgrove potentially more useful to archaeologists than either of the upper two units at this site or the very plentiful finds recovered from Swanscombe?

Question 2.7

(a) Which type of geological deposits can be used for K–Ar dating and magnetic reversal studies?

(b) Which type of date (i.e. absolute or relative) do these techniques provide for the geological layers analysed and the archaeological artefacts positioned either above or below these layers?

Part 1 Activity 2.9   Geomorphological evidence and its use in archaeology

(The estimated time needed to complete this activity is 15 minutes.)

Main learning outcomes developed: KU3 and KS3.

Now read *Greene* Chapter 5, Section 4.2 (pp. 188–90) and complete Table 2.2, summarising the different types of information that can be obtained from soils. (The first row is completed for you as a guide to the type and level of information expected.)

Table 2.2 The range of archaeological information that can be obtained from soil studies. *(Use the blank version of Table 2.2 in the back of the Study Guide to complete your answer to Part 1 Activity 2.9.)*

Feature	Archaeological implication or type of information available
colour	different colours (and textures) between layers can be used to recognise human activities or changing environmental conditions
climate	
soil profiles (e.g. podsols, brown earths)	
earthworks	
composition	

The biosphere

Read the introduction to *Greene* Chapter 5, Section 5 (p. 190).

Question 2.8

What significant development altered the diet and source of food eaten by humans at the end of the Palaeolithic Period (~10 000 years BP), and what impact did this have on how and where societies lived?

The following sections in *Greene* on plants, animals, shells and insects contain detailed information about the types of evidence that are useful in archaeology. As you read each section, bear in mind that you will return to this chapter in Part 2 of this Study Book, where much of this information will be put into context.

- Section 5.1 'Plants' (pp. 190–1), up to 'Pollen and phytoliths'.
- Section 5.2 'Animals' (p. 196), up to 'Interpretation'.
- Section 5.4 'Shells' (pp. 201–3).
- ·Section 5.5 'Insects and other invertebrates' (p. 203).

Part I Activity 2.10   Plants, animals, shells and insects

(The estimated time needed to complete this activity is 20 minutes.)

Main learning outcomes developed: KS2 and KS4.

After reading the above four sections of *Greene*, complete the flow diagram in Figure 2.8, which summarises the different types of archaeological information that can be obtained from plants, animals, shells and insects. To help you see the type and level of information to include, the plants entry is completed for you.

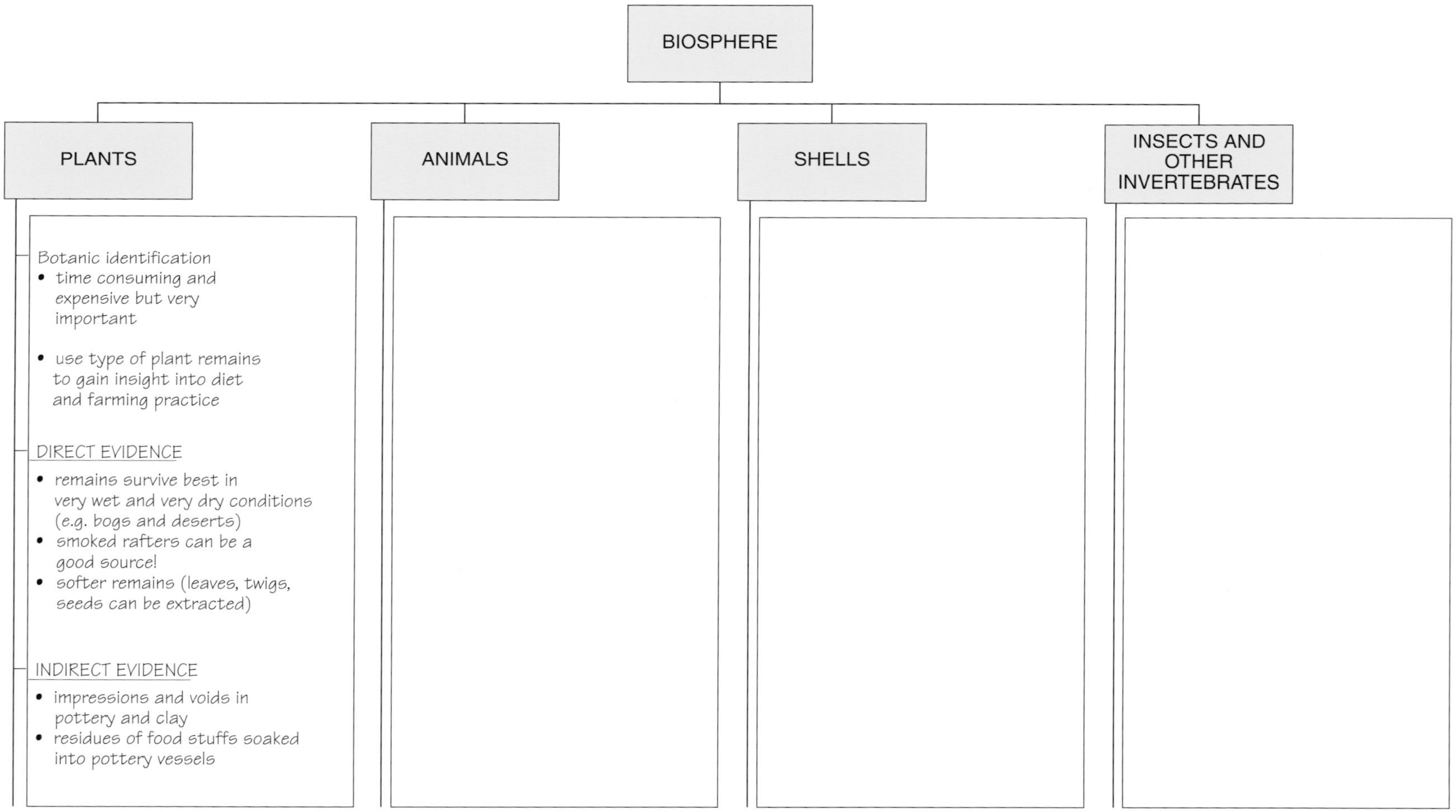

BIOSPHERE

PLANTS

Botanic identification
- time consuming and expensive but very important
- use type of plant remains to gain insight into diet and farming practice

DIRECT EVIDENCE
- remains survive best in very wet and very dry conditions (e.g. bogs and deserts)
- smoked rafters can be a good source!
- softer remains (leaves, twigs, seeds can be extracted)

INDIRECT EVIDENCE
- impressions and voids in pottery and clay
- residues of food stuffs soaked into pottery vessels

ANIMALS

SHELLS

INSECTS AND OTHER INVERTEBRATES

Figure 2.8 Flow diagram showing the complexity of the biosphere and the type of archaeological information that can be obtained from plants, animals, insects and shells. (To be completed in Part 1 Activity 2.10.)

2.5 Summary of Part 1

After completing Part 1 you should now be able to:

1 State what is meant by the terms 'archaeology, 'archaeological science' and 'anthropology', and describe how the main foci of these three areas of study differ from but also complement each other (CS1).

2 Describe how the concept of time can be subdivided into historical, prehistorical and geological periods, and how archaeologists can compare the age of objects and events using relative and absolute dating techniques (CS2, CS3).

3 Give examples of how social, cultural and historical influences have changed people's perceptions of and attitudes towards archaeology over time (KU3, CS2).

4 Describe how human activities have altered the natural environment (e.g. landforms, plants and animals), as well as how the natural environment has controlled the range of human activities within an area, over time (KU1, CS3).

5 Use basic arithmetical, graphical and textual information and methods to solve various archaeological problems (KS1).

6 Describe some of the different strategies that can be used to develop learning effectively (KS4).

Remember, each summary statement relates to several of the learning outcomes developed in this course; only the most important one or two outcomes are listed above to help emphasise which ones they are specifically addressing. You may find these references useful when reviewing the activities and working towards your End of Course Assessment (ECA).

PART 2   THE INVESTIGATIVE TOPICS

Topic 1
Reading the archaeological landscape

1.1   Introduction

Say the word 'archaeology' and the first thing most people think of is an excavation, with archaeologists digging away to reveal layer upon layer of evidence of past civilisations. In reality, excavation is not the only method of investigation, and is only used when it has been demonstrated to be the most effective technique for the situation. Furthermore, given the large number of archaeological sites that have already been excavated over the past 100 or so years, and the wealth of information collected about certain features and people in particular parts of the world, it is difficult to justify excavating even more similar-aged features without a valid reason. As such, archaeologists have to justify *why* they need to excavate in relation to the importance of the site and *how* this will contribute to current scientific and historic understanding.

In this topic, you will investigate how field archaeology is carried out from the initial discovery, reconnaissance (e.g. field walking) and surveying stages, to the excavation and conservation of archaeological finds. You will also consider some of the ethical issues that professional archaeologists have to deal with as part of their daily lives, before considering how archaeology is perceived by the wider community.

Throughout this topic, you will be asked to read relatively long sections of *Greene* (flagged by 📖 in the margin), each of which is accompanied by some study prompts in this book, to help you identify the key points of each section. You will also need to complete each of the related activities, which are either in this book, on the DVD in the 'Topics' section (indicated by 💿 in the margin) or in the 'Activities' section on the course website (indicated by 🖱 in the margin). In each activity, you will examine and apply some of the field techniques used at the three main case studies, which (in order of size) are as follows.

- **The city mound of Tell es-Saʿidiyeh, Jordan** (Figure 1.1a and b): the initial phase of work on this large double-mound (tell) settlement was carried out by James B. Pritchard (University of Pennsylvania) in 1964–7, followed by a second phase of excavations led by Jonathan Tubb (British Museum) in 1985–96. The site of Tell es-Saʿidiyeh is situated between major transportation routes in the Jordan valley, with the Wadi Kufrinjeh immediately to the north and the River Jordan approximately 1.5 km to the west. Excavations show that a settlement existed on this site as early as the fifth millennium BC and that because of its strategic location, this developed into a major urban settlement in the Early Bronze Age (~3200 BC), covering the entire site. After the destruction and abandonment of this major settlement around 2500 BC, a new period of development began on the eastern side of the upper mound (i.e. the upper tell), while the lower tell became the site of the city's cemetery. To date, over 400 graves have been excavated in the cemetery within an area of only ~120 m². As a consequence of deteriorating physical and political environments, the population of Tell es-Sa'idiyeh started to wane after the 8th century BC, the site finally being abandoned in the seventh century AD (the Early Islamic Period) (Part 1, Figure 2.7). Overall, the double-mound structure covers approximately 13 hectares and is of significant archaeological and historic importance, as it provides an insight into an almost continuous period of occupation of about 6000 years between the fifth millennium BC and the seventh century AD.

A hectare (abbreviated to ha) is equal to 10 000 square metres (10 000 m²), which is the same as a square that measures 100 m by 100 m.

- **The Hungate Dig, York, England** (Figure 1.1c): scheduled to run from 2006 until 2012, the Hungate Dig is the largest excavation to be carried out in the City of York during the last 25 years, covering an area approximately 320 m long by 150 m wide. As this inner city centre site has been scheduled for urban regeneration into a prime residential and commercial centre, the Hungate Dig can be described as a rescue excavation, with a large proportion of the site being gradually revealed to allow ~2000 years of habitation in this part of York, to be investigated. The excavation also has the important task of finding the exact location of a medieval cemetery known to have occupied part of the site.

- **Wetwang Woman, East Yorkshire, England** (Figure 1.1d and e): in March 2001, preliminary archaeological excavations carried out as part of the standard planning process at the eastern end of Wetwang village, East Yorkshire, discovered an important type of Iron Age grave called a square barrow. Given the importance of the site, English Heritage asked a team of expert archaeologists from the British Museum to carry out a detailed rescue excavation. While excavating the barrow, the remains of a wooden cart decorated with cast and hammered bronze, red coral (most probably from the Red Sea) and red glass were recovered, beneath which lay an Iron Age woman (dated to ~300–200 BC), carefully buried with a rare iron mirror and some pig joints (to aid her journey into the next world). Once the remains of the woman, cart and other finds had been removed from the ~9 m² grave, construction work resumed.

Figure 1.1   The case studies: (a) the double mound at Tell es-Saʿidiyeh, Jordan and (b) one of its unusual Egyptian-style burials; (c) excavations at Hungate, in the summer of 2007; (d) excavating the square barrow at the corner of Chariot Way, Wetwang and (e) the remains of the Iron Age woman and her mirror.

You will find the full list of learning outcomes and their codes at the back of this Study Book and in the Study Guide.

Part 2 Activity 1.1   Background to the case studies

(The estimated time needed to complete this activity is 30 minutes.)

Main learning outcomes developed: KU2, KU3, KS2 and KS4.

In this activity, you will familiarise yourself with each case study used in this topic, before going on to compare and contrast some of the logistical and practical aspects of each site. As you work through Topic 1, you will return to look at issues relating to the planning, surveying, excavation and preliminary interpretations of each site.

Now go to the DVD, click on 'Topics', find Topic 1 and complete Part 2 Activity 1.1.

1.1.1   Using the correct terminology: finds, sites, projects and landscapes

So far this topic has already referred to archaeological sites, finds, artefacts, remains and projects, while the title of this topic includes 'the archaeological landscape'. Before proceeding any further, it is important to define each of these terms and some others, so you can use them correctly.

- The **archaeological landscape** refers to the wider social, political, cultural and environmental context of an archaeological object or site, and uses information from other archaeological evidence in the region to see the 'bigger picture'. The archaeological landscape considers issues relating to the natural geography, topography, geomorphology and geology of the environment, as well as the ecology and climatic conditions under which the area or object of interest was formed and used. It then combines all of this with documented information about past social, political and cultural issues to understand *why* the site or object was used. The archaeological landscape is therefore the broadest level context; it is the natural and social environment in which a study needs to be based, allowing the results to be put into context with other studies.

- An **archaeological** (or field) **project** is an entire study. This may consist of several locations (e.g. sites) of interest and be carried out over an extended period of time (with each period of activity called a *field season*, e.g. the Tell es-Saʿidiyeh project in 1985–1996, or the Hungate Dig scheduled for 2006–12), or it may consist of one site, investigated in one season (e.g. the rescue excavations at Wetwang). The project outlines the overall aims and objectives of the study during the field-work and post-excavation research phases. It therefore describes what the archaeologists want to do, why they want to do it and how this will enhance current levels of understanding.

- An **archaeological site** is a place or an area that preserves evidence of past human activity. Sites can exist at various scales from a relatively small area (e.g. recovery of an individual object or grave such as the Wetwang barrow or the graves in the Tell es-Sa'idiyeh cemetery) to large dispersed areas consisting of a major settlement, a series of related smaller settlements or several features of interest (e.g. the city of Tell es-Sa'idiyeh, or the Hungate Dig). Large sites are often divided into smaller manageable areas (sub-sites) which can be studied more efficiently. A site therefore relates to the physical area of interest studied during a specific survey or excavation.

- **Context** is extremely important in archaeology and relates to a discrete 'activity in time', which produced some evidence that has been preserved in the archaeological record. (Archaeological deposits form as a result of everyday activities; as people live their daily lives, they leave evidence for future investigators to find and interpret, i.e. they set the context.) For example, the construction of a defensive structure, burial of a person, digging of a post-hole or filling of ditch are all contexts; they represent activities in the past that have been preserved in the archaeological record.

- **Archaeological features** are fixed (non-portable) evidence of human activity, found in the ground. These include *constructed features* such as building foundations, post-holes, ditches, fish ponds (i.e. anything that has been purposely constructed) and *cumulative features*, which develop through the repeated use of an area (e.g. compacted soil relating to commonly used routes through a settlement or a floor in a building; the baked region of a fire hearth; discoloured soils caused by the presence of latrine waste).

- The terms archaeological **finds** and **artefacts** are often used interchangeably. They refer to any portable archaeological object that has been *manufactured or modified* by humans, including both inorganic materials (e.g. stone axes, buildings, glass, pottery, metal objects) and organic materials (e.g. wooden objects, textiles, paper).

- In this course, the term **remains** is used to refer to any *naturally occurring or modified organic material* (e.g. human and animal bones, large plant fragments) that has been preserved in the archaeological record, and is prefaced by a descriptive term (e.g. human remains, animal remains, plant remains, environmental remains).

It is important to note that the term 'archaeological remains' can also be used in a more generic sense to refer to any object or feature in the archaeological record (e.g. the remains of a medieval building, the skeletal remains of an individual, the remains of a midden); therefore, you should always look at how this term is used.

Question I.I

Match each of the descriptions in Table 1.1 with the correct descriptive term (e.g. archaeological landscape, project, site, area, feature, artefact or human remains).

Table 1.1 Examples of different archaeological landscapes, projects, sites, areas, features, artefacts and human remains from the four main case studies. (For use with Question 1.1.)

Description	Term
Tell es-Sa'idiyeh cemetery	
the skeleton of a person, recovered from a grave at Tell es-Sa'idiyeh	
the horse bits recovered from the Wetwang cart	
the iron mirror, brooch and pig bones recovered from the Wetwang grave	
the scooped-out hollow into which Wetwang Woman was placed	
determining the location of the cemetery at Hungate	
the square barrow (grave) at Wetwang	
the Iron Age of East Yorkshire	
the Hungate Dig	

1.1.2 A question of size …

As you read through the introduction, you probably noticed that several references were made to the size (area) of each site.

■ Which three different styles of measurement were used to describe the size of the case studies sites? (Box 1.1)

Box 1.1 Pause for thought: study tip reminder

It is good practice to write down your answer to this type of 'pause for thought' question *before* reading the suggested answer. This will help you develop your critical thinking skills and allow you to check how well you are learning.

☐ Some of the sites were referred to in terms of their approximate length and breadth (e.g. Hungate covers an area approximately 320 m long by 150 m wide), while others were described in terms of their square metre coverage (e.g. the grave at Wetwang occupies ~9 m^2) or coverage in hectares (e.g. Tell es-Sa'idiyeh covers ~13 ha).

All archaeologists need to be able to work with different types of measurement across a range of scales (e.g. millimetres, centimetres, metres and kilometres). In addition, they need to ensure that they take, record, use and interpret all measurements as accurately as possible. As you work through this topic, you will practise working with data on a range of scales, in relation to field measurements and recording data from archaeological finds and features.

The SI system is the International System of Units (e.g. m, kg, s, °C); the term 'SI', is derived from its French name – *Système International d'Unités*.

In science, all measurements of length and area use the SI metric system, part of which you will already be very familiar with: for example, millimetres (mm), centimetres (cm), metres (m) and kilometres (km) (Table 1.2).

Table 1.2   Summary of SI units of length, comparing the size of each relative to 1 m.

SI Unit	Symbol	Equivalent in metres	To convert to metres
1 kilometre	km	1000 m	× 1000
1 metre	m	1 m	× 1
1 centimetre	cm	0.01 m (one-hundredth of a metre)	÷ 100
1 millimetre	mm	0.001 m (one-thousandth of a metre)	÷ 1000

To convert a number from a larger to a smaller unit, you need to *multiply* by the relevant conversion factor; whereas to convert a number from a smaller unit into a larger unit, you need to *divide* by the relevant conversion factor (Table 1.3). In other words, to change the unit shown in any one of the *rows* in Table 1.3 to one of the other units in each column, you need to use the conversion factor shown. For example, to convert 35 mm into metres (m), locate the 'mm' row on the left-hand side of Table 1.3 and then find the 'm' column along the top of the table. Now follow the millimetre row across the table and where it intersects with the metre column, this shows the conversion factor you need to use (e.g. 35 mm ÷ 1000 = 0.035 m).

Applying the same process, 2.45 km can be converted into centimetres (cm) as follows: 2.45 km × 100 000 = 245 000 cm.

Table 1.3   Summary of the conversion factors for changing units of length from kilometres (km) to millimetres (mm).

		Units getting smaller ⟶			
		km	**m**	**cm**	**mm**
Units getting smaller	**km**	–	× 1000	× 100 000	× 1 000 000
	m	÷ 1000	–	× 100	× 1000
	cm	÷ 100 000	÷ 100	–	× 10
	mm	÷ 1 000 000	÷ 1000	÷ 10	–

In fieldwork, archaeology operates on the millimetre to kilometre scale: for example, scales that are visible to the unaided eye (i.e. millimetres to metres), or can be measured on maps (e.g. distances up to kilometres in length). When carrying out detailed examinations of archaeological finds in the laboratory using high-powered imaging or analytical techniques (e.g. optical or scanning electron microscopes, chemical analyses), measurements are typically at the sub-millimetre scale.

Returning to field archaeology, areas are measured in square metres (m^2) and, occasionally, as square centimetres (cm^2) or square kilometres (km^2). A square metre is a square measuring 1 m × 1 m = 1 m^2, so 100 m^2 consists of 100 squares, each 1 m × 1 m in size. An area of 100 m^2, comprises an area measuring 10 m × 10 m or 20 m × 5 m (both of which equal 100 m^2), but *not* 100 m × 100 m, as this equals 10 000 m^2 (Figure 1.2).

Figure 1.2 Calculating areas: the difference between 1 cm², 1 m², 100 m² and 10 000 m² (1 ha).

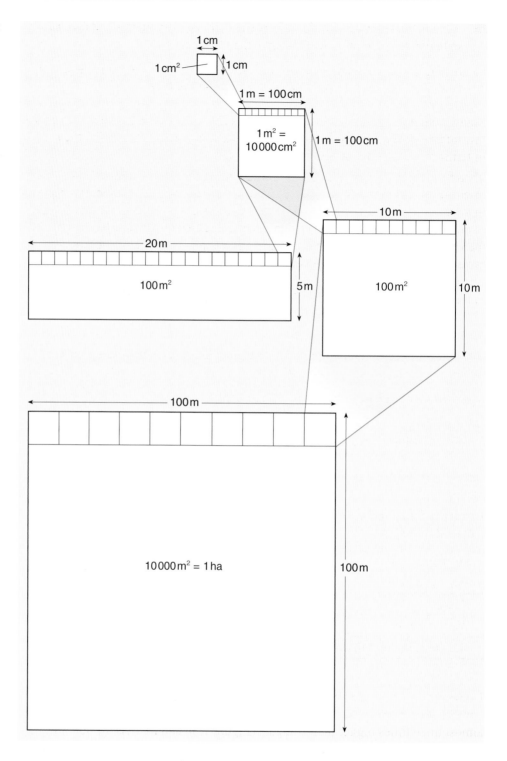

Working on the same basis, 1 cm² is equivalent to a square measuring 1 cm × 1 cm; so an area extending 6 cm by 15 cm is equal to 90 cm² (e.g. 6 cm × 15 cm = 90 cm²). As there are 100 cm in 1 m, 1 m² (1 m × 1 m) is equal to 100 cm × 100 cm = 10 000 cm².

■ What is the length of the side of a square kilometre in metres and how many square metres are there in a square kilometre (km²)?

☐ A square kilometre equals 1 km × 1 km = 1 km². As a kilometre is equal to 1000 m, 1 km² equals 1000 m × 1000 m = 1000 000 m².

Many medium to large scale archaeological sites are within the size range of a few hundreds of metres in length, and so archaeologists often describe these sites in terms of the number of hectares (ha) they cover.

Remember – I hectare (ha) = 10 000 m² (e.g. 100 m x 100 m).

Therefore, if you know the length and breadth of a site (in m or km), you can calculate its area by multiplying the two sides together (to produce a measurement in m², ha or km²); likewise, if you know the total coverage of the site and the length of one side, the length of the other side can be calculated by dividing the area by the known length. In all cases, you need to check that all units being used are the same (e.g. if the area is given in km² or ha and the length in m, the area needs to be converted to m² first, to allow you to do the correct division). *(You can find additional help on working with numbers in the Maths Skills ebook on the course website.)*

Question 1.2

The entire field site (including the double mound and the surrounding land) at Tell es-Sa'idiyeh covers an area of 13 ha.

(a) How many square metres does this represent?

(b) Knowing that 1 km² equals 1000 000 m², what is the equivalent size in square kilometres (km²) for Tell es-Sa'idiyeh?

Question 1.3

Using the following summary table of field measurements, calculate the missing values (Figure 1.3).

Field site	Length	Breadth	Area
Tell es-Sa'idiyeh	500 m		13 ha
Hungate	320 m	150 m	
Wetwang grave		2.6 m	~9 m²
individual grave, Tell es-Sa'idiyeh	160 cm		~2 m²

Converting all four sites into the same unit of area (e.g. m² or ha) allows direct comparisons to be made. This reveals that the entire site at Tell es-Sa'idiyeh is almost three times bigger than Hungate (Figure 1.3a and b), over 14 000 times bigger than the Wetwang grave (Figure 1.3d) and 65 000 times bigger than an individual grave at Tell es-Sa'idiyeh (Figure 1.3c)! Comparing the size of a single grave from Tell es-Sa'idiyeh (Figure 1.3c) with a complete city (Figure 1.3a) obviously does not make sense. More sensible comparisons are between the two areas of settlement (e.g. Tell es-Sa'idiyeh and Hungate; Figure 1.3a and b) and the two single graves at Wetwang and the Tell es-Sa'idiyeh cemetery (Figure 1.3d and e). Direct comparisons between the graves at Wetwang and Tell es-Sa'idiyeh cemetery reveal the 9 m² grave of the Iron Age woman at Wetwang is 4.5 times larger than the individual grave in Tell es-Sa'idiyeh.

Figure 1.3 Comparing the relative size of (a) the double mound, which forms part of the Tell es-Saʿidiyeh site; (b) the entire construction site at Hungate; and (c) a single grave from Tell es-Saʿidiyeh, all drawn at the same scale. Comparing the relative size and style of single occupancy graves at (d) Wetwang and (e) Tell es-Saʿidiyeh, both drawn at the same scale.

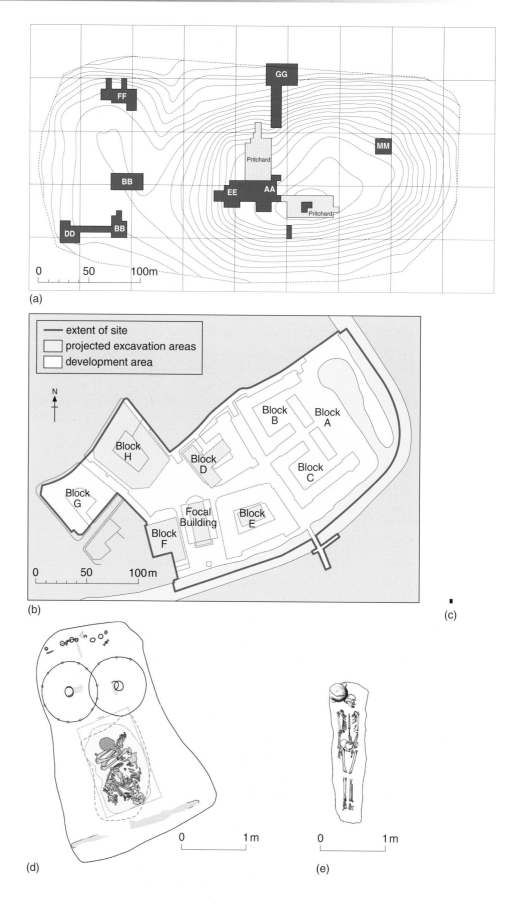

(a)

(b)

(c)

(d)

(e)

1.2 Surveying the archaeological landscape

The first step in an archaeological field study is to identify the area or site of interest. Some of the ethical considerations involved in field archaeology include the preference for using non-destructive surveying techniques rather than excavation unless the site is known to be at risk of destruction or there is a particular reason why excavation would enhance current understandings (see *Greene* Chapter 2, Section 2.1, p. 55). So, unless there is a valid archaeological reason to excavate, the preferred option is often to accurately log the presence and physical extent of a site or feature, but to leave it intact.

■ How are archaeological sites and features of interest found?

☐ Every year, a significant number of archaeological finds and features are discovered by accident (by the general public as well as by archaeologists) and through systematic field investigations (by amateur and professional archaeologists).

The majority of these finds will not be of great scientific or historical importance (although each one is still important in its own right, and in furthering understanding of the local archaeology). Occasionally finds, remains and features are uncovered in different situations that do enhance current understandings of different aspects of archaeology the development of that particular area, and so merit further investigation and the potential of a detailed field-site survey and/or excavation.

The broad *types* of sites can be thought of in three ways.

1 Sites that are discovered by accident, which may require a more systematic investigation of the area (e.g. road construction or building excavations exposing an unknown feature or find; natural weathering processes or farming activity bringing an object to the surface).

2 Sites that are known from references in historical documents, but for which the exact location is unknown or uncertain (e.g. the Mayan cities in Belize; the extent of the different occupation periods at Hungate).

3 Known sites or structures that are clearly visible and/or form distinct features on the physical landscape that may or may not have been investigated as part of an archaeological survey (e.g. Tell es-Sa῾idiyeh; Stonehenge in southern England; the Egyptian pyramids in Giza; the Hills of Tara, Co. Meath, Ireland; less visually impressive building foundation walls, etc.).

Potentially interesting archaeological sites can be assessed using a combination of the following reconnaissance techniques:

• Desk-top surveys where information from historical and modern documentary evidence (e.g. maps; written personal records; books; official documents, records and tax returns; engravings, painting, photographs; previous archaeological surveys) is combined with verifiable oral accounts, to develop a picture of what may be discovered in a specific area.

• Field, ground or surface surveys where individuals systematically walk over a site, looking for exposed archaeological objects or discarded materials (e.g. ash, middens), and note the location of archaeological features (e.g. walls, foundations, defensive stone and earth structures).

- Aerial surveys using aerial photographs to identify physical features of interest.

- Geophysical surveys used to investigate shallow-level features within the ground that may or may not be visible on the surface.

- More rarely, geochemical surveys where soil samples can be collected for laboratory-based analysis to identify the presence of past human activity and occupation (although it is important to note that these surveys are very susceptible to contamination, such as animal burrowing and agricultural seeps).

The exact type of reconnaissance work depends on a variety of logistical and practical issues, including: (a) the main objective of the investigation (e.g. the questions the archaeologist wants to answer); (b) the amount of time and resources available for this work (e.g. the number of people working on the project, the type of equipment available, the amount of funding backing the project and the time period each of them can be accessed); (c) the physical geography (i.e. terrain), size and location of the area (e.g. if the area covers tens of hundreds of square metres, field walking across the whole area is not logistically possible in one field season; likewise, there is no point in doing an aerial survey of a site that covers only a few square metres or is not visible from the air); (d) prior knowledge of the area (including documented and local spoken information); (e) any ethical considerations (e.g. social, cultural and political sensitivities associated with working at specific sites, features and remains). Most archaeological sites have several scales of surveying, including an *initial rapid survey* of the whole area (see the next section), to create a base grid reference system against which all measurements and finds can be logged relative to each other. This is followed by an *intermediate landscape survey*, where the physical location of each archaeological feature (including its depth below or above ground surface) is accurately measured and recorded against fixed reference points. The final stage of surveying involves a *detailed survey* of a small area of the site, an interesting feature or an individual find, to record its exact location and its appearance in the field.

- ■ Using the above information, when is surveying done during an archaeological dig?

- ☐ Surveying is an ongoing process that happens throughout the duration of a dig. The dig starts with an initial survey to set up the main reference grid, allowing the more detailed landscape surveys to be put into geographic context with each other and so aid cross-matching between excavated layers in terms of their historic context. As the dig progresses, new areas may need an initial survey to allow the base reference grid to be extended or to allow new exploration areas to be linked to those already completed. As each excavation area is investigated, detailed surveys may be necessary to allow the exact location of a feature or an object to be accurately logged, so that the archaeologist can determine the importance of the historical and geographical context of the site.

Part 2 Activity 1.2 Surveying the skeleton at Wetwang

(The estimated time needed to complete this activity is 15 minutes.)

Main learning outcomes developed: KU1, KU3 and KS2.

When the skeleton at Wetwang was exposed, it was clear that removing it from the grave was going to be difficult because of the fragility of the bones, their arrangement in the grave and the overlying grave goods. The archaeologists also wanted to collect as much information as possible so that they could reconstruct the grave in three dimensions to learn more about this form of burial.

Now go to the DVD, click on 'Topics', find Topic 1 and complete Part 2 Activity 1.2, which examines the different stages of surveying carried out at the Wetwang site.

When doing an initial survey, it is vital that all data (e.g. observations, descriptions and measurements of the features of interest) are collected and recorded systematically and without bias or any preconceptions of what the data might show. This is possibly one of the most important skills that all archaeologists need to develop: noting down exactly what they find and see, rather than jumping to conclusions about what this may represent. By recording information about an object or feature as it is found in the field, anyone can use this 'raw' data during the project or future investigations without the risk of being misled by incorrect assumptions or interpretations. Only once all of the data for a particular study has been collected should any interpretation of what it means be carried out, with this interpretative work clearly differentiated from the original field observations.

It is important to realise that in reconnaissance surveys the vast majority of techniques are non-destructive and non-invasive (with the exception of geochemical surveying, which removes soil samples, and some field-walking surveys, which may remove finds from the site). In other words, they do not physically destroy, remove or disturb the archaeology. In the rest of this section, you will examine some field-based surveying techniques and consider the type of information each one produces and how this can be used to determine whether a site or feature is worthy of further investigation.

1.2.1 Field walking: systematically walking the line

Start by reading *Greene* Chapter 2, Section 2.2 (pp. 55–7); as you read, make notes on the following key points:

- the main purpose of field walking
- how it is done
- what is done when a find is made
- how field-walking surveys are used on very large sites
- why scattered finds or the lack of finds does not necessarily mean there was no occupation in the past.

Field walking is commonly used when looking for evidence of past human activity or occupation (e.g. when looking for new, unknown archaeological sites). Typical finds discovered on the ground surface include shards of ceramics, pottery and worked stone, although metal finds including solitary or scattered collections of coins, bone fragments and evidence of hearths (from baked rocks) can also be found. Changes in the topography of a field and/or variations in the soil texture, colour or drainage can also be used to identify the potential location of archaeological features (e.g. buried walls, foundations or ancient drainage ditches).

Question 1.4

Using the additional information below, which of the four case studies is suitable for a field-walking survey?

- **Tell es-Sa'idiyeh**: a large site (~13 ha) in the centre of the Jordan valley. The valley had been used for agriculture throughout the 20th century, and is currently occupied by numerous agricultural poly-tunnels and rapidly growing urban developments.

- **Hungate**: an urban site (~4.5 ha) that was a tarmac-covered car park before the start of excavation. As the excavation proceeds, each successive layer will be stripped away to reveal a new surface.

- **Wetwang**: a small grassy site at the end of a village in which the topsoil was removed at the start of construction revealing a more compacted soil layer surrounded by a filled ditch.

- **Tell es-Sa'idiyeh cemetery**: a densely packed area measuring ~120 m^2, containing hundreds of graves dug into underlying pre-existing building foundations and floors. Some graves contain several occupants, and many individuals were buried with the entire or upper part of their body in a large clay pot.

Part 2 Activity 1.3   Devising a systematic sampling technique

(The estimated time needed to complete this activity is 20 minutes.)

Main learning outcomes developed: KU1, CS3 and KS1.

Now go to the DVD, click on 'Topics', find Topic 1 and complete Part 2 Activity 1.3, in which you will discover how different systematic sampling approaches are used in field walking.

1.2.2   Remote sensing from the air: aerial surveys

Remote sensing means any reconnaissance method that is used at a distance to locate and study archaeological features. This includes the use of aerial (and satellite) images to look for features on the Earth's surface, ground-penetrating geophysical techniques to find objects or structures buried below the surface and airborne geochemical sampling techniques.

The main aerial surveying techniques include: vertical and oblique aerial photography, which can be used to identify large features not visible from the ground, including shadow sites, crop marks and soil marks; multispectral and thermal prospecting; and photogrammetry.

Aerial photography and photogrammetry

Read *Greene* Chapter 2, Section 3.1 (pp. 62–7), up to 'Multispectral and thermal prospecting', followed by the short sections 'Photogrammetry' and 'Interpretation of aerial images' (pp. 68–9). As you read, make notes on the following key points:

- how optical aerial photography helps in archaeological fieldwork (there are two key points to note here)
- how high altitude and low altitude vertical images are used
- the range of information (relating to the physical environment, time of year and possible interference from weather) that needs to be considered before carrying out aerial reconnaissance
- how aerial photography can supplement observations of visible and invisible sites on the Earth's surface and how shadow sites, crop marks and soil marks form, as well as what can influence how clearly they appear on photographs
- how photogrammetry is used to convert oblique photographs into maps.

There is further information about vertical and oblique aerial photography, along with how crop and soil marks form, under 'Photogrammetry' in the 'Techniques' section on the DVD, which you should refer to now.

At Tell es-Saʿidiyeh, the archaeologists used low altitude aerial photography by attaching a remotely operable video camera to a long pole on the site. This provided oblique (i.e. angled) views across the site, along with a 'bird's eye view' of the excavations.

Question 1.5

Compare the oblique photograph of part of the site at Tell es-Saʿidiyeh (Figure 1.4a) with a copy of the field map (Figure 1.4b). What do you notice about the shape of features and the apparent distances between identifiable features?

This question illustrates one of the problems of using oblique photographs to create ground maps. Although a mixture of geometry and trigonometry can be used to correct for obliquity in the photographs, you will be pleased to know you won't be asked to do this here!

(a)

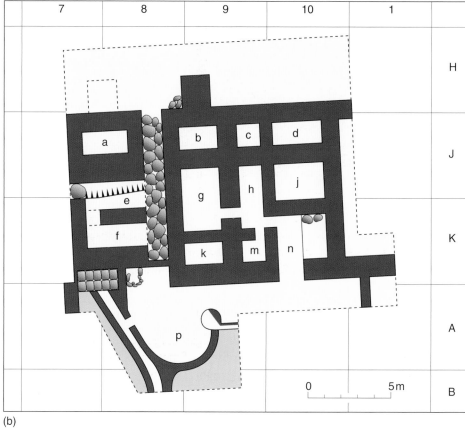

(b)

Figure 1.4 (a) Oblique photograph of part of the excavations at Tell es-Saʿidiyeh. (b) Vertical map of the same area constructed by ground surveying.

Multispectral and thermal prospecting

Light can be divided into three main types (Figure 1.5): (a) visible light, also known as the visible or coloured spectrum, which ranges from red to violet (i.e. the rainbow colours), and combines to form white light, all of which can be detected by the human eye; (b) ultraviolet (UV) light and (c) infrared (IR) light. Neither (b) nor (c) are visible to humans without the aid of special sensors; together (a), (b) and (c) form part of the electromagnetic spectrum. All three types of light are characterised by different measurable wavelengths. By filtering images so that they only record certain wavelengths (or wavebands), it is possible to emphasise different types of features that are either not visible to the unaided eye or are masked by the full range of light.

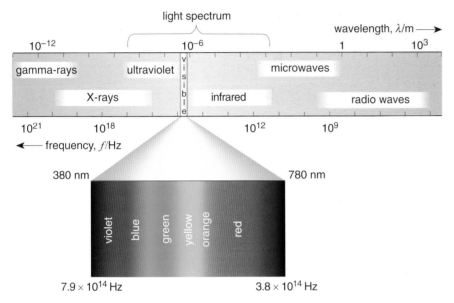

Figure 1.5   Schematic diagram of the electromagnetic spectrum from gamma to radio waves, which includes the light spectrum (ultraviolet to infrared), showing the relative wavelengths for all parts of the spectrum.

Now read the short section 'Multispectral and thermal prospecting' in *Greene* Chapter 2, Section 3.1 (pp. 67–8), making notes on how multispectral scanners work, the types of features they can be used to investigate, and the type of environment that is best suited for this surveying technique.

1.2.3   Remote sensing from the ground – geophysical surveys

Unlike the geophysical surveys used to investigate large geological structures located deep within the Earth (at depths of tens of metres to thousands of kilometres), at most archaeological sites geophysical surveys are used to investigate relatively small structures located in the top few metres of the ground. These structures are found by looking for physical changes in the soil, which produce detectable magnetic, electrical or electromagnetic anomalies (where an anomaly is simply something that is different from what is expected).

To be able to detect such anomalies, the equipment needs to be sensitive enough to enable small changes within a restricted depth range to be detected, but must also be of a high enough resolution to allow the operator to distinguish between archaeological features and natural disturbances (e.g. roots, natural cobbles and boulders). This is a difficult task and not always one that is possible. In practice, this means that the equipment must be physically small and portable to allow distinct readings to be taken over relatively short distances (e.g. on the scale of tens of centimetres rather than several metres).

The most common geophysical techniques used in archaeology include electrical resistivity (which measures how easily an electrical current can pass through the ground), magnetometry (which examines variations in the magnetism in the ground), metal detection (which relies on the induction properties of objects causing a disturbance to the magnetic field of the detector and so set off a sensor; Figure 1.6), and ground-penetrating radar (GPR, which sends pulses of microwaves through the ground and measures the reflections that come back; Figure 1.7). These techniques are described in the 'Techniques' section on the DVD, which you should work through now before reading *Greene* Chapter 2, Section 3.2 (pp. 69–76), up to the section 'Underwater location devices'. As you read pp. 69–76 of *Greene*, make notes on the following points:

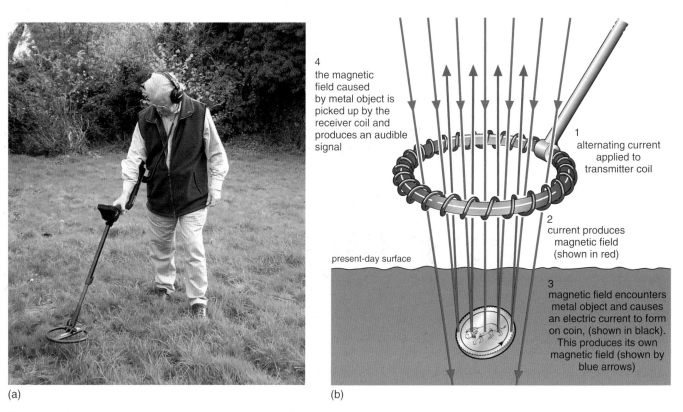

Figure 1.6   (a) A metal detectorist surveying a site; (b) schematic diagram showing how objects are located using a metal detector. (There is a full explanation in the 'Techniques' section on the DVD.)

- why geophysical (and geochemical) surveying is used in addition to oblique photography and field-walking surveys before starting an excavation
- the main purpose of geophysical surveying
- what operators need to know before carrying out a survey (and why this is important)
- the type of measurements taken and how these are compared with the survey grid
- the different ways of presenting the results
- how resistivity works (e.g. what is being measured and the type of objects that cause resistance)
- the equipment needed and how this is arranged to take readings
- the features that resistivity is most suited to measure.

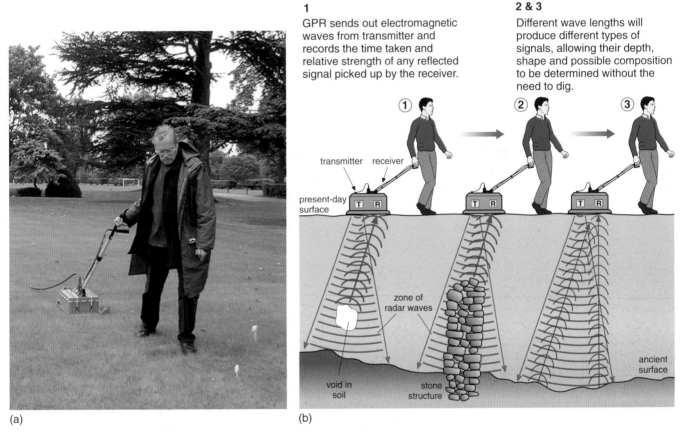

1
GPR sends out electromagnetic waves from transmitter and records the time taken and relative strength of any reflected signal picked up by the receiver.

2 & 3
Different wave lengths will produce different types of signals, allowing their depth, shape and possible composition to be determined without the need to dig.

(a)

(b)

Figure 1.7   (a) Carrying out a survey by ground-penetrating radar (GPR); (b) schematic diagram showing how GPR works. (A full explanation can be found in the 'Techniques' section on the DVD.)

Magnetometry and metal detection

Magnetic surveying is perhaps the most commonly used geophysical technique in archaeology. It works by looking for local variations in the Earth's magnetic field (Figure 1.6). You may think this technique is only suitable for detecting metal objects that contain iron and are therefore magnetic. In reality, many other archaeological objects and materials can be detected by this method (e.g. pits and ditches filled with different material from the surrounding soil, fired clay and ceramics, ancient hearths). This is because variations in the *magnetic susceptibility* of these objects and features can be detected: in other words, by disturbing or heating the objects and features, they have taken on a distinctive magnetic polarity, the impact of which causes the local magnetic field to rise or dip accordingly). Where an area is devoid of highly magnetic materials, subtle changes caused by the presence of decaying organic material can also be detected by a magnetometer.

■ What could prevent magnetic readings being obtained from archaeological structures or features?

☐ Magnetometers detect any changes in the local magnetic field so, if the operator is wearing something containing iron, this will cause a local disturbance and affect their readings! Power cables will also show on a survey (as the electricity creates a magnetic field around the cables), with the density of cables in some urban areas preventing the subtle variations produced by archaeological features from being seen. Likewise, the local geology can affect whether a magnetic survey can be used, as certain types of igneous rocks rich in iron, will swamp minor fluctuations produced by the archaeology.

The most basic type of metal detector can be thought of as a mini-magnetometer. It works by producing a current which forms a magnetic field around the base of the detector, the strength of which is directly proportional to the size of the current (Figure 1.6b). As the detector is moved across the ground, any metal object that enters its magnetic field causes a disturbance, which generally triggers an audible alarm, alerting the detectorist to the presence of something metal (or containing metal). Although metal detection is popular with many amateur as well as professional archaeologists, it is important to note that in certain countries (e.g. Northern Ireland, France and Sweden) and on certain types of ground (e.g. historical sites in Scotland), it is illegal to use metal detectors without a licence.

Now read the sections in *Greene* 'Magnetic surveying' and 'Metal detectors' (pp. 74–5), and make notes on:

- why heating objects, and digging and refilling ditches, alters their magnetic reading
- the different types of magnetometers and the range of equipment (and people) needed to take readings
- what the changes in magnetic susceptibility of a localised area can indicate.

Ground-penetrating radar

Read *Greene*, p. 75 'Ground penetrating radar (GPR)'.

GPR works by emitting electromagnetic pulses into the ground and analysing the types of reflections that are returned to the sensor and is particularly good for locating voids as well as solid features in the ground (Figure 1.7).

■ The Wetwang grave contained several voids left by the decayed wood, so why did the archaeologists on this site not use GPR?

☐ The simple answer is that this technique was not readily available to archaeologists in 2001.

This is a good example of why it can be useful to leave some sites and features unexcavated if they are not at risk from destruction (unlike the case of Wetwang), as the development of new techniques in the future may allow more detailed information to be extracted from sites than is available using current techniques. It also illustrates how quickly technology and the availability of different techniques are changing. Another aspect of reconnaissance surveying that is changing rapidly is the use of global information systems (GIS), in which information and data from a range of different sources are combined to form a three-dimensional overview, allowing scientists to investigate how historic and current land-use relate to a range of natural features. GIS is not covered in this course; however, if you would like to know more about it, read *Greene* Chapter 2, Sections 4 and 5 (pp. 77–84).

To complete this review of the more common surveying techniques, read *Greene*, 'Seismic prospecting and geochemical examination of soil' (pp. 75–6) and Section 6 (p. 84).

Part 2 Activity 1.4   Surveying the case study sites

(The estimated time needed to complete this activity is 20 minutes.)

Main learning outcomes developed: KU2, KS2 and KS3.

In this activity, you will use your notes from the introductory films in Part 2 Activity 1.1, as well as extract information from the 'Case Study' descriptions on the DVD about the different surveying techniques used at the three main field sites.

(a) Complete Table 1.4, which summarises the range of surveying techniques used at the three field sites, noting the specific type of technique used in each case (e.g. low altitude photography would be recorded under aerial survey; magnetometry under geophysical survey; if no related techniques were used, write 'not used').

Table 1.4 Summary of surveying techniques used at the case study sites. *(Use the blank version of Table 1.4 in the back of the Study Guide, to complete your answer to Part 2 Activity 1.4.)*

	Field-walking survey	**Aerial survey**	**Geophysical survey**
Tell es-Saʿidiyeh			
Hungate			
Wetwang			

(b) Using your knowledge of each surveying technique described in this section (and referring back to your notes and the case study summaries), briefly state why the archaeologists chose to use the geophysical technique(s) they did at each site, but rejected others. (Your answer should be one or two sentences for each site.)

1.3   Planning an archaeological project

Ultimately, excavation is a destructive and irreversible process so, before starting a dig, it is vital to devise a project plan stating the exact type of work to be done, where it will be done, what techniques will be used, how the data and any finds will be recorded and conserved as the project proceeds, as well as what will be done with the data and finds at the end of the excavation phase of the project. Similarly, before the project plan can be devised, the archaeologist needs to have an understanding of what the site is like and hence which surveying techniques are best suited to the terrain and the types of finds and features likely to be discovered. They also need to think about what can be achieved based on the likely staffing, funding and duration of the project.

From this description, you will hopefully have realised that a reconnaissance survey is required, followed by a planning stage, before moving on to the excavation. In the excavation stage, further surveys must be carried out, alongside adjustments to the project plans if unexpected finds or features are discovered or if there are significant logistical changes such as the need for specialist staff, different surveying or excavation techniques, less or more funding, etc.

■ Refer back to the introductory films for the case studies (in Part 2 Activity 1.1) and compare the sequence of events at Tell es-Saʿidiyeh and Hungate, with that at Wetwang. Is this sequence of events (reconnaissance–planning–excavation) always true for all archaeological sites?

☐ Both Tell es-Saʿidiyeh and Hungate were known to be sites of archaeological interest before work started. At both digs, the projects began with a comprehensive desktop survey using information from previous digs (at Tell es-Saʿidiyeh) and historical documents (Hungate), which were used to inform the aims of the project and its planning stage, leading to requests for permission and funding to dig over extended time periods (11 years at Tell es-Saʿidiyeh and 6 years at Hungate). Once the preliminary desktop survey and planning stages were completed, ground surveys were carried out, allowing the excavations to begin.

Although archaeologists were working at Wetwang when the grave was discovered, they did not expect to uncover such a feature, so an immediate response was needed to ensure the remains could be recovered as quickly as possible before they were damaged. As the time and resources available to work on this discovery were limited, an initial ground survey was done rapidly and an emergency plan of action drawn up to enable the excavation to start as soon as possible.

So, although the sequence of events at all three sites is similar, there were differences in terms of the amount of prior knowledge gathered about each site, the ability to carry out a preliminary desktop survey and the amount of time (and resources) available to complete the dig.

Now read *Greene* Chapter 3, Section 3.1 (pp. 99–100), paying particular attention to the ethical issues that archaeologists need to consider when excavating a site, before attempting the following questions on the Institute of Field Archaeologists' (IFA) Code of Conduct (*Greene*, Table 3.1, p. 100).

Question 1.6

Table 3.1 (*Greene*, p. 100) sets out the five principles of the IFA code of conduct (used by most professional UK archaeologists), along with a selection of rules used to explain each principle.

You can access the full code of conduct via the 'Documents' section on the course website.

Read each of the five principles in turn (the key points of which are summarised in Table 1.5 below), before identifying the main points from each rule. Principle 1 is completed for you as an example.

Table 1.5 Summary of the key points of the five principles of the IFA's Code of Conduct and the main points extracted from the associated rules. *(Use the blank version of Table 1.5 in the back of the Study Guide, to complete your answer to Question 1.6.)*

Principle	Key points	**Main points from rules:** *All archaeologists should …*
1	Standards of ethical and responsible behaviour	1.2: present results responsibly; avoid exaggerating results or making misleading statements 1.4: not do work they are not qualified for
2	Responsible for conservation	
3	Reliable information and results can be collected and recorded	
4	Results will be made available to others	
5	Safe employment conditions and the chance for ongoing development	-

Now read *Greene* Chapter 3, Section 3.2 (pp. 101–4), paying particular attention to the following key points while thinking how they relate to the three case studies.

- Why it is not acceptable to excavate every archaeological site discovered around the world.
- How aerial and geophysical remote-sensing techniques have helped archaeological investigations.
- The issues surrounding excavations in densely populated areas and the potential conflicts that can arise, based on who is funding the work.
- The guidance issued by government bodies to help determine whether a site should or should not be excavated (and the three stages devised by English Heritage).
- Ethical issues about how 'general sites' and 'unique sites' are dealt with by different organisations and governmental bodies, and the type of archaeological information both can provide about a historical period or population.
- The four types of archaeological investigation.

As you go on to read *Greene* Chapter 3, Section 3.3 (pp. 104–5), bear the following additional points in mind:

- The legislative policy PPG 16 Archaeology and Planning and the associated policy, PPG 15 Planning and the Historic Environment, are only relevant to archaeological sites in England.
- The equivalent planning policies in Scotland are the National Planning Policy Guideline 5 (NPPG 5) and Planning Advice Note (PAN) 42 Archaeology – the planning process and scheduled monument procedures (Scotland).

- Sites in Wales are covered by the Planning Policy Wales and Welsh Office Circular 60/96 Planning and the Historic Environment: Archaeology (Wales).

- In Northern Ireland, archaeological sites and historic monuments are protected by a series of Planning Policy Statements (PPS), in particular PPS 6 *Planning, Archaeology and the Built Heritage*. In the Republic of Ireland, the National Monuments Act 2000 and the Planning Act 2000 are used by the Heritage Council to develop the guidelines *Archaeology and Development: guidelines for good practice for developers*.

See the 'Documents' section on the course website for links to these planning policy documents.

As you read this section of *Greene*, note how this approach can help to preserve archaeological sites for future investigations and in turn, how it relates to the four types of archaeological investigation listed in *Greene* Section 3.2 (pp. 101–4). You should also consider the restraints this policy guidance places on the types of sites that are now typically excavated (e.g. think back to the example of site selection from 20 Roman sites described in *Greene*, Chapter 3, Section 3.2 (p. 101)).

Now move on and read *Greene* Chapter 3, Section 3.4 (pp. 105–7) and Chapter 2, Section 2.4 (pp. 60–1), making notes on:

- the type of information that can be usefully gathered as part of a desktop survey and how this can direct the landscape survey

- the type of information and techniques that can be used to investigate features on and below the Earth's surface

- the legal and logistical issues that need to be resolved before starting a dig

- how the staffing needs and types of data collected may change during a dig

- the type of information that is stored on the database of the Sites and Monuments Records (SMR), and how it can be used as part of the planning process for different archaeological projects.

Note: the SMR, which was only relevant to England, was replaced by the Historic Environment Record (HER) in 2003, and applies to historic sites in England, Scotland and Wales. Northern Ireland and the Republic of Ireland maintain their own SMR databases.

Part 2 Activity 1.5   Planning a dig: the case for Hungate, Wetwang and Tell es-Saʿidiyeh

(The estimated time needed to complete this activity is 30 minutes.)

Main learning outcomes developed: KU4, CS3 and PS1.

In this activity, you will review some of the key stages and people involved in planning the Hungate Dig, before comparing and contrasting this information with how the Wetwang and Tell es-Saʿidiyeh projects were planned.

Now go to the DVD, click on 'Topics', find Topic 1 and complete Part 2 Activity 1.5.

1.4   Excavating an archaeological site

There is no avoiding the fact that the excavation stage of an archaeological project is the part that has most 'public appeal' and raises general interest in the subject as a whole. It is unlikely that the UK's television programme *Time Team* would continue to attract viewing figures in the millions if the programmes focused on desktop surveys rather than geophysical surveys and site excavations! However, it is equally important to remember that every archaeological excavation effectively destroys the very area it is investigating (once the soil is disturbed, it can never be put back exactly as it was), so solid scientific, social and historical evidence needs to be used to justify why an excavation should take place, rather than a field evaluation or certain types of watching briefs.

■ How does an archaeological excavation differ from a field evaluation or watching brief?

☐ Referring to *Greene* (pp. 103–4), an excavation is used to examine, obtain and interpret archaeological finds and features through a variety of destructive field techniques in which deposits are disturbed and removed from a specified site. A field evaluation assesses a site in terms of the type, quality, extent and significance of archaeological features, while causing minimal disruption and simultaneously comparing its importance with other regional, national and international sites, for future reference. A watching brief is carried out in any building development, where archaeological features could be put at risk of destruction or damage.

The discovery of the square barrow (grave) at Wetwang was the result of a watching brief, carried out as part of the housing development work. As you will see shortly, a watching brief is also carried out every time a layer of deposits is removed from the Hungate site when opening a fresh surface for investigation.

1.4.1   Developing an excavation strategy

The initial surveys have been carried out, the project plan is in place, the logistical issues over staffing, equipment and finances have been resolved, and the ethical arguments about the need to excavate have been discussed and justified, so the excavation is ready to start. But where and how do you start to dig?

There are no set rules about where and how to dig in an archaeological investigation, hence the development of the IFA's Code of Conduct (see the 'Documents' section on the course website) and the need for a well thought-out project plan. How to dig however, can be resolved by referring to the initial (desktop and geophysical) surveys, using this information to pinpoint a place to start, with the exact style and method of digging depending on: the aims and objectives of the project; the type and abundance of finds and features that are expected; the terrain and size of the site; the physical environment (e.g. the likely weather conditions, the soil-type, the amount and type of vegetation); and the time, staffing and equipment available.

Irrespective of the style of excavation, one of the most important concepts to grasp in field archaeology is that the exact horizontal and vertical locations of all finds and features need to be observed, measured and recorded to develop a complete picture of the site. Investigations of a *horizontal plane* will provide information and insight into a specific period of occupation and the spatial relationship between finds, for example: the relative arrangement of different buildings and working areas in a settlement; the floor plan of a house; the road leading into a town; the layout of a grave or a cemetery. In contrast, by studying the *vertical sequence* of deposits, information can be obtained for an extended period of time allowing the *stratigraphic relationship* of the area to be determined, for example: the change in land use of an area; evidence for variations in diet over time extracted from successive layers in a midden; the construction of new buildings on the foundations of older ones; the reuse of graves in a cemetery. By examining the horizontal and the vertical extent of a feature and recording data in both planes, its provenance can be compared with every other find, allowing it to be placed in a geographic as well as a historic context (Figure 1.8).

Figure 1.8   Schematic block diagram indicating how information from the horizontal and vertical planes at an archaeological site are related.

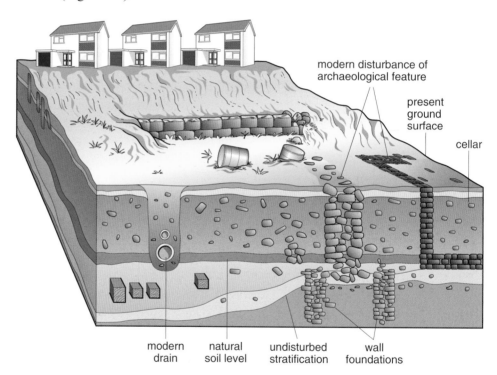

modern disturbance of archaeological feature

present ground surface

cellar

modern drain

natural soil level

undisturbed stratification

wall foundations

Some of the earliest excavations in the late 19th and early 20th centuries unfortunately did more (unintentional) damage than is imaginable, by cutting right through archaeological features to create vertical transects (Figure 1.9) or to simply reach the artefacts believed to be buried in its core. Although these attempts at excavation are now viewed as being crude, without these early pioneers, the science of excavation would not be where it is today. The rest of this section describes the three main excavation methods currently used by archaeologists, each of which has its own benefits and disadvantages, depending on the size and terrain of the site being investigated and the type of features likely to be discovered.

Figure 1.9 Early excavations in the City of Troy, western Turkey, cutting straight through the archaeological site.

Before looking at each excavation technique in detail, start by reading *Greene* Chapter 3, Section 4 (pp. 107–8), which describes the *depositional sequence of events* that occur at a site (referred to as *taphonomy* by Greene) and the importance of setting the results in context. As you read, make notes on:

- the type of observations an archaeologist makes as they proceed with an excavation

- what the terms 'context' and 'unit of stratification' mean

- the type of evidence that can be used to confirm the chosen excavation strategy is appropriate or needs to be changed

- issues of safety in the field.

Greene uses *taphonomy* to describe how an archaeological site has built up over time; this is referred to as the *depositional sequence of events* in this course, while taphonomy is used exclusively to describe how organic remains are buried and become preserved.

The horizontal approach: open area excavation

This is the most common approach to excavation. It involves stripping away complete layers from an archaeological site, allowing the horizontal extent and spatial relationships between finds and structures of the same age to be investigated. In saying this, it is important to realise that deposits rarely form truly horizontal layers. This is because the layers follow older surfaces or the underlying topography of the area, and will slope at points, be of irregular thickness, or disappear entirely in different parts of the site.

An open area excavation does not, however, mean that the whole site is excavated all at once. Depending on the size of the site and the associated logistical issues (e.g. staffing, ease of working, and the time available to do the work), the whole area can be excavated at once, or worked as a series of smaller, open area sites (Figure 1.10). Within each open area excavation, as interesting finds and features are encountered, they are excavated separately with the vertical dimensions accurately measured and recorded by means of a detailed survey, allowing it to be reconstructed in three dimensions at a later stage.

Figure 1.10 Two separate open excavations at Tell es-Saʿidiyeh cemetery.

■ In which of the case studies have you already encountered this horizontal and vertical approach to excavation, to allow the features and stratigraphy of the site to be reconstructed in three dimensions?

☐ The grave at Wetwang was very carefully excavated, with the relative depths of all features (including the skeleton) accurately recorded to allow the structure of the burial to be visualised in three dimensions.

The advantages of this approach are most apparent when complete features need to be excavated or the relative spatial relationship between different features from a single time period are of paramount interest to the investigation. Open area excavation therefore allows a complete view of a specific point in archaeological time. The disadvantages of this approach however, are that when the overlying layers are removed, so are any opportunities to view the vertical stratigraphy of the site to recheck the physical location of units or finds, relative to the others. It is therefore paramount that an accurate and reliable method of detailed surveying and data recording is used, and that this includes an internal checking system so that if errors do creep in, corrections can be applied to the data.

Before doing the next activity, go to the 'Techniques' section on the DVD and work through the background information on 'Levelling, spot heights and reference points'.

Part 2 Activity 1.6   Setting up a reliable grid reference system

(The estimated time needed to complete this activity is 20 minutes.)

Main learning outcomes developed: KU1, KS1 and KS2.

While working on the Iron Age grave at Wetwang, Tony Spence discovered the hard way how good his grid reference system was. After measuring numerous survey points across the excavated grave, a regular spot height check indicated that one of the fixed reference points was no longer where it was supposed to be according to the readings! An error had crept in at some point.

Now go to the DVD, click on 'Topics', find Topic 1 and complete Part 2 Activity 1.6, in which Tony Spence describes how the surveying error was spotted and how the problem was resolved.

Another problem with open area excavation is the need to remove significant amounts of material from the site without damaging the archaeological evidence; so on very large areas, baulks (i.e. unexcavated strips) must be left, to allow access across the excavation area (Figure 1.11). Furthermore, if the site consists of layers with no useful archaeological information (either because there was no occupation of the site at that time, or because agricultural practices and/or natural processes have destroyed the original context in the layer), it is not an effective use of time or resources for the archaeologists to excavate this by hand. Such layers (divided into a series of spit levels) are therefore often removed by mechanical digger.

baulk

baulk

baulk

Figure 1.11   An extended, open area excavation at Tell es-Sa'idiyeh, separated by a series of baulks across the section, allowing ease of access across the site.

■   What can be done to ensure that the mechanical digger only removes the unwanted layer and does not destroy important archaeological information?

☐   A watching brief must be carried out, with the watching brief officer in charge, monitoring progress and checking for the first sight of any archaeological features that will require a more careful approach to be used.

The vertical approach to excavation: opening trenches and test pits

A trench is any linear form of excavation that cuts down through successive layers and, although they can be any shape, most are rectangular (Figure 1.12). Trenches can be used as a rapid investigative tool or for more detailed and prolonged studies. For example, exploratory trenches and test pits (which are 1 m^2 and typically run through the whole soil horizon, down to the bedrock), can offer a quick and effective method of determining the stratigraphy of part of the site, and deciding whether a potentially interesting feature or area identified by geophysical surveys or from historical maps and documents, is worthy of more detailed excavation, without the need to disturb the whole site. Exploratory pits and trenches can also help archaeologists answer intriguing questions they may have about why a particular feature or structure is where it is, such as the origin of the double mound at Tell es-Saʿidiyeh.

Figure 1.12   A trench excavation carried out as part of a *Time Team* investigation in October 2007, at Dungannon, Northern Ireland.

The most effective position to locate a trench is perpendicular to (or across) the feature of interest, as this allows a complete cross-sectional view to be obtained. In the case of buildings or defensive structures, a trench can allow the archaeologist (if they are lucky) to determine which is the inside and which is the outside of the feature – something that is not always easy to establish!

Part 2 Activity 1.7   A tale of two tells

(The estimated time needed to complete this activity is 15 minutes.)

Main learning outcomes developed: KU2, CS1 and CS2.

The site of Tell es-Saʿidiyeh is unusual in that it consists of a large upper tell and a smaller lower tell. However, before excavation, it was not clear why these two areas existed or whether they were related.

Go to the DVD, click on 'Topics', find Topic 1 and complete Part 2 Activity 1.7, to discover how Jonathan Tubb and Rupert Chapman used a trench-excavation approach to resolve this issue.

The major benefit of a trench system therefore, is that it offers a relatively quick mechanism of obtaining potentially useful information about a specific area or feature with minimal disturbance to the context of the rest of the site (or indeed the rest of the feature). As a single exploratory trench can be opened (and closed) within a matter of hours, they are also a cost- and time-effective method of preliminary excavation. One of the disadvantages of a trench system is that it allows access to only a small part of the site or feature, so it is uncertain whether the finds and data obtained are typical of the rest of the site. The shape of the trench is also restrictive and not good for understanding features with a large horizontal extent or variable in form. (One analogy is to think of the trench system as like looking through a keyhole, while an open area excavation gives an 'open door' view.)

The combined approach to excavation: box-grid and sectional systems

The box-grid system was originally devised by British archaeologist Mortimer Wheeler (1890–1976) in the early 20th century, and consisted of a series of square trenches separated by narrow baulks (Figure 1.13a). Although the baulks allowed a comprehensive record of the vertical stratigraphy to be retained throughout the excavation, as well as offering an easy system by which to remove the spoil deposits from the site, they were found to impede preliminary interpretation of the site as a whole. This is an important issue as the continued progress of an excavation relies on being able to interpret the archaeology as it is uncovered to ensure that the context of significant layers and finds is recorded properly. This allows educated decisions to be made about whether to remove a unit to allow the underlying archaeology to be investigated, or whether further horizontal excavations are needed first. To understand the layout of the site and enable the horizontal context of features to be investigated fully, it was necessary to remove some or all of the baulks at the end of the project to create an open area excavation. For these reasons, plus the high costs involved in creating such a system, box-grid systems are no longer widely used.

Figure 1.13 (a) Example of a box-grid system. (b) Sectional excavation of a small round feature at Hungate.

(a)

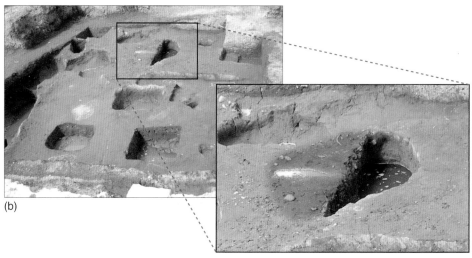
(b)

In contrast to the box-grid system, the sectional system is still used and is particularly useful when excavating round structures (e.g. post-holes, barrows and settlements) (Figure 1.13b). In this case, the site or feature is divided into two or four quadrants and half of it is excavated (with opposite quarters excavated in a quadrant system). In theory, this approach enables enough of the horizontal and vertical structures to be seen to decide whether a full excavation is merited or whether this approach has revealed enough information about the feature to allow it to be interpreted. It also allows sections to be drawn to reveal the stratigraphic sequence of the section being excavated.

Part 2 Activity 1.8 Digging Hungate through sectioning, test pits, trenches and open area excavation

(The estimated time needed to complete this activity is 20 minutes.)

Main learning outcomes developed: KU1, CS1 and CS3.

As excavations are ongoing at Hungate, you should check the 'Dig Hungate update' section on the course website regularly for the latest examples of trench, open area and sectional excavations across the site. Meanwhile, go to the DVD, click on 'Topics', find Topic 1 and complete Part 2 Activity 1.8, in which you will watch a series of short training films on setting out a trench and using different surveying and excavation techniques on site.

Question 1.7

Safety is paramount when working on an archaeological site and in particular when working in a trench.

(a) List the different precautions taken at a site such as Hungate to ensure all of the archaeologists can work safely within and around the multitude of trenches on site.

(b) Although most trenches are less than 2 metres deep, Trench 3 in Block H at Hungate was considerably deeper. What mechanism did the archaeologists use to ensure its sides did not collapse?

1.4.2   Unravelling the stratigraphy of a site

Tools of the trade

The mechanism for physically opening an excavation depends on several factors including the size of the site, the type of soil being worked and the abundance and type of archaeological features and finds found. In general, the topsoil is removed by a mechanical digger (e.g. at Hungate) or by hand (e.g. at Tell es-Sa'idiyeh), and deposited well away from the site to avoid contamination with the archaeologically rich layers below. Once the topsoil has been cleared, the archaeologists can start the more detailed excavations by hand.

■   What types of tools does an archaeologist need for an excavation?

☐   The most obvious tools that you might have thought of include: various sized trowels for removing soil deposits and to collect samples for environmental analysis; buckets and wheelbarrows to remove the soil from the site; variably sized sealable bags and containers to collect samples; marker pens to write on each sample bag; different sized picks to dig out large features and break up large resistant layers; a (mason's pointing) trowel for scraping off layers of soil, breaking smaller resistant patches of material or gently scraping between small features; variously sized brushes (e.g. large hand brushes down to paint brushes) to sweep loose dry material off a surface or feature; dental tools or spatulas to excavate around fragile finds such as pottery, metal and bones; a tape measure; string and a spirit level for marking off features of interest; a variety of scale bars to use in photographs and field sketches; a GPR, magnetometer and/or metal detector to check the areas for potential finds and disturbed areas as the excavation proceeds; a laptop, PDA (personal digital assistant) or, at the very least, a field notebook and some recording sheets to log the data; and so on!

As each layer is excavated, in addition to the range of observational information that needs to be recorded, any soil samples or finds that are removed from each unit need to be numbered and measured so that they can be put into their geographic and historic contexts (Box 1.2).

Box 1.2 Understanding the rules of stratigraphy

■ What is the difference between the depositional sequence of events and stratigraphy in an archaeological section?

☐ The depositional sequence of events describes the series of actions that caused an archaeological site to develop, whereas stratigraphy refers to the sequence of layers (or deposits) that make up a site, with older deposits lying below more recent ones.

As described in the previous section, an archaeological sequence is not as simple as one horizontal layer being deposited on top of another to form a series of uniform layers (Figure 1.14a). Instead, it consists of a series of overlapping layers, cuts and fills, each of which may represent a distinct context in the history of the site. For example, imagine the scenario of a person in the past digging a post-hole in an archaeological sequence (contexts 1–3, Figure 1.14). Digging the hole (a cut) will result in materials from different contexts (units) being mixed together (Figure 1.14b). The action of digging the hole represents a context (4), as does filling it with the mixed-up materials (5), which now represent a stratigraphically younger unit than the original sequence, the creation of the hole and the post. This new fill forms a sharp (possibly near-vertical) boundary with the older layers, while any surplus material from the hole is dumped elsewhere (to form another context). Over time, the post decays to leave a new hole (another context, 6) (Figure 1.14c) that

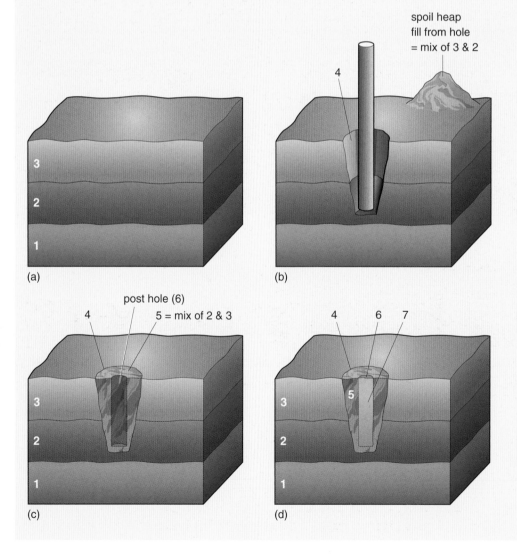

Figure 1.14
(a) Schematic cross-section through a stratigraphic sequence of distinct layers (contexts 1–3). (b) A post-hole has been dug, forming a new cut context (4), into which is placed a post, held in place by a mixture of soil from the hole (forming a fill context (5). (c) Time passes, and the post decays, forming a new hole (and new context, 6), which (d) is subsequently filled by materials from elsewhere (another context, 7).

is filled by more materials or the collapse of surrounding pit walls (7) (Figure 1.14d). From an archaeological perspective, the action of digging the post-hole to form a cut context is as important as the deposition of material in the hole or the mixing of material from the hole and its redeposition as a fill context.

Archaeological sequences therefore consist of a series of distinct layers (or deposits) but, to understand the full depositional sequence of events, the *interfaces* (or boundaries) between cuts, fills and layers need to be taken into account as well.

To help put the different archaeological layers (which can also be called units, deposits or strata) and interfaces into a stratigraphic order, Edward Harris created a new system in the 1970s of visually recording and representing stratigraphic sequences according to the timing of their formation, which he

called the 'Harris Matrix' (see *Greene*, Figure 3.10, p. 97). He also recommended that the term 'unit of stratification' be used to describe any distinct archaeological event or deposit.

Although a full explanation of how a Harris Matrix is constructed is beyond the scope of this course (see the introductory description in the 'Techniques' section on the DVD), it is sufficient to say that this approach allows the full depositional sequence of events of a site to be constructed, with all units of stratigraphy ordered chronologically. The system also allows any number of complex vertical sections from across a site or several sites to be related to each other. This provides a comprehensive overview of the stratigraphic history of events across the whole area, and permits every event to be placed in a relative time frame.

Now work through the section 'Cuts and fills' in the 'Techniques' section on the DVD, before reading *Greene* Chapter 3, Section 2 (pp. 96–9).

Putting it all into an archaeological context

To conclude this section, an important part of understanding a site's stratigraphy is putting everything into a relevant context. This includes recognising *positive contexts* and features (e.g. earthworks, banks and mounds, which have involved the build-up of material at some point) and *negative contexts* and features (e.g. holes, pits and ditches, in which material has been removed, often to create positive features).

Now read *Greene* Chapter 3, Section 4.3 (pp. 119–21) before completing the next activity.

Part 2 Activity 1.9   Putting excavations into an archaeological context

(The estimated time needed to complete both parts of this activity is 15 minutes.)

Main learning outcomes developed: KU2, KU3, CS2 and KS2.

In this activity, you will hear two different accounts of how a combination of surveying, excavation and historical data was used to put the finds from two very different sites into their relative contexts. (You may also want to return to Part 2 Activity 1.7 and review how the small 4 m² exploratory trench between the double mounds at Tell es-Saʿidiyeh helped to put the two mounds into context with each other.)

Now go to the DVD, click on 'Topics', find Topic 1 and complete Part 2 Activity 1.9.

1.5   Saving, sampling and recording the evidence

'**Principle 3:** The archaeologist shall conduct his/her work in such a way that reliable information about the past may be acquired, and shall ensure that the results be properly recorded.'

Institute of Field Archaeologists, 2006[2]

1.5.1   Recording and context sheets

Start by reading *Greene* Chapter 3, Section 5.1 (pp. 132–5), which describes some of the important background as to why archaeologists in the UK typically record all site information on recording and context sheets. As you read, pay particular attention to:

*   why single context recording became the favoured approach for UK archaeologists

*   the reasoning behind the design of pre-printed forms and the type of information logged on them

*   how the relationship between different units (layers) is noted (and how the stratigraphy can be represented in a Harris Matrix)

*   what else recording sheets are used for, besides excavated units.

Recording (or context) sheets provide a mechanism of systematically logging and cross-referencing detailed information about individual contexts that make up a stratigraphic sequence. *You will find examples of completed recording sheets from Hungate in the 'Documents' section on the course website.*

Part 2 Activity 1.10   Completing a recording sheet

(The estimated time needed to complete this activity is 30 minutes.)

Main learning outcomes developed: CS1, CS3, KS2 and KS3.

In this activity, one of the Hungate archaeologists will show you how to fill in a recording sheet, before you complete your own sheet for a feature of interest.

Now go to the DVD, click on 'Topics', find Topic 1 and work through Part 2 Activity 1.10.

1.5.2   Detailed plans, section drawings and photographs

One of the most effective ways of describing different features or finds and their context, is to measure and draw them *in situ* (e.g. in place in the field). Each drawing must have a scale, geographic direction (e.g. location of north) and a key for any patterns or symbols used on the sketch.

---

[2] By-laws of the Institute of Field Archaeologists, *Code of Conduct*, revised edition, October 2006.

Detailed plans

Detailed plans of a site or feature of interest are normally produced by a specialist illustrator who will produce architectural grade drawings to an exact scale (Figure 1.15). On these plans, all features are positioned relative to the main grid reference system and accurately plotted by standard triangulation techniques or GPS. Detailed plans are typically constructed by placing a small wire grid across the feature, carefully measuring each component *in situ* and transferring this at the appropriate scale to the drawing. Detailed plans therefore provide a record of the *horizontal spatial relationship* between different features.

(At this point you may find it useful to refer to 'Creating a plan', 'Wire grids in field surveying' and 'Triangulation' in the 'Techniques' section on the DVD.)

(a)

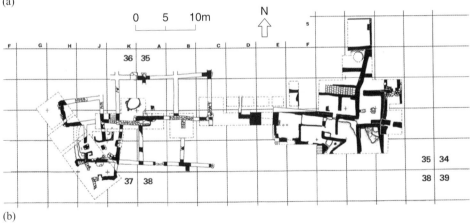

(b)

Figure 1.15   (a) Preparing a detailed plan and (b) the final detailed map of the cemetery at Tell es-Sa'idiyeh.

Section drawings

Section drawings (also known as section profiles) are used to record the *vertical* and *horizontal* features within a sequence, i.e. they are used to show the *relative stratigraphic relationships* between different units. Annotated black-and-white sections are normally drawn to a standard scale (usually 1:10 or 1:20) on graph paper by the excavator or another field archaeologist. They are used to highlight differences in the colour, texture or composition of successive layers, as well as illustrate the relative context of artefacts and features within and between stratigraphic units.

A scale of 1:10 means that 1 'unit of measurement' on the drawing is equivalent to 10 units in the section, where the units can be mm, cm, m, etc. So, at a scale of 1:10, 1 cm on the drawing equals 10 cm in the section.)

Question 1.8

(a) If a scale of 1:20 is used, what does 100 mm on a drawing equal in the section?

(b) A pottery sherd is measured as being 84 mm long and 10 mm thick. What are the dimensions of this feature on a section drawing if it is drawn at a scale of (i) 1:10 and (ii) 1:20? (iii) Which scale is more appropriate in this example?

Before starting a drawing, the section is often cleaned by scraping the vertical surface with a trowel and lightly spraying it with water to improve the visibility and definition of each unit, and to increase colour contrasts. In some instances, colorimetry equipment may also be used to accurately determine colour changes between units. Where different people are involved in doing the excavations and section drawings, or when there is a time gap between these two processes, each unit in the section is labelled with a context number. This can help to ensure all of the units identified during excavation are included on the drawing.

Part 2 Activity 1.11   Constructing a section drawing

(The estimated time needed to complete this activity is 25 minutes.)

Main learning outcomes developed: CS1, KS2 and KS3.

Now go to the DVD, click on 'Topics', find Topic 1 and work through Part 2 Activity 1.11, where you will learn how a section drawing is constructed, before creating your own profile for a trench at Hungate.

Section drawings are also used to represent the complete stratigraphic sequence of a site, in which a series of drawings is compiled into one large cross-section.

Part 2 Activity 1.12   Summarising the site stratigraphy in a section drawing

(The estimated time needed to complete this activity is 15 minutes.)

Main learning outcomes developed: KU3, CS2 and KS2.

In this activity, listen to Rupert Chapman as he talks you through a drawing for a section at Tell es-Sa'idiyeh. As you listen, make notes on how the stratigraphic relationships between different units have been interpreted in this example.

Now go to the DVD, click on 'Topics', find Topic 1 and work through Part 2 Activity 1.12.

Photographs

■ What is the name of the technique in which photographs are used to help construct a site plan? What can affect its accuracy in determining the relative location of different features?

☐ The technique is photogrammetry (see Section 1.2.2 and the 'Techniques' section on the DVD). Unless the photographs are perfectly vertical, the apparent distances between features on the photograph will appear to be greater than they are, requiring these distortions to be corrected mathematically.

In addition to being used to make site plans, photographs provide a useful visual record of finds and features, discovered throughout an archaeological project.

■ What must be included in a photograph to make it scientifically useful?

☐ It should include an appropriate scale bar to allow the size of the feature to be determined.

The photograph must also be numbered appropriately, so that it can be cross-referenced with other information about the find or feature and its original context. Additional information about the orientation of the photograph (e.g. looking northwards) should accompany the image, which can then be added to the recording sheet for the find or feature.

■ What other factors need to be considered that may affect the reliability of the image as a true representation of the feature?

☐ The lighting will affect the range and depth of colours recorded by the photograph (e.g. colours look different on dull versus sunny or rainy days), so some details apparent to the unaided eye may not be visible on the photograph. If the photograph is taken at an angle, some distortion in the relative proportions of the object will occur. The photograph also needs to be taken at an appropriate scale to show the features of interest.

Although digital photography has gone some way to give colour consistency, the other issues highlight why section drawings and sketches are still the main method of visually recording field information.

1.5.3   Collating finds and samples

An important part of any excavation is the identification, sampling and collation of finds, each of which must be given a unique reference number that allows it to be cross-referenced with the rest of the site.

Recovering archaeological finds

Once a find has been discovered, its relative importance needs to be assessed. If it is one of many similar finds (e.g. fragments of medieval pottery recovered from a 14th century AD layer at Hungate), it is classified as a *common find* (or bulk find), and recorded as belonging to a specific archaeological unit (context). It is then grouped with other common finds from that context (Figure 1.16a), before being passed on to the Site Finds Officer.

Figure 1.16   (a) Some of the common finds and (b) a small find of twisted blue Victorian glass, recovered from the Hungate Dig.

(a)

(b)

■ Common finds from a single context can consist of a mixture of objects and materials (e.g. stone, pottery, glass, metal and bone), some of which will be physically competent whereas others will be fragile. What would happen if they were all placed in the same finds tray or container?

☐ More fragile finds could be damaged or destroyed by more robust or heavier ones. Different common finds should therefore be placed in different trays or containers, each of which must be clearly labelled as belonging to the same context.

In contrast to common finds, if the find is rare, unique or unusual for the context from which it was recovered, it is classified as a *small find* (Figure 1.16b) and given a unique reference number with its exact context logged, before being described in detail on a separate finds recording sheet. Before the small find is excavated, it may be sketched and/or photographed *in situ*, both of which will be numbered and logged on the recording sheet.

Sieving and sorting soil samples

In addition to finds that are visible to the unaided eye, finer material on the millimetre to sub-millimetre scale can be recovered from each unit by sorting soil samples. This is done either by sieving a quantity of soil from each unit (Figure 1.17) or by flotation, both of which are sorting techniques. Now go to the 'Techniques' section on the DVD to find out how these techniques work.

In addition to sieving and screening materials, whole soil samples can be collected from sites for environmental analyses. The method of sampling varies depending on the type of site being worked (e.g. different approaches are needed when working on dry, sandy soil compared with peat bogs). All samples must however, be collected in a way that minimises any contamination from the present-day environment, with samples placed in sealable bags or containers, and stored appropriately before being sent for analysis in a specialist laboratory.

Figure 1.17   Soil sampling at Hungate.

■   Why is contamination a problem when collecting soil samples?

☐   Environmental scientists are interested in separating macroscopic (large) to microscopic fragments (e.g. wood, charcoal, soot, seeds, hair and insect remains) from the soil to determine the original environmental conditions at the time of deposition (e.g. how cold, warm, wet or dry it was; what type and relative abundance of plants were present). As all of these fragments can be readily transported by animals, birds, wind and water if the sample is taken from an exposed part of the unit or left out in the open, present-day equivalent fragments will start to collect on its surface, contaminating the original evidence (Box 1.3).

Box 1.3 Using pollen to unravel past environmental conditions

In addition to the evidence described above, pollen analyses are also used to investigate past environmental conditions, with pollen samples generally collected by coring soils to prevent the possibility of present-day contamination. Pollen studies do however have two major drawbacks. Firstly, pollen only survives in acid soils and can be transported long distances by water, wind and animals, so may not reflect the local environmental conditions. Secondly, different trees, shrubs and plants produce different amounts of pollen, so the abundance of different pollen types in a sample may not be representative of the relative abundance of different plant types and hence the past environmental conditions.

Now read *Greene* Chapter 4, Section 4.4 (pp. 155–6) and the subsection 'Pollen and phytoliths' in Chapter 5, Section 5.1 (pp. 191–3) to find out how pollen can be used successfully to investigate past environmental conditions.

The role of the Site Finds Officer and emergency conservation

In addition to the Project Director, specialist archaeological and scientific staff, and general field assistants and workers, many sites will also have a Site Finds Officer, whose job is to ensure all finds are appropriately cleaned, labelled, bagged and logged on the finds database. Common finds from a single context are cleaned, sorted and frequently bagged under one reference number, while more distinctive small finds are logged separately, and given a unique reference number, linking them back to the exact location of recovery. Each find must

Figure 1.18 Working in the finds repository at Hungate.

be assessed in terms of its current preservation state and the likelihood of whether it will decay or degrade in storage. If this is the case, the Site Finds Officer, in association with on-site conservators (where present), need to ensure the find has the correct type and level of emergency conservation, so that its present physical state is maintained. Once all finds are logged, they must be boxed up, numbered and placed in either temporary storage on-site or permanent storage off-site, where they will stay until needed for post-excavation research. Determining the correct storage conditions for the multitude of finds recovered in different states of decay presents yet another significant challenge that the Site Finds Officer needs to resolve! (Figure 1.18)

Part 2 Activity 1.13   The role of the Site Finds Officer

(The estimated time needed to complete this activity is 20 minutes.)

Main learning outcomes developed: KU4, KS3 and PS1.

You have had a quick insight into some of the work carried out by the Site Finds Officer. Now go to the DVD, click on 'Topics', find Topic 1 and complete Part 2 Activity 1.13, to gain a better understanding of this role.

As you listen to Geoff Krause, the Site Finds Officer at Hungate talk about his role, make notes on:

*   how the finds are passed on from the field
*   who works in the finds repository
*   how different types of finds are initially sorted and classified
*   the range of cleaning processes for different types of finds
*   the decisions involved in sending a find for emergency conservation or further investigation
*   bagging, logging and storing finds.

1.5.4   After the dig: closing the site and publishing the results

As part of the planning process, decisions about what happens to a site at the end of the excavation should have been made. These will depend on the original reasons for the project, the features uncovered, the archaeological importance of the site, and any future planned land use.

Question 1.9

What has happened to the sites at Tell es-Saʿidiyeh and Wetwang since their excavations ended? What is the intended land use for the Hungate site once excavation ends in 2012?

Completing the excavation stage of a project does not mark the end of the work on a site as, in accordance with principle 4 of the IFA's Code of Conduct: 'The archaeologist has responsibility for making available the results of archaeological work with reasonable dispatch.'

Now read *Greene* Chapter 3, Section 5.2 (pp. 135–8), which outlines how data is commonly recorded during a project, and how this facilitates rapid dissemination and publication of the results. As you read, pay particular attention to:

- the use of digital equipment and systems to record and store information
- how the style of site reports has been changed to make them more accessible to non-specialists
- the advantages and disadvantages of making all of the data obtained during an excavation publicly accessible online and only publishing a short summary statement of the site.

1.6 Summary of Topic 1

By completing this topic you should now be able to:

1 Use the appropriate terminology correctly (e.g. archaeological landscape, project, site, context, feature, artefacts and remains), when describing different aspects of field archaeology (KS3).

2 Give examples of the different scales at which archaeologists work, and be able to convert measurements of length and area from one scale to another (KS1).

3 Explain, with examples, the difference between non-destructive and destructive field techniques (KU1).

4 Outline some of the ethical and logistical reasons why a full-scale excavation is not appropriate at all archaeological sites (PS1).

5 Describe the survey processes and most common surveying techniques used when evaluating the archaeological potential of an area of interest (KU1, CS1).

6 Explain how magnetometers, metal detectors, GPR and resistivity meters detect archaeological features, and what can affect the reliability of data collected (KU1, CS2).

7 List the processes involved in planning an archaeological project, give examples of some of the main legislative policies that protect archaeological sites in the UK and Ireland, and briefly describe the IFA code of conduct adhered to by many UK-based professional archaeologists (KU2, CS3).

8 Explain why it is important to record the horizontal and vertical context in an excavation and describe the four different excavation methods commonly used to do this (KU1, KS2).

9   Describe and show how context sheets and section (plan) drawings are used to record information on site, and why it is important to accurately measure and describe what can be seen, rather than combining this with interpretive comments (KU1, KS2).

10 Describe the role of the Site Finds Officer in collating all data and finds on site, for ease of access and use during an excavation and the post-excavation work (KU4).

Remember, only the most important one or two learning outcomes are listed after each summary statement above, to emphasise the ones they are specifically addressing. Each summary statement does however, relate to several of the learning outcomes developed in this course, and you should bear this in mind when reviewing the topic and working towards your End of Course Assessment (ECA).

Topic 2
From bog bodies, skeletons and mummies to forensic archaeology

2.1   Introduction

The discovery of human remains is one aspect of archaeology that consistently attracts much attention, but why? Archaeological human remains provide a brief, but real glimpse of the past and enable us to understand what our distant ancestors were like. They also offer a tangible link with past societies and cultures, including an insight into the level of care provided to individuals during life and death, and give associated artefacts a sense of belonging. In other words, the discovery of archaeological human remains helps us understand where our ancestors came from and how they lived.

The most common human remains discovered by archaeologists are bones. If a body is carefully buried, the bones can stay articulated (i.e. in life position) to form a complete skeleton. Fragments of disarticulated and burned bones are frequently discovered from cremations relating to mortuary rites or post-burial disturbance. In exceptional circumstances, more complete bodies can be preserved naturally (e.g. in waterlogged sediments or by glacial ice) or as the result of deliberate embalming and mummification. These bodies are important because the preservation of skin, hair and more rarely, stomach contents provide a level of insight that cannot be obtained from just skeletal remains.

Using different investigative methods at the macroscopic, microscopic and molecular levels, archaeologists can extract a wealth of information from different types of human remains. This includes the sex, height, weight, state of health at time of death, and biological age (i.e. an estimation of the *relative* age at time of death, categorised as infant, child, adolescent, adult or old age, and obtained by studying bones or teeth) of the person or people represented. This can be achieved using observational and imaging techniques (i.e. non-destructive and non-invasive techniques) and/or various destructive techniques, including tissue sampling and biochemical analyses, with the methods depending on the physical and chemical state of the remains, and the reason for the study. In addition, it is sometimes possible to gain information about the time-of-year of death, what was done to the remains at this time, the living conditions and the environment the person inhabited, and how long ago the death occurred, from other associated evidence such as pollen or soil samples collected directly from or alongside the remains. When remains for a large number of individuals are recovered from one area (either from the same time period or extending over a definable period of time), a broader picture of the social and cultural environments can be determined, providing a better insight into the population dynamics over time.

Macroscopic objects are visible to the unaided eye. Objects on the microscopic scale must be viewed with imaging equipment, while on the molecular scale, investigations are done chemically.

Throughout this course, the terms 'find' and 'artefact' are used interchangeably to refer to any portable object in the archaeological record that has been manufactured or modified by humans. Meanwhile, the term 'remains' is used to describe all natural organic portable objects from the archaeological record, with the type of remains usually indicated (e.g. human remains, plant remains, animal remains, environmental remains).

As you work through this topic, you will investigate four key themes:

1 why the physical and the chemical state of human remains differ depending on the environment of preservation

2 how the biological age, sex, stature and state of health of individuals can be established (and how this can be used in certain circumstances to gain an insight into population dynamics)

3 the cultural inferences that can be made from the mode and method of burial

4 key ethical considerations that must be considered when working with human remains.

You will do this by investigating a variety of case studies (which are in this book, on the DVD in the 'Topics' section, under Topic 2, and in the 'Activities' section on the course website). Arranged by archaeological age, the Topic 2 case studies include:

- **Krapina Neanderthal bones:** between 1899 and 1904, over 800 human bone fragments (dating from ~130 000 years BP) were discovered in a cave in northern Croatia, the majority of which are broken and have cut marks made by stone tools. A debate has arisen about whether these represent cannibalistic or mortuary practices.

- **Lapedo Child:** discovered in 2001 in the picturesque region of Lagar Velho, in the Lapedo Valley, central Portugal, the 24500-year-old skeleton of a young child has contributed to changes in current theories about the relationships between Neanderthal and modern humans.

- **Tell es-Saʿidiyeh cemetery:** located on the lower of two mounds (tells), excavations within the cemetery have recovered skeletal remains from over 400 individuals in single and multiple occupancy graves, with one of the most fascinating aspects being the different styles in which some individuals were buried.

- **Nesperennub:** an Egyptian mummy from Luxor, dating back to ~800 BC, Nesperennub was discovered in the 1890s and was sent to the British Museum in 1899, intact inside his mummy wrappings and outer casing, in which he still resides.

- **Wetwang Woman:** in 2001, while carrying out an archaeological survey as part of the standard planning process during the construction stage of some new houses in East Yorkshire, an important Iron Age square barrow was discovered. This contained the skeleton of a woman dating to ~300–200 BC, who had been carefully buried beneath her cart.

- **Lindow Man:** in 1984, a prehistoric body was recovered from the Lindow Moss bog, near Manchester, northwest England. Named 'Lindow Man', he dates to between AD 20 and 90, and provides an intriguing insight into Iron Age Britain.

- **Hungate cemetery:** one objective of the Hungate Dig is to find the medieval cemetery that occupied part of the site; the problem is that its exact location is unknown.

- **Llullaillaco** (pronounced '*you-yeh-yako*') **mountain children:** discovered in 1999, these three 500-year-old, frozen mummies were recovered from the summit of Llullaillaco volcano in the High Andes, northwest Argentina. They give a unique insight into some of the past cultures and practices of the Inca people.

As you work through this topic, you will test your understanding of a variety of scientific and ethical issues by completing a series of associated activities. You will also develop a range of academic literacy skills (Box 2.1), including working with scientific papers, summarising and extracting information and recognising why different styles of writing (e.g. technical, academic and popular) are used in distinct contexts. You are also likely to encounter various biological and chemical terms, processes and techniques that are new to you. These are presented on a 'need to know' basis, with terms and processes described in this book and the Glossary (which is in the 'Course Resources' section on the course website and on the DVD), while the investigative techniques are described in the 'Techniques' section on the DVD.

Box 2.1   Scanning and skim reading

One of the best ways to learn is by *active reading*; this is where you systematically work through the text, pausing to make notes, answering questions, and reviewing what you have learned, to help you make good academic progress. Two other very useful reading approaches include scanning and skim reading.

- Scanning is a useful approach to use before studying something in detail. It involves looking over a section of text (in a book or online) quickly but carefully, looking at the subheadings, key words, diagrams and tables, to get an overview of what it covers. You should scan all text before using active reading approaches to study it more systematically.

- Skim reading is useful in two ways: it can be used when searching for specific information in material you have already worked through systematically; and it can be used to skim-read material that is new to you to check its relevance to your studies. If skim reading indicates that a new source of material is of interest, you should start by scanning its structure and content, making notes of key points of interest, before studying it more systematically.

You can find more advice on developing active reading skills in the section 'Learning with the OU' on the course website; go to 'Develop your study skills'.

You will find a full list of learning outcomes and their abbreviations in the back of this Study Book and in the Study Guide.

Greene uses the term 'osteological development', this relates to the structure and function of bones.

Part 2 Activity 2.1   Getting to know the case studies

(The estimated time needed to complete this activity is about 25 minutes.)

Main learning outcomes developed: KU2, KU3, KS2 and KS4.

If you have not already done so, go to the DVD, click on 'Topics', find Topic 2 and complete Part 2 Activity 2.1, *scanning* each of the case-study summaries to get an overview of the range of types of remains you will work with.

Now read *Greene* Chapter 5, Section 5.6 (pp. 203–5), up to the end of 'Burials'.

Don't forget to make notes while you read.

When studying human remains, it is important to consider: (a) the *type* of human remains being studied; (b) the *number* of individuals these represent; (c) whether they originate from the same *location* and *time period*, or originate from a range of locations and/or an extended time period; and (d) the type of *information* that can be extracted from the remains.

2.1.1   Which types of human remains are useful?

■ Referring back to *Greene*, pp. 203–5, list the *type* of human remains that are useful in archaeological investigations. (See Box 2.2.)

Box 2.2 Pause for thought: study tip reminder

When you meet this type of 'pause for thought' question, you should try to answer it first (jotting down your answer) *before* reading the suggested answer. This will help develop your critical thinking skills and allow you to check that you understand the issues being discussed.

☐ The short answer is basically any type of remains, although their size, form and relative completeness will affect the investigative methods used and the type of information available. In terms of the actual types of remains, you might have listed some or all of the following: an intact body (including the skin, bones, hair and internal organs); dismembered body fragments (e.g. the torso, lower body, a leg, an arm) which will contain bones and soft tissues; a complete skeleton; individual large bones or bone fragments (e.g. the skull, a leg or arm bone, the pelvis). You might also have included individual hairs, human excrement and chemical secretions from the decayed body, all of which can provide different types of useful archaeological information.

There is no doubt that intact or nearly intact bodies can provide the most information. This includes *artificially preserved mummies*, where the body has been deliberately treated at the time of death to prevent or reduce the amount of decay that occurs after deliberate burial, and *naturally preserved bodies* that survived as a result of the depositional environment preventing decomposition. The latter includes bodies preserved in waterlogged conditions (e.g. bogs), where the lack of oxygen impedes bacterial and other forms of decay.

Even when human remains are no longer physically present, forensic methods of investigation can be used to gain a chemical insight into the individuals once present. For example, in situations where a skeleton buried in acidic soil has completely decayed, the position of the body can still be detected by examining any staining of the sediment. In such circumstances, careful recording and chemical analyses of these traces can provide evidence of the sex, build and burial position of the individual.

2.1.2 Ethical considerations when working with human remains

All archaeologists, conservators and scientists are expected to abide by strict regulations when working with human remains at all stages of their investigations including the initial discovery, excavation, conservation, preservation and storage of remains, and the forms of invasive and non-invasive analyses used. Although the exact regulations vary between countries, the underlying principles are generally similar to those set out by the UK's Church Archaeology Human Remains working group, which was set up jointly with English Heritage to develop a policy for human remains recovered from Christian burials in England, dating from the 7th to 19th century AD. Their report states:

- '... human remains should always be treated with dignity and respect
- burials should not be disturbed without good reason, however ... the demands of the modern world are such that it may be necessary to disturb burials in advance of development
- human remains are an important source of scientific information
- there is a need to give particular weight to the feelings and views of living family members when known
- there is a need for decisions to be made in the public interest, and in an accountable way.'

Church Archaeology Human Remains Working Group Report, 2001

You can access the full report in the 'Documents' section on the course website.

In the UK, the overarching legislative policies on the use of human remains from living and deceased individuals is governed by the Human Tissues Act 2004 in England, Wales and Northern Ireland, and by the Human Tissues (Scotland) Act 2006 in Scotland (see the 'Documents' section on the course website). These two documents underpin many other policy and guidance documents. For example, the UK Department of Culture, Media and Sport (DCMS) has produced a reference policy document based on the Human Tissues Act 2004, entitled 'Guidance for the care of human remains in museums', which describes the legal and ethical framework all organisations must follow, along with instructions on the curation, care and use of human remains, and how museums should deal with requests for the return of human remains. Meanwhile, Heritage Scotland (which is directly responsible to the Scottish Executive for the preservation of the historic environment) has produced a reference document based on the Human Tissues Act (Scotland) 2006 called 'The treatment of human remains in archaeology'.

Rather than use these complex, legal documents (which were not designed for general use), most public and professional organisations working with human remains prefer to write their own procedures based on the policy documents. This ensures that the relevant sections of the Human Tissues Acts and associated legal documents can be brought to the attention of their members in a style and format that is easily understood and applied. Now complete the next activity in which you will examine extracts from a range of policy documents and guidelines devised by different organisations for working with human remains.

Part 2 Activity 2.2   Working with human remains policy documents

(The estimated time needed to complete this activity is 20 minutes.)

Main learning outcomes developed: KU4, CS3, KS4 and PS1.

In this activity, you will compare and contrast the style and complexity of language used in the human remains policy documents from the British Museum and the Institute of Field Archaeologists (IFA).

(a) Go to 'Activities' section on the course website, find Part 2 Activity 2.2 and locate the extracts from the British Museum policy on 'Human Remains' and IFA Paper No. 7 'Guidelines to the Standards for Recording Human Remains'.

You can access the full human remains policy and IFA guidelines in the 'Documents' section of the course website.

(b) Skim-read the two extracts (pages 1 and 2 of the British Museum document and pages 5 and 6 of the IFA document).

Note: you are not expected to understand the content of these documents, but to get a sense of who they are aimed at and the issues discussed.

(c) After you have examined the extracts, make some brief notes (one or two sentences each) on:

- the style of language used (e.g. 'plain English'; technical, scientific or archaeological terms; legal terms)
- how easy it is for you to understand
- which, if any, of the Human Tissues Acts or government documents are referred to.

Question 2.1

The two policy documents cover similar issues about working with human remains; however, the style and complexity of language in each document varies greatly.

(a) What single reason explains why the style and formality of the language used varies so much?

(b) Using the style of language and the structure of the documents as a guide, decide whether the documents are aimed at: government departments or professional archaeological organisations; non-archaeological organisations needing specialist help; or the 'general public'.

2.1.3   One-off finds or multiple burials?

Start by reading 'Cemeteries' in *Greene* Chapter 3, Section 4.1 (pp. 111–3).

Locating Hungate cemetery

As part of the standard planning requirements within the City of York, the site at Hungate is currently being excavated to ensure an accurate record of its archaeology is made before the construction of a new commercial and residential development. The development will include a large underground car park, several multi-storey buildings and an open-air plaza.

Historical documents suggest that during medieval times, part of the site was occupied by a church and a cemetery. In accordance with the guidelines of the Church Archaeology Human Remains working group and IFA, this raises various ethical issues that need to be resolved by the construction companies (Crosby Lend Lease, Evans Property Group and Land Securities Group plc), York City Council and York Archaeological Trust archaeologists carrying out the dig (see Section 2.12).

The key question facing the organisations working on this site is whether or not to disturb and remove all of the human remains in the cemetery as part of the excavation process. This would require contingency plans to deal with the long-term storage or re-interment of the exhumed graves. Alternatively, the decision could be taken to leave the cemetery undisturbed, which would limit the area available for the planned construction work.

The problem is that the exact location of the cemetery on the Hungate site is uncertain, an issue that is explored in the next activity.

Part 2 Activity 2.3   In search of the Hungate cemetery

(The estimated time needed to complete this activity is 15 minutes.)

Main learning outcomes developed: KU3, CS1, CS3 and PS1.

As you listen to Peter Connelly (Director, Hungate Dig) talk about the various issues involved in searching for the cemetery, make notes on the following key points:

- the age and expected location of the cemetery
- why its exact location is unclear
- the ethical and logistical considerations that everyone involved with the site must address during the dig and subsequent construction period
- what the local council, archaeologists and site owners have decided to do once it has been located.

Now go to the DVD, click on 'Topics', find Topic 2 and work through Part 2 Activity 2.3.

As well as the type of remains being studied (Section 2.1.1), the *number* of remains recovered from an area and the *timescale* over which they were deposited must also be considered.

■ Why are these issues important?

☐ Although the discovery of a single body or a fragment may give an insight into the life of that individual, it will not allow inferences to be made about the overall age range, life expectancy or state of health of their population. Likewise, it may not be apparent how representative this individual was, in terms of their age, physical stature, social status and state of health, compared with the rest of the population.

Therefore, although a one-off burial can give an insight into the life and death of an individual person along with evidence about the social and cultural practices at the time of death, this type of find cannot be used to understand the population dynamics of the time.

■ Why might a cemetery and/or mass burial site not provide an accurate insight into the structure and composition of a particular society?

☐ Referring back to *Greene*, depending on the age and original purpose of the burial site, it may contain only certain sections of society, while excluding others according to their age, religion, sex or social status.

Even in prehistoric times, cemeteries and burial sites might have been the preserve of a particular, possibly elite section of society, and so will provide only a very limited view of the population dynamics. In many Roman cemeteries, although the remains of adults from all sections of society have been found, newborn babies and young infants are frequently absent, with recent studies indicating these remains were sometimes disposed of through the sewers. In contrast, in some cemeteries, high levels of infant mortality and deaths associated with childbirth during historical times have resulted in the average age and sex being skewed, implying that a higher proportion of these two groups (infants and young women of child-bearing age) existed than was present in the population at their time of death. Meanwhile, human remains from mass burial sites associated with warfare might consist primarily of young, healthy males who died as a result of fatal, traumatic injuries rather than old age or the prevalent diseases of the time, whereas remains resulting from genocide may produce a death assemblage that is a true reflection of the actual living community. The sectors of society recovered from a burial site will also depend on whether it was used for a single event or over an extended period of time, as extended usage may reflect changes in social practices and the influx of different communities.

Therefore, in contrast to one-off finds, burial sites (especially those used over an extended time period) can provide a better understanding of the population dynamics and the wider social and cultural practices of that time. Given the above, it is still important to remember that the range of information available from multiple burials may be limited, so overgeneralisations should not be made. In all cases, human remains represent a *specific sample* of the population, but do not necessarily equate to a representative cross-section of the whole population.

Question 2.2

What other source(s) of information could be used to supplement that obtained from human remains, to gain a better understanding of the age of the site, and the social and cultural practices at the time of death?

Question 2.3

Complete Table 2.1 by categorising each of the main case studies used in this topic as (a) a 'unique or one-off find' or (b) 'part of a multiple find'.

Part 2 Activity 2.4   Archaeological importance of unique and multiple finds: Wetwang versus Tell es-Sa'idiyeh

(The estimated time needed to complete this activity is 30 minutes.)

Main learning outcomes developed: KU2, CS1 and KS2.

In this activity, you will compare and contrast the range of archaeological evidence obtained from the single skeleton recovered at Wetwang in East Yorkshire with the numerous individuals exhumed from the Tell es-Sa'idiyeh cemetery in Jordan (Figure 2.1).

(b)

(a)

Figure 2.1   (a) Examining the remains of the Iron Age woman at Wetwang. (b) Excavating in the cemetery at Tell es-Sa'idiyeh.

Now go to the DVD, click on 'Topics', find Topic 2 and work through Part 2 Activity 2.4.

2.1.4   How the cause of death impacts on the type of burial

Greene Chapter 5, Section 5.6 (pp. 204–5) lists three common *categories* of death and burial: (i) intentional burial (e.g. the Egyptian mummies, the Medieval Inuit from Greenland); (ii) ritual murder, sacrifice or execution (e.g. Lindow Man); and (iii) accidental death (e.g. Ötzi, 'the Neolithic ice man', from the Italian–Austrian border).

■ What impact will the *category* of death have on how the remains have been buried?

☐ An intentional burial implies that some level of care has been taken to dispose of the human remains and that the people who buried them had feelings and/or a sense of responsibility for the individual who died. Intentional burials may involve different rituals such as the careful positioning of the body and burial of grave goods with the remains, relating to beliefs in an 'after life'. With ritual murders (e.g. sacrifices and executions), the reason for death will dictate how carefully the remains are disposed of. Some sacrificial victims may be carefully positioned and buried with culturally significant artefacts as offerings to the gods, whereas others, including those who were randomly murdered, will be disposed of with less care and respect. Accidental deaths are at the mercy of the environment in which the individual(s) died; they may be found in the same position as in death, or in various states of disarray, if they have been scavenged or reworked by natural processes.

To recap, so far you have considered the number of individuals recovered from a burial site (contrasting unique 'one-off' and multiple human remains sites), the type of remains that have been recovered (e.g. intact bodies, skeletons and fragmental remains) and the three most common styles of burial (intentional, sacrificial and accidental), and have started to compare and contrast information from some of the case studies. You have also started to build up a wealth of information about the different case studies and examples used in this topic, and need a way to easily compare and contrast all of this (Box 2.3).

Box 2.3 Using summary tables

Summary tables are an effective way of working with large amounts of information that you may need to refer to periodically. For example, Table 2.1 compares and contrasts information about the date, location and types of human remains in each case study in this topic.

As you work through the rest of this topic, you should complete Table 2.1 and Table 2.2, which compare and contrast the different observational and analytical techniques used to investigate each case study. Start by returning to your answer to Question 2.3 and add this information to the table. *You will find a blank version of Table 2.2 to complete at the back of the Study Guide or can download an electronic version from the 'Documents' section on the course website.*

Table 2.1 Summary of the date, location, type and cause of death experienced in each case study in Topic 2.

Case study	Approximate age of remains	Period	Location	Type of find	Unique find (UF) or part of multiple find (MF)	Cause of death
Krapina bones	130 000 yrs BP	Palaeolithic	Krapina, N. Croatia	skeletal fragments		various – natural?
Lapedo Child	24 000 yrs BP	Upper Palaeolithic	Lapedo Valley, Portugal	nearly complete skeleton		unknown – natural?
Tell es-Sa'idiyeh	13th–12th and 8th–4th centuries BC	L. Bronze Age and E. Iron Age: Persian Period	Jordan	more than 589 graves		various
Nesperennub	800 BC	L. Bronze Age	Thebes, Egypt	intact mummy		natural–ill health
Wetwang Woman	300–200 BC	Iron Age	Wetwang, E. Yorks.	intact skeleton		unknown – natural?
Lindow Man	AD 20–90	L. Iron Age– E. Roman Period	near Manchester	intact upper body		intentional – execution?
Hungate Cemetery	13th century AD	Medieval	York city centre, Yorks.	unknown		various causes
Llullaillaco children	AD 1500	L. Intermediate Period	Llullaillaco mountain, S. America	intact frozen bodies		intentional – sacrificial?

Table 2.2 Summary of the observational and analytical techniques used to investigate the case studies in Topic 2. *(Use the blank version of Table 2.2 in the Study Guide to complete the missing information as you work through Topic 2.)*

Case study	Approximate age of remains	Imaging techniques used	Information obtained	Analytical (chemical) techniques used	Information obtained
Krapina bones	130 000 years BP				
Lapedo Child	24 000 years BP				
Tell es-Sa'idiyeh cemetery	13th–12th and 8th–4th centuries BC				
Nesperennub	800 BC				
Wetwang Woman	300–200 BC				
Lindow Man	AD 20–90				
Hungate Cemetery	13th century AD				
Llullaillaco Mountain Children	AD 1500				

2.2 Preservation and decomposition of human remains

After death, all organic material, including human remains, starts to decompose. The rate of decomposition depends on: the nature of the remains (e.g. structure and composition); the composition of the surrounding material; the depth of burial; the temperature and humidity of the environment of decomposition; the presence and percolation of water through the site (e.g. whether water can pass through the remains); whether there is an ample supply of oxygen, which is needed for decomposition to occur; and the amount of physical, biological and chemical actions by any scavengers or insects that will break down the remains more quickly and more efficiently. Other factors that affect the rate at which organic remains decay include: whether they have been preserved (e.g. by embalming); whether they are enclosed in a protective layer (e.g. a coffin or clothing); if there are open wounds, which increases access to softer tissues by percolating fluids, scavengers, insects and bacteria; the time-of-year of death; and the size and weight of the body. The fastest rate of decay is in warm, humid environments where the body is exposed to the open atmosphere, whereas in arid (hot or cold) conditions, decomposition may stop altogether because of desiccation (drying out). Desiccated remains will only decay when they are exposed to moisture.

The process of decomposition is caused by:

Enzymes are a type of protein (i.e. large organic molecule) that act as a catalyst to speed up chemical reactions, and convert one substance to another.

(a) the chemical breakdown of tissues by enzymes from within the body, resulting in autolysis (which is from the Greek for 'self', *auto-* and 'digestion', *-lysis*)

(b) the biochemical actions of bacteria, resulting in putrefaction (i.e. the breakdown of organic materials into different compounds), which is the main source of gases and noxious odours released from decaying bodies.

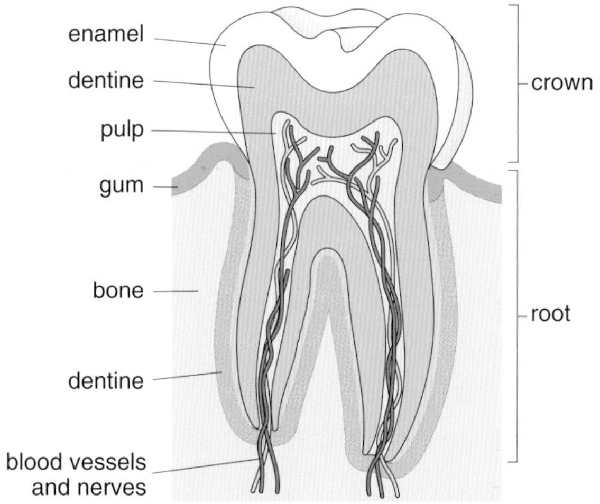

As a body decays, the soft tissues preferentially decompose first as the fatty substances in the body break down to form what is rather evocatively called 'grave grease', leaving the more resistant skeleton (e.g. teeth and bones). Teeth comprise of enamel (e.g. the crown, which is the visible white part of the tooth – a hard, resistant inorganic crystalline material made of calcium phosphate), dentine (e.g. the root of the tooth – a mass of inorganic calcium phosphate, soft and less resistant organic connective collagen-like tissues and water), and dental pulp (e.g. the interior of the tooth, consisting of soft tissue that is progressively replaced by dentine as the tooth ages) (Figure 2.2). When teeth decompose, the dentine decays more rapidly than the enamel, although both have been recovered from very ancient teeth.

Figure 2.2 Schematic cross-section through a human tooth.

Bones consist of a mixture of calcium phosphate and connective tissues of collagen (a long, fibrous protein molecule that gives bones their strength and flexibility) (Figure 2.3). Bones do not have a solid structure, but typically consist of an outer, harder layer of dense bone (comprising ~80% of the bone mass) and an internal spongy bone core surrounding the bone marrow (although the exact structure varies between different types of bones, e.g. long bones and ribs). Bone marrow decomposes more rapidly than bone, which is why many bones found in graves are hollow.

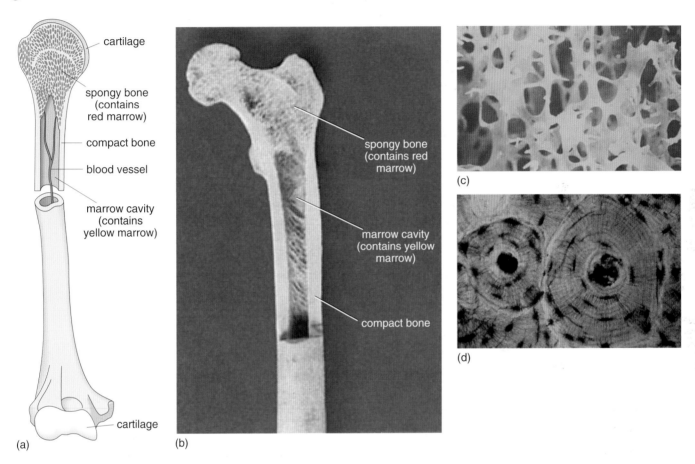

Figure 2.3   (a) Schematic cross-section and (b) photograph through a partially sectioned bone, showing its internal structure. Microscopic structure of (c) spongy bone and (d) compact bone.

Under suitable environmental conditions, teeth and bones can maintain their physical integrity for significant periods of time (e.g. the skeleton of Lapedo Child, ~24 500 years BP; the Krapina bones, ~130 000 years BP). However, in acidic environments (e.g. a peat bog, certain types of sandy soils), teeth and bones break down more rapidly, as the inorganic mineral component is lost by acid dissolution. Acid attack can be recognised by the physical change in appearance of teeth and bones, which become eroded and pitted, and in extreme cases may become more rounded, leaving very fragile and light remains (e.g. the bones of the Lapedo Child and Wetwang Woman).

When decomposition proceeds so that no physical trace of the body remains, chemical tracers can still be found. In some cases, these may stain the surrounding sediment but where no trace can be seen under normal lighting, UV light can be used to check dissolved phosphate from the teeth and bones, which fluoresces under this type of light, revealing the past presence of skeletal material. Soil samples can also be analysed for specific organic compounds including amino acids (which are the building blocks of proteins, found in bones and tissues), cholesterol (found in many internal organs and cell membranes) and steroid hormones (produced from cholesterol and useful for identifying the sex of the individual), all of which identify the presence, at some point in the past, of human or animal tissue.

2.2.1   Natural preservation and artificial mummification processes

The vast majority of archaeological human remains consist of skeletal fragments. More rarely, exceptionally well naturally and artificially preserved remains are discovered (e.g. Nesperennub, Lindow Man and the Llullaillaco mountain children mummies). By studying such remains (including their skin, hair, nails, internal organs and skeletons) and any cultural artefacts buried with them, it is possible to determine their appearance, stature, diet, state of health and cause of death, as well as make inferences about their social and cultural status, and the environment in which they lived. This section investigates the physical and chemical conditions necessary to allow intact human remains to be preserved.

Natural preservation processes – preservation in peat bogs

The lack of drainage and throughput of fresh water causes peat bogs to be stagnant, acidic environments where all life and aerobic activities (i.e. those requiring oxygen, such as the decomposition of organic material) is limited to the bog surface. Below this, the environment quickly becomes anaerobic (i.e. lacking free oxygen), slowing down the decomposition of matter by bacterial decay. It is these special anaerobic conditions that lead to the remarkable preservation of organic remains in peat bogs, including the natural preservation of human bodies that have fallen in or been disposed of in a bog.

Bog bodies are typified by the retention of their skin, hair, nails, internal organs and skeletons. The cold, anaerobic, acidic waters chemically preserve the skin and internal organs by natural tanning processes through the build-up of tannins that come from the peaty water.

Tannin is a chemical substance released by plant matter. It is used in the tanning industry to preserve hides and produce leather.

■ Based on what you know about the decomposition of bones in acidic environments, would you expect to find well-preserved skeletal remains in bogs?

□ No – although several bog bodies have retained all or some of their skeleton, the acidic bog conditions cause the bones and teeth to preferentially dissolve more rapidly, while leaving the chemically tanned and preserved soft tissues intact. The skeletal remains of bog bodies are therefore often soft and fragile compared with normal bones and teeth.

Part 2 Activity 2.5   The case of the Irish bog bodies

(The estimated time needed to complete this activity is 20 minutes.)

Main learning outcomes developed: KU2, CS2, KS2 and KS4.

(a) Read the following news item about the discovery of two bog bodies –
    Clonycavan Man and Old Croghan Man – which were found in Ireland in 2003
    (Figure 2.4). As you read, pay particular attention to the highlighted text. This
    emphasises the range of scientific information and methods of analysis used
    during the initial archaeological investigations of these bog bodies.

(a)

(b)

Figure 2.4   (a) Clonycavan
Man and (b) Old Croghan Man,
recovered from two bogs in
Ireland in 2003.

BBC News Article: Iron Age 'bog bodies' unveiled

Archaeologists have unveiled two Iron Age 'bog bodies' which were
found in the Republic of Ireland. The bodies, which are both male
and have been dated to more than 2000 years old, probably belong
to the victims of a ritual sacrifice. In common with other bog bodies,
they show signs of having been tortured before their deaths. The
first body dropped off a peat cutting machine in February 2003 in
Clonycavan, near Dublin. The forearms, hands and lower abdomen
are missing, believed to have been hacked off by the machine. The
second was found in May the same year in Croghan, just 25 miles
(40 km) from Clonycavan. Old Croghan Man, as it has become
known, was missing a head and lower limbs. It was discovered by
workmen clearing a drainage ditch through a peat bog.

Tanned skin

Although the police were initially called in, an inspection by the state
pathologist confirmed that this was an archaeological case. Both
bodies were subsequently taken to the National Museum of Ireland
in Dublin. A team of experts from the UK and Ireland has been
examining the bodies to learn how they lived and died. Radiocarbon
dating, for example, would show that both had died at similar times –
around 2300 years ago. One of the experts is Don Brothwell, the
York University archaeologist who led the scientific investigation of
Lindow Man, the bog body found in Cheshire in 1984. Hundreds of
bodies have been recovered from peat wetlands across Northern
Europe. The earliest accounts date back to the 18th Century. The
unique chemistry of peat bogs essentially mummifies bodies.

Summer death

The peat-building sphagnum moss embeds remains in cold, acid and oxygen-free conditions that immobilise bacteria. 'The way peat wetlands preserve bodies has been described as a process of 'slow-cooking' which tans them dark brown,' *Timewatch* producer John Hayes-Fisher told the BBC News website.

Clonycavan man was a young male no more than 5 ft 2 in tall (c. 1.6 m). Beneath his hair, which retains its unusual 'raised' style, was a massive wound caused by a heavy cutting object that smashed open his skull. Chemical analysis of the hair showed that Clonycavan man's diet was rich in vegetables in the months leading up to his death, suggesting he died in summer. It also revealed that he had been using a type of Iron Age hair gel; a vegetable plant oil mixed with a resin that had probably come from south-western France or Spain.

Dismembered body

Old Croghan man was also young – probably in his early to mid 20s – but much taller than his counterpart from 25 miles away. Scientists worked out from the length of his arms that he would have stood around 6 ft 6 in tall (2.0 m). He had been horrifically tortured before death. His nipples had been cut and he had been stabbed in the ribs. A cut on his arm suggested he had tried to defend himself during the attack that ended his life. The young man was later beheaded and dismembered. Hazel ropes were passed through his arms before he was buried in the bog.

Food remains in his stomach show that Old Croghan man had eaten milk and cereals before he died. But chemical analysis of his nails showed that he had more meat in his diet than Clonycavan man. This suggests that he died in a colder season than Clonycavan man, when vegetables were more scarce. It may also explain why his remains are better preserved.

Hopeful offering

The researchers used digital technology to reconstruct the distorted face of Clonycavan man.

From his studies on these bog bodies and others, Ned Kelly, keeper of Irish antiquities at the National Museum of Ireland, has developed a new theory which explains why so many remains are buried on important political or royal boundaries. 'My belief is that these burials are offerings to the gods of fertility by kings to ensure a successful reign.' Mr Kelly told the BBC's Timewatch programme. 'Bodies are placed in the borders immediately surrounding royal land or on tribal boundaries to ensure a good yield of corn and milk throughout the reign of the king.'

BBC News, 7 January 2006

■ What does this tell you about these men and their cause of death?

☐ You know their sex; their approximate biological age (both 'young'); their height; their last meal and what their recent diet consisted of; the season when they died (based on their diet); that neither appear to have died of natural causes; and the approximate date of their death (from radiocarbon dating).

All of this information is based on the systematic scientific investigations of the bodies, which has allowed verifiable (i.e. provable and repeatable) scientific data to be obtained. The results have then been used to present a scientific case of what the evidence tells us.

(b) Now go to the DVD, click on 'Topics', find Topic 2 and complete Part 2 Activity 2.5, and watch the short film about the discovery of Clonycavan Man and Old Croghan Man, before continuing with this activity.

■ Are the comments by Ned Kelly (Keeper of Irish Antiquities at the National Museum of Ireland in Dublin) highlighted in the news item above and in the short film based on scientific facts?

☐ Yes and no! Ned Kelly has used scientific facts and information to devise a theoretical hypothesis of why the bodies were murdered and placed in the bogs. As there are no written documents or other forms of evidence to prove this theory as fact, he has combined evidence from the location of the finds with other archaeological knowledge about the culture at that time to propose a plausible explanation for the deaths.

We will never know for certain whether Ned's theory is correct. Someone else using the same data may suggest a different hypothesis. The job of the archaeologist, scientist and historian is to demonstrate which is the most plausible based on the information currently available.

Professional conservation of bog bodies by artificial freeze-drying

If bog bodies were left in the state they were recovered in, they would quickly decompose under normal environmental conditions as a result of bacterial decay and shrinkage through water loss (with up to 50% shrinkage possible for some waterlogged remains). All bog bodies therefore must be professionally conserved so they can be kept for future research or public display in museums.

The remains of Clonycavan Man and Old Croghan Man were preserved by soaking them for several weeks in a pre-treatment solution of polyethylene glycol (PEG) and water, before they were frozen and then artificially freeze-dried.

Soaking in PEG solution reduces the effect of expansion caused by the waterlogged tissues freezing, and helps to bond the deteriorated collagen molecules together. The PEG solution also acts as a humectant (moisturiser) after freeze-drying. The freeze-drying process results in ice in the tissues being rapidly removed as a vapour. Sublimation (i.e. conversion of solid ice straight to water vapour), prevents drying stains forming on the body, which may happen if left to dry naturally. By putting bog bodies through this process of soaking, freezing and freeze-drying, the remains become softer, fuller and more flexible, and are preserved without any shrinking or warping occurring which in turn allows some of the finer features of the individual to be seen more clearly. In the next activity you will use some of the information and approaches developed during your examination of Clonycavan Man and Old Croghan Man to investigate the life, death and conservation history of Lindow Man.

Part 2 Activity 2.6   Who was Lindow Man and how did he die?

(The estimated time needed to complete this activity is 40 minutes.)

Main learning outcomes developed: KU3, KU4, CS1 and KS4.

(a)   Start by reading the following summary (extracted from the British Museum website) about Lindow Man (Figure 2.5). As you read this text, highlight any relevant information about: (i) the man (e.g. his size, age, diet); (ii) the scientific techniques used during initial investigations; and (iii) the range of scientific data collected by British Museum staff.

Figure 2.5   The conserved remains of Lindow Man, dating from the Iron Age (first century AD), found in Lindow Moss, Cheshire, England, in 1984.

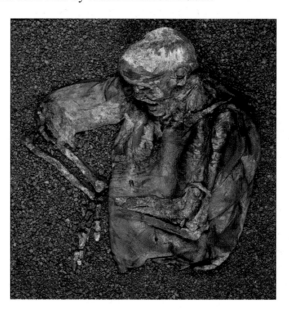

British Museum Article: Lindow Man: Victim of sacrifice?

The body of this man was discovered in August 1984 when workmen were cutting peat at Lindow Moss bog in north-west England. It was carefully transported to the British Museum and thoroughly examined by a team of scientists. Their research has allowed us to learn more about this person – his health, his appearance and how he might have died – than any other prehistoric person found in Britain.

The conditions in the peat bog meant that the man's skin, hair and many of his internal organs are well preserved. Radiocarbon dating shows that he died between AD 20 and 90. He was about 25 years of age, around 168 cm tall and weighed 60–65 kg. He had probably done very little hard, manual work, because his finger nails were well manicured. His beard and moustache had been cut by a pair of shears. There is no evidence that he was unwell when he died, but he was suffering a severe case of parasitic worms. His last meal probably included unleavened bread made from wheat and barley, cooked over a fire on which heather had been burnt.

The man met a horrific death. He was struck on the top of his head twice with a heavy object, perhaps a narrow bladed axe. He also received a vicious blow in the back – perhaps from someone's knee – which broke one of his ribs. He had a thin cord tied around his neck which was used to strangle him and break his neck. By now he was probably dead, but then his throat was cut. Finally, he was placed face down in a pond in the bog. This elaborate sequence of events suggests that his death may have been ritual killing, with some people arguing that he was the victim of a human sacrifice. Before dying, the man had consumed a drink containing a mixture of ingredients and ingested some mistletoe pollen.

British Museum website, accessed 2 November, 2007

(b) Now go to the DVD, click on 'Topics', find Topic 2 and complete Part 2 Activity 2.6, during which you will investigate the life, death and preservation histories of Lindow Man.

Natural preservation processes – desiccation and natural freeze-drying

As decomposition is directly related to the temperature and humidity of the surrounding environment, when these two factors decrease, so does the rate of decomposition, eventually reaching a point where it stops. Under extremely hot or cold arid conditions, human and animal remains can become desiccated or freeze-dried by natural processes. Desiccation results in the gradual removal of moisture from the soft tissues and bones, while natural freeze-drying results in the rapid removal of water from the body, with both processes resulting in dehydration of the tissues. Desiccation processes will alter the physical structure of cells and tissues, whereas natural freeze-drying allows the original physical structure to be retained.

Human remains can also be frozen without first being dehydrated. Such bodies are very rare, the most famous being Ötzi, the Neolithic 'Ice Man', discovered in the Italian Alps in 1991; Juanita, the Inca 'Ice Maiden', dating from the 15th century AD, discovered in 1995 in southern Peru; and most recently, the 16th century AD mummies of the Llullaillaco mountain children (Figure 2.6), discovered in 1999 in northwest Argentina.

■ What would happen if a desiccated or naturally freeze-dried body was left in warmer and more humid conditions?

☐ As the remains have been dried, increasing the temperature would not affect the physical state of the body as long as the conditions remained arid. In contrast, increasing humidity would have a detrimental effect on the body, and may result in the tissues absorbing water and starting to decay.

Part 2 Activity 2.7   The frozen children of Llullaillaco volcano

(The estimated time needed to complete this activity is 35 minutes.)

Main learning outcomes developed: KU1, KU3, CS2 and KS2.

In this activity, you will discover how a wide range of non-destructive and destructive analytical techniques were used to investigate the age, state of health and cause of death of the three Inca children recovered from the Llullaillaco volcano, in northwest Argentina (Figure 2.6).

Figure 2.6   The exceptionally well-preserved remains of the 'Llullaillaco Maiden', the oldest of the three children recovered from the top of the volcano.

 Now go to the DVD, click on 'Topics', find Topic 2 and work through Part 2 Activity 2.7.

Artificial mummification – the process of embalming

In archaeology, the term 'mummy' (derived from the Latin word *mumia*, which itself is derived from the Arabic or Persian word *mūmiya*, meaning bitumen) describes a deliberately preserved body, which has been embalmed or treated with preservatives before deliberate burial. The name *mummy* originates from the fact that the ancient Egyptians were thought to use bitumen as part of the embalming process because of the blackened colour of the corpses when they were unwrapped.

Several past cultures around the world practised mummification, the most famous being the Egyptians. In Egypt, the process involved the ritualistic removal of all internal organs, which were then dried, embalmed separately and either stored in canopic jars or put back inside the embalmed body; the exception was the heart and sometimes the kidneys, which were left in place, and the brain, which was removed and discarded. After the internal organs had been removed, the body was packed internally and externally with a natural drying agent called natron (sodium carbonate), to remove all traces of moisture and so stop the decaying process. Once dried, the embalming was completed by cleansing the body with aromatic oils and coating it with resins before wrapping the corpse in linen bandages. The whole process is believed to have taken about 70 days to complete.

In China, the mummification process started with the ritual washing of the body with aromatic lotions, after which it was dressed and wrapped in various cloths. The body was then placed in the first of several coffins and submersed in an acidic liquid believed to contain the mineral cinnabar (mercury sulfide, which is commonly used in traditional Chinese medicines for a variety of purposes).

■   What was the purpose of placing the body in this acidic liquid?

☐   It served a similar role to acidic waters in peat bogs, preventing decomposition by bacterial activity and preserving the body.

Unlike Egyptian mummies, Chinese mummies typically kept all their internal organs.

Part 2 Activity 2.8   Looking inside mummies – the ethical way

(The estimated time needed to complete this activity is 15 minutes.)

Main learning outcomes developed: KU1, CS3 and PS1.

A well-preserved mummy can give archaeologists an unprecedented amount of scientific and social information about the life, health and cause of death of the individual. In the past, the only way of doing this was to unwrap the mummy, which destroyed a lot of evidence and limited the potential for future investigations using yet-to-be-discovered investigative methods. Although there are instances where unwrapping is the most effective method to improve certain types of research, the current general preference is to use non-destructive and non-invasive techniques such as X-rays and computerised tomography (CT scans) to see what is inside the mummy (while in the recent past, xeroradiography was also used).

In this activity, you will look at some of the non-invasive imaging techniques used by staff at the British Museum and University of Manchester to study the 9th century BC Egyptian priest Nesperennub (Figure 2.7), without unwrapping a thing!

Now go to the DVD, click on 'Topics', find Topic 2 and work through Part 2 Activity 2.8.

 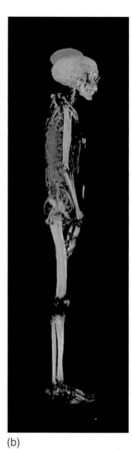

(a)   (b)

Figure 2.7   (a) The exquisitely decorated cartonnage protecting Nesperennub's mummy. (b) Three-dimensional composite scanning image of Nesperennub's skeleton.

Research on Nesperennub shows how advances in science and the development of imaging techniques traditionally used in medicine have created new methods of archaeological investigation. These non-invasive techniques produce highly detailed information, some of which may have been missed or lost when using conventional destructive techniques. They also allow the remains to be conserved for future research, where more advanced investigative techniques may reveal even more detailed evidence about the life and death of the mummified body.

You will revisit Nesperennub later in this topic and look at his state of health and nutrition in more scientific detail.

Question 2.4

What happens to the following types of human remains when they are exposed to normal atmospheric conditions (e.g. normal temperatures and moderate levels of humidity)?

(a) Bog body

(b) Desiccated or naturally freeze-dried mummy

(c) Egyptian mummy still intact in its linen wrappings (but not its protective outer sarcophagus and inner cartonnage casings).

2.3   What were they really like? Getting to know our ancestors

In this section, you will discover how the physical characteristics of skeletal remains can be used to build up a picture of the sex, biological age, stature and state of health of an individual, and start to unravel some of the genetic information held within these remains.

2.3.1   It's all in the bones …

In marvelling at all that can be discerned from naturally preserved and mummified bodies, it is easy to forget that the most common type of human remains recovered is bones. Throughout much of prehistory (from 2.5 Ma to 10 000 years BP), human remains were not typically deposited in graves, with intentional burials not starting until about 120 000 years BP. As a result, complete skeletons such as that of the ~1.5 Ma-old boy from Nariokotome, Kenya are exceptional, whereas disarticulated skulls, teeth and limb bones are more usual. The study of how such bones are preserved at a site is called taphonomy (derived from the Greek for 'burial [ta͵ɔhos] study'). It involves studying each of the processes that have affected the bones, from the time an animal or a human died, through the process of deposition, burial, fossilisation and eventual discovery and excavation (Figure 2.8).

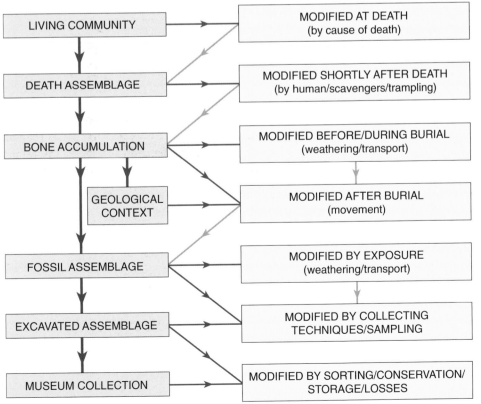

Figure 2.8   The taphonomic stages involved in the accumulation and modification of bone assemblages, from the time of death to excavation.

During a taphonomic study, archaeologists examine the physical appearance of bones, looking at their surface texture as well as any breaks, cut marks and scratches, to help determine what happened to the bones during life, death and the burial and exhumation processes. For example, the presence of accidental and intentional trauma to bones (e.g. fractures and deformities) can give an insight into the life and possible death of an individual. If a bone has been broken but then healed, this indicates the trauma occurred during life and the individual had time and peace to heal. It may also give an insight into the level of care from the community, as people with serious fractures would need to be tended by others for a considerable period of time. In contrast, fractures that have not healed imply they were formed prior to or after death. Determining whether bone damage was a result of a one-off, repeated or continuous event can also provide useful information about the type of environment the individual lived in, and the level of risk of trauma they encountered. The physical appearance, structure and chemical composition of the bones can also be used to determine whether the cause of death was due to disease or blood poisoning, causing abnormalities to develop in the bone.

If a body is not buried quickly after death or becomes exhumed, it may be scavenged by animals, and in some cases, it is possible to determine which animals did this from the character and size of the tooth marks made. Random scratches, scuffs and scrapes as well as breaks to bones can also result from trampling or natural reworking processes, while mortuary practices may cause breakages, leave cut marks and traces of burning on the bones (Figure 2.9). Finally, bones can also be broken or damaged by machinery or heavy equipment at the time of excavation, if not exhumed carefully.

Figure 2.9   Scanning electron microscope images of: (a) naturally formed random scratches on the surface of a bone that were produced by rock abrasion and are characterised by a linear shape; (b) deliberately formed cut marks, produced by a stone tool to cut this animal bone, characterised by a variable shape, shallow on one side, with a ridge of bone on the opposite side. Note that (a) is at ×1.5 the scale of (b).

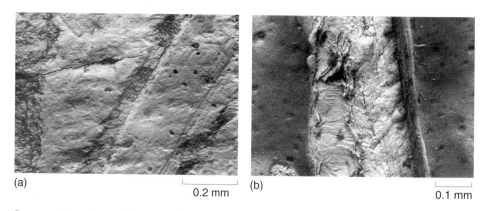

(a) 0.2 mm   (b) 0.1 mm

Determining the taphonomic history

To determine the life history of a bone, it is necessary to 'read' the layers of marks that are on its surface and to 'interpret' the nature of breaks and other modifications to discover whether they are a result of natural or artificial processes.

Compare the two images in Figure 2.9. Figure 2.9a shows random, superficial scratches on the surface of a bone that was moved around by natural processes, across a rocky surface. Figure 2.9b shows a cut mark made in an experiment using a stone tool on fresh bone. This mark is well defined and asymmetric, showing displacement of bone on one side of the cut along with internal striations. Cut marks are non-random and occur where it is necessary to cut through tough muscles and dismember joints. When such marks are discovered on human remains, they can cause controversy about whether they represent ritual mortuary practices involving the defleshing of the corpse, or are due to cannibalism. By building up a library of images of marks produced by known causes through present-day experimentation on animal bones, it is possible to interpret archaeological cut marks on all types of bone.

For example, Seianti Hanunia Tlesnasa was an important Etruscan woman from Tuscany, in northern Italy, who died aged 50–55, around 150–140 BC. In this part of Italy, the Etruscans practised a variety of funerary rites involving cremation or burial. A study of Seianti's remains reveals her body was initially buried to increase the rate of decomposition of the flesh. Her skeleton was then exhumed, cleaned and dismembered and the bones carefully interred in her sarcophagus. Each stage of these ritualistic practices left a series of cut marks on the bones, which in turn have enabled archaeologists to gain a better insight into these funerary rites. Her remains were finally laid to rest in a spectacular sarcophagus, (now housed in the British Museum), which shows her exquisitely dressed and reclined on a bed, with a mirror in her left hand, adjusting her cloak with her right hand.

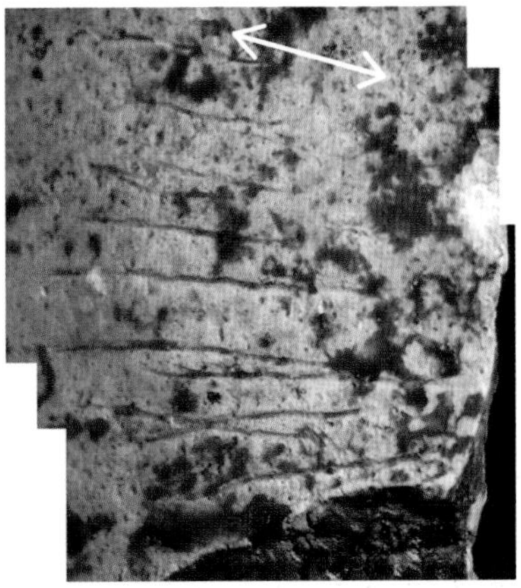

Part 2 Activity 2.9   Interpreting the 876 bones from Krapina

(The estimated time needed to complete this activity is 25 minutes.)

Main learning outcomes developed: KU1, CS2, CS4 and PS1.

The remarkable site of Krapina is situated in the sandstone hills north of Zagreb in Croatia. It was discovered in 1899 and, over a period of five years the geologist and palaeontologist Dragutin Gorjanović-Kramberger (1856–1936) excavated 876 human bones, which is still the largest known sample of Neanderthal remains recovered from a single site. The majority of these human remains were recovered from the lower levels of the site, now dated to about 130 000 years BP, although the site spans a longer period. Many of the bones are broken, some are burnt and many are marked with cuts and scratches, including a distinctive ladder-like pattern of marks on the skull of a woman (Figure 2.10). This and other cut marks started a debate in the scientific community: were they the result of a respectful burial ritual or evidence of cannibalism?

Now go to the DVD, click on 'Topics', find Topic 2 and complete Part 2 Activity 2.9, in which Jill Cook describes the research work she has been doing on these Neanderthal bones, before you work through the evidence to decide the cause of the cut marks.

Figure 2.10   Ladder cut marks identified on the skull of a Neanderthal woman, Krapina Cave, Croatia.

Determining the sex of a skeleton

A wealth of evidence can be extracted from the skeleton of an adult human to help determine their sex. Starting from the top of the skeleton (Figure 2.11), the diagnostic bones include:

- skull – in males, the skull typically has a more prominent brow and larger lower jaw bone (mandible) than in females
- clavicle (collar bone) – males typically have straighter, thicker clavicles than females (who may have a more V-shaped collar bone)
- rib cage – females generally have a shorter rib cage than males of similar height
- sternum – the central breast bone is typically broader and longer in males than in females

- pelvis – the female pelvis is wider and has a much larger cavity compared with the male pelvis, which is typically more enclosed
- tibia (shin bone) – females generally have thinner tibias than males.

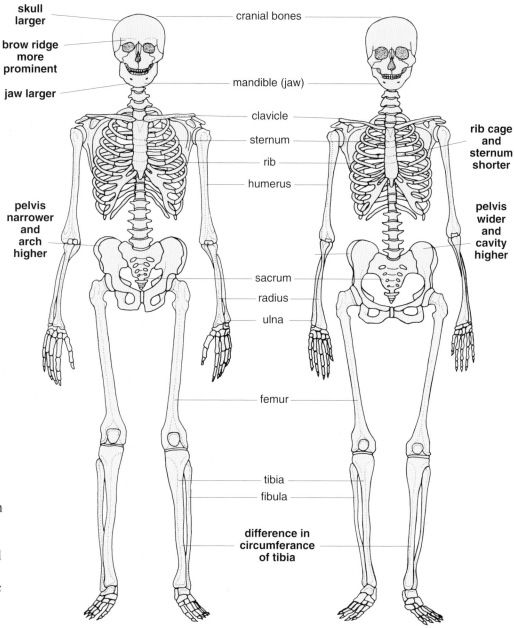

skull larger

brow ridge more prominent

jaw larger

pelvis narrower and arch higher

cranial bones

mandible (jaw)

clavicle

sternum

rib

humerus

sacrum

radius

ulna

femur

tibia

fibula

difference in circumference of tibia

rib cage and sternum shorter

pelvis wider and cavity higher

MALE

FEMALE

Figure 2.11 Comparison of a male and a female human skeleton, highlighting the anatomical location and different shapes and sizes of specific bones that can be used to determine the sex of the individual.

A relatively high level of certainty can be obtained by carefully measuring and comparing the size and shape of skeletal components from adult human remains with modern-day records, as a means of determining the sex of an individual. Although the sex of an individual cannot be definitively determined from measurements of a single bone, by combining evidence from several bones, or using this evidence in conjunction with other evidence, it is possible to improve the certainty of sex identification of adult human remains. In contrast, it is not generally possible to determine the sex of adolescents and children from the size and shape of the bones, as the skeleton continues to grow at varying rates until late adolescence (or early adulthood). To resolve this problem, a small group of archaeologists and molecular geneticists have been working since the 1990s on a method of determining the sex of infants from bone fragments by ancient DNA analysis (aDNA) (see Box 2.4).

Box 2.4 What is DNA and how does genetic fingerprinting work?

DNA (deoxyribonucleic acid) is a large, complex molecule that occurs in the nucleus of most cells. It carries the genetic information that is copied and transferred into each new cell that forms within a body and is passed down through the generations as part of the reproductive process. In eukaryotic organisms (i.e. organisms characterised by complex cell structures, which includes humans, all other animals, plants, fungi and some forms of algae), each individual DNA molecule forms a single chromosome (where a chromosome is simply a very long strand of DNA that is wrapped up on itself; Figure 2.12), and in each cell, there is a set number of chromosomes, the number being diagnostic for that particular organism. For example, all human cells (except red blood cells, which do not have a nucleus and therefore no DNA), contain 23 pairs of chromosomes – half of which come from the mother and half from the father. Of these 23 pairs, one pair determines the sex of the individual (these are the X and Y chromosomes, where females have an XX pairing and males an XY pairing), while the other 22 pairs of chromosomes carry the bulk of information involved in transferring hereditary traits and characteristics.

Each chromosome is comprised of a series of genes, which can be thought of as the 'basic units of heredity' or 'coding' units separated by varying amounts of non-coding units (Figure 2.12a). Regulatory processes switch genes on and off to control particular functions in cells. Genes influence the behavioural traits of an organism and are involved in transferring hereditary diseases in the form of genetic mutations and recessive genes. The order of the coding and non-coding components that make up a gene, in addition to the complete sequence of genes that make up a particular organism, is called the genome. The DNA of the human genome (which is relatively simple compared with some organisms) consists of ~100 000 different genes. With the exception of identical twins, everyone's genetic make-up (i.e. the order of the coding units and sequence of genes in their DNA) is unique to them.

Genetic fingerprinting is a technique used to distinguish between the DNA of different individuals from the same species. It can be done by analysing DNA from any number of different biological samples, such as skin, hair, bones and blood (separating DNA from the white blood cells). DNA analysis is typically done by a technique called gel electrophoresis, which separates molecules according to their size, shape and electrical behaviour.

If you are unfamiliar with this technique, go to the 'Techniques' section on the DVD, and read about how it is used in 'Genetic fingerprinting'.

In archaeology, DNA analyses are used in various ways, for example to: (a) establish the sex of human remains; (b) identify the presence of human remains at some point in the past in a soil sample; (c) compare genetic sequences in specific populations over time; (d) track the movement of populations over time as they migrated and interacted with others; and (e) track the geographic spread of certain diseases over time. One of the biggest problems archaeologists face however, is that over time, the DNA molecule breaks down, resulting in many archaeological samples containing little or no usable genetic material.

To counteract this problem, a new method of analysis called ancient DNA (aDNA) has been developed. As archaeologists are generally interested in using DNA to answer more general questions (e.g. the sex of an individual, which population they belonged to, whether they have common genetic ancestors, and the occurrence and spread of diseases) rather than definitively identifying one individual from another (as required in modern forensics and molecular biochemistry), using lower-quality genetic information is entirely acceptable within an archaeological time frame.

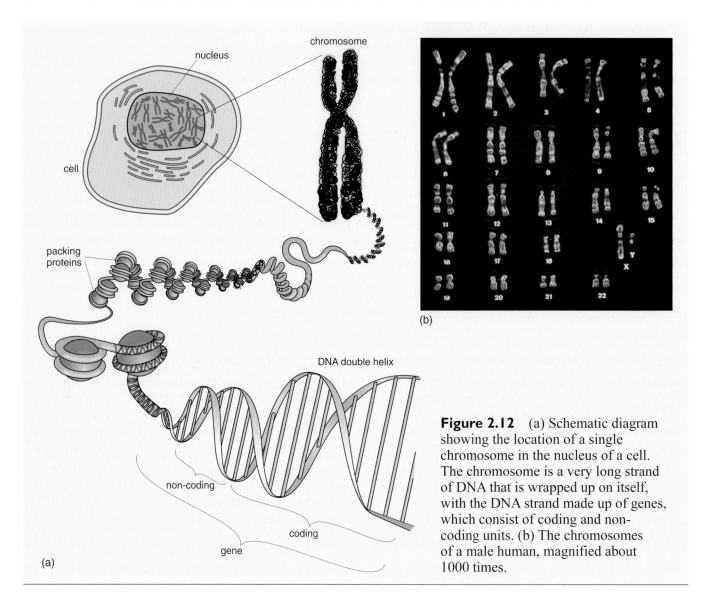

(b)

(a)

Figure 2.12 (a) Schematic diagram showing the location of a single chromosome in the nucleus of a cell. The chromosome is a very long strand of DNA that is wrapped up on itself, with the DNA strand made up of genes, which consist of coding and non-coding units. (b) The chromosomes of a male human, magnified about 1000 times.

Now read *Greene* Chapter 5, Section 5.6 'Genetics' (pp. 208–10), which summarises some of the key ways genetic and DNA analyses are used in archaeology.

Sizing up stature: height and weight

There are several means of determining the height and weight of an individual from intact human remains, whole skeletons and certain skeletal fragments.

Establishing the height of an individual from intact adult human remains or a skeleton is relatively easy – all you have to do is measure them! However, it is important to remember that bodies shrink slightly upon death (although water-saturated remains can shrink by up to 50% if they dry out), so the height of the living individual will be slightly greater than that measured directly from the dead body.

When dealing with partial adult skeletons, an accurate method of determining the height is to measure the length of specific *long bones* (i.e. the three long leg bones – femur, tibia and fibula, and the three long arm bones – humerus, radius and ulna; Figure 2.11). This method assumes that different parts of the adult body are in proportion with each other, and that the relative proportions between height and leg or arm length vary according to the sex and the ethnicity of the individual. By averaging measurements from many individuals in a specific ethnic group (and dividing them into male and female), the average relationship between height and limb length can be established. This is then used to calculate the full body height of any other individual from that group, by applying a method called *regression analysis* (see Box 2.5).

Box 2.5 What is a regression analysis?

In regression analysis, measurable changes in one item (called a variable) are used to accurately predict how a related variable will change (in this case, changes in the length of a long bone can be used to determine an individual's full height).

The relationship between long bones and full height was determined by taking numerous measurements of different long bones in modern-day adult corpses, and comparing them directly with the individual's measured height. By doing this, a mathematical equation was devised that links the changes in bone length to overall height, with the multiplying factors used in the equation changing depending on (i) the type of long bone used, (ii) the broad ethnic origin and (iii) the sex of the individual being investigated (Table 2.3). (When the ethnicity or sex of an individual is unknown, an averaged equation can be used to allow an approximate height to be calculated.)

Table 2.3 Equations for calculating full adult height for males and females from different ethnic groups, using long bone measurements.

Bone type	Ethnicity	Male equation	Female equation
femur (thigh bone)	Caucasian	(Length × 2.32) + 65.53 cm	(Length × 2.47) + 54.13 cm
	African	(Length × 2.10) + 72.22 cm	(Length × 2.28) + 59.76 cm
tibia (shin bone)	Caucasian	(Length × 2.42) + 81.93 cm	(Length × 2.90) + 61.53 cm
	African	(Length × 2.19) + 85.36 cm	(Length × 2.45) + 72.56 cm
fibula (calf bone)	Caucasian	(Length × 2.60) + 75.50 cm	(Length × 2.93) + 59.61 cm
	African	(Length × 2.34) + 80.56 cm	(Length × 2.49) + 70.90 cm

(Source: adapted from http://forensics.rice.edu/pdfs/activity_nine.pdf)

For example, if the fibula of a Caucasian (white) female is measured as 33.25 cm, her height can be calculated as follows.

- The correct equation from Table 2.3 is: (length × 2.93) + 59.61 cm.
- Substituting the measured length gives: (33.25 cm × 2.93) + 59.61 cm.
- In mathematics, values *within* brackets are always calculated first, which gives: (97.42 cm) + 59.61 cm = 157.03 cm or 1.57 m (to the nearest cm).

Question 2.5

Calculate the relative height of the individuals from the following bone measurements.

(a) The shin bone (42.34 cm) of a white male

(b) The femur (50.19 cm) of a black male

The mathematical relationship between the length of long bones and height of the individuals can also be shown graphically, with the measurable value (the independent variable) plotted on the horizontal x-axis, and the predicted value (dependent variable) plotted on the vertical y-axis. For example, the length of the long bones (the measurable or independent variable) is plotted on the x-axis, and the height of the individual (the predicted or dependent variable) is read from the y-axis, at the point where the measured length of the bone intersects the regression line (Figure 2.13).

You can get help with working with graphs in the Maths Skills ebook on the course website.

Question 2.6

(a) The following skeletal remains of a male human were recovered from a grave at Tell es-Saʿidiyeh: the skull, some rib bones, the clavicle (35.34 cm), the right side of the pelvis, the left tibia (35.89 cm), the lower half of the right fibula (11.2 cm) and the right femur bone (44.67 cm).

Referring to Figure 2.13, estimate the full height of this individual.

(b) Now repeat the exercise by calculating his height using the most relevant equation(s) in Table 2.3.

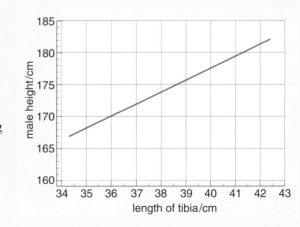

Figure 2.13   Graph of calculated height against length of tibia (shin bone) for males. This graph can be used to estimate the height of an individual by plotting the measurement of the shin bone (as accurately as possible) on the x-axis and drawing a vertical line up to the diagonal (red) regression line. At the intersection point with this line, a horizontal line should be drawn extending across to the y-axis. The point where this horizontal line cuts the y-axis is the expected height of an individual with a bone of the measured length.

Your values for (a) and (b) in Question 2.6 might be slightly different even though you used the same data. This is because the level of accuracy involved in the two processes differs. Reading from the graph is less precise in this case because the scales on each axis are fairly large, which means the height can be estimated only to within 1 cm. In contrast, by putting values into the correct equation, the height of this individual can be calculated down to one-tenth of a millimetre (which is more accurate than you could probably measure in person!).

■   What about the weight of individuals? Can this be determined from intact mummies, skeletons or skeletal fragments?

☐   Yes, studies show that intact mummies lose an average of 70–75% of their body mass, so an approximate estimation of the living weight of the individual can be estimated by weighing the intact remains. For skeletons and skeletal fragments, archaeologists can use estimates of the individual's height (from the process above) to determine the body mass index (BMI) and estimate the expected normal weight for an adult of that particular height and sex.

This technique is the same as that used by present-day doctors to establish whether a person has a 'healthy' weight for their size. In terms of archaeological remains, weighing mummies and measuring long bones will not indicate whether the person was overweight or malnourished; all they can do is say what the approximate 'healthy' weight would be in relation to modern-day standards.

Throughout this discussion, references to the height and weight of individuals from intact remains or skeletal fragments are accompanied by descriptive terms such as 'approximately' and 'estimation'. This is because each value is obtained from *absolute data* (i.e. values obtained by physically measuring or weighing the remains), to calculate the most *probable answer* based on detailed studies of modern humans and associated regression analyses (see Box 2.5). In other words, modern-day analogies that can be measured and compared, can be used to establish the most probable answer for combinations of variables from archaeological examples.

Assessing age

In archaeology (as well as forensic science and pathology), estimating the age of an individual at the time of death is subject to the same limitations that affect the calculation of height and weight. Only an approximation of the biological age can be determined (e.g. the broad divisions of infant, young, adolescent, adult and old age), which can also be stated in age spans such as 30–40 years old, rather than the exact chronological age (e.g. 35 years old). The biological age of an individual depends strongly on their genetic susceptibility to ageing and the harshness of the environment they live in. In archaeological remains, one of the most useful ways of determining the biological age is to investigate the physical structure of the bones and teeth.

Assessing age from bones

As a person ages, the structure, strength and connectivity of their bones will change. These changes allow the level of development or degeneration of an individual to be estimated, which can then be used to estimate their biological age. For example, in infants and young and adolescent children, the amount of connectivity between bones in the skull and the body can infer an approximate age. As an infant develops, separate bones in the skull fuse, while throughout childhood, adolescence and into early adulthood, the shafts of long bones fuse with the growing (articulating) joints, reaching completion by the mid-twenties to early thirties. As an adult continues to develop and enter old age, most bones start to decrease in density (because of osteoporosis and resorption of calcium into the body), losing strength and becoming more fragile, while the ends of the rib cage become irregular as they thin. In contrast, the skull bones continue to thicken with old age. Changes in the physical structure and strength of bones can be easily determined by examining skeletal remains; when working with intact bodies and mummies or to investigate the density of bones, the most commonly used techniques include X-ray analysis and computerised tomography (CT) scans.

 If you are uncertain how these non-destructive techniques work, you should go to the 'Techniques' section on the DVD, and read about how they are used in archaeology.

Assessing age from teeth

■ Thinking back to your own experience, what distinctive events in the development of your teeth could be used to determine your biological age?

☐ The most obvious indication of biological ageing from teeth is the replacement of the milk or baby (primary) teeth by the adult (permanent) dentition, which occurs from mid childhood to early adolescence, and the presence of the third molars (i.e. the wisdom teeth), which generally erupt in late adolescence to early adulthood.

The shape of the tooth's root tip (Figure 2.2) can also be used to determine biological age, as newer teeth have pointed root tips, while older teeth have more rounded root tips.

In addition to looking at the type of teeth present in a skull, the amount of wear on the teeth can be used to estimate an approximate age (although the exact type and extent of wear depends on the individual's diet). As wear occurs naturally, the upper surface of the tooth (i.e. the enamel, Figure 2.2) is continuously replaced at a steady rate throughout an individual's lifetime. As it forms, microscopic ridges develop on the surface, with the frequency and spacing between these ridges useful for identifying periods of ill health and poor nutrition (this topic is revisited in Section 2.4.1).

As with bones, changes to the surface of the teeth can be studied by direct observations or with a scanning electron microscope, in which the actual tooth or an exact replica can be examined at very high magnifications. Where there is no direct access to the teeth (e.g. in a mummy), or the area of interest is embedded in the skull (e.g. the root), X-ray analyses can be used.

Teeth can also be used to date human remains chemically, by measuring the relative abundance of a naturally forming amino acid within the tooth by a technique called amino acid racemisation (AAR) (see the 'Techniques' section on the DVD). The particular amino acid of interest occurs in two forms, which are compositionally identical but have different physical structures (e.g. similar to the differences between your right and left hands); substances with the same chemical composition but different structure are called *isomers*. In this case, the isomers of interest are called the L- and D-isomers. Studies show that the relative amount of L- and D-isomers found in human teeth changes in a predictable way, with the L-isomer constantly produced throughout an individuals lifetime, transforming at a steady state to the D-isomer after death. The D/L ratio can therefore be used to establish an approximate *archaeological* age by regression analysis (i.e. the date of death rather than the age of the person when they died).

Part 2 Activity 2.10   Determining the Late Bronze Age population dynamics of Tell es-Saʿidiyeh – evidence from the graves

(The estimated time needed to complete this activity is 25 minutes.)

Main learning outcomes developed: KU4, CS1, KS2 and PS1.

An interim report was published on excavation work at Tell es-Saʿidiyeh cemetery, in which the sex, age at death, average height from long bones, and cause of death of a number of individuals from two areas (BB and DD) in the cemetery were compared.

In this activity, you will use this data to compare and contrast the types of individuals buried in each site, and devise scientifically valid reasons to explain any differences that exist. Now go to the DVD, click on 'Topics', find Topic 2 and complete Part 2 Activity 2.10.

What did they look like?

Start by reading 'Pathology' in *Greene* Chapter 5 (pp. 205–7).

When faced with exceptional finds such as the extremely well-preserved, 500 year-old Llullaillaco mountain children, there is no difficulty in imagining what they looked like when alive (Figure 2.6). (The difficulty in this case is accepting they died so long ago.) With many of the bog bodies such as Clonycavan Man (Figure 2.4a) and Lindow Man (Figure 2.5), although their skulls were deformed during burial and the skin discoloured by the tannins, it is still possible to visualise what they looked like. Other remains may be accompanied by physical artefacts placed alongside the body at the time of burial that can help reveal what the individual looked like, such as the outer covering of Nesperennub's mummy (Figure 2.7) and Seianti Hanunia Tlesnasa's elaborate sarcophagus.

- ■ What other approach can be used in archaeology to gain an understanding of what an individual might have looked like?

- ☐ Figure 5.13 (p. 207) in *Greene* shows an archaeological pathologist at work, reconstructing the facial features of a Viking man from the ninth century AD, by using the anatomical structure of the skull as a guide.

If you have watched any recent forensic science programmes, you will be well aware that anthropologists can use a variety of techniques to reconstruct heads. The same techniques can be used in archaeology to help with interpretations about the scientific relevance of specific human remains (see Box 2.6).

Box 2.6 Reconstructing faces from the past

Traditionally, anthropologists start by reconstructing the skull (if it is broken or only partially present) and produce a plaster cast into which marker pegs are inserted at between 20 and 35 key anatomical points (Figure 2.14a). The appropriate length of each peg is determined by using tissue depth data collected from living subjects, and related to the most probable ancestry group, sex and approximate biological age of the deceased individual. Once in position, the pegs are used as guides to the relative thickness of the underlying facial tissues and skin (Figure 2.14b).

The size and location of the major facial muscles are determined from the shape and structure of the skull and are modelled in clay. Although many facial features (such as the shape of the nose and eyes, and how the lips close) can be estimated from skeletal and dental details, some features (including the shapes of the lips and ears) cannot be easily determined. In some instances however, mummified soft tissues can help provide a great deal of facial information, as the ears and hair will often be well preserved. Superficial aspects such as the colour of the skin, eyes and hair, and styling of the hair, can not be extrapolated from skeletal material and can only be estimated from population probabilities or historical documents (Figure 2.14c).

More recently, faces have been reconstructed with the help of technology. By laser scanning skull fragments, a skull can be reconstructed virtually and used to produce an exact replica carved by laser, from a hard foam substance or plastic onto which the anthropologist can build up the muscle structure as above. Alternatively, the scanned skull fragments can be transformed into a virtual three-dimensional model on which the muscle structure, skin and facial features can then be constructed digitally. As well as laser scanning, radiologists can use CT scanning to produce a series of digital slices through a skull, enabling the external and internal anatomy of the skull to be viewed. The resulting three-dimensional virtual model can then be used to produce an exact virtual or real model on which the facial reconstruction can be developed.

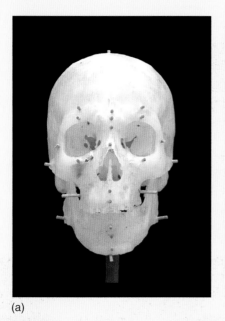 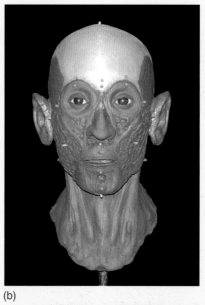 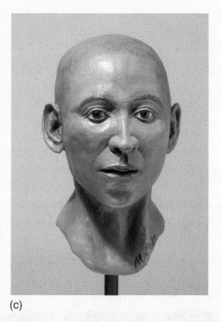

(a)   (b)   (c)

Figure 2.14   (a) The modelled plastic skull of Nesperennub (reconstructed from evidence collected from a series of CT scans) with tissue depth pegs inserted at key anatomical locations. (b) Adding the muscle structure to the plastic model. (c) The finished reconstruction of Nesperennub, produced by Caroline Wilkinson. Images courtesy of the University of Manchester.

So far, you have encountered facial reconstructions for four of the case studies: Nesperennub (Figure 2.14c), Lindow Man (Figure 2.15a), Clonycavan Man (Figure 2.15b) and Wetwang Woman (Figure 2.15c), the last three all being from the Iron Age.

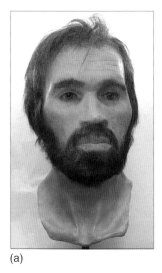

(a)   (b)   (c)

Figure 2.15   Facial reconstructions of (a) Lindow Man, (b) Clonycavan Man and (c) Wetwang Woman.

In the next activity, you will examine how reconstructions of the external and internal morphology of a skull were used to investigate the origins of a Palaeolithic child found in the Lapedo Valley, Portugal. You will also see how studies of the mode of this child's burial have provided new insights into the meaning of society at that time.

Part 2 Activity 2.11   The Lapedo Child: a hybrid 'love child' or just a 'chunky' infant?

(The estimated time needed to complete this activity is 1 hr 20 mins.)

Main learning outcomes developed: KU2, CS3, KS2 and PS1.

This activity is based on parts of a 50-minute television programme produced in 2002 by the BBC for The Open University. In it, the archaeological significance of the Lapedo Child was examined, before some of the implications of this discovery in relation to the emergence of modern humans across Europe were discussed (Figure 2.16). For the purpose of this activity, you will focus

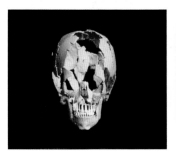
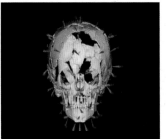
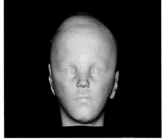
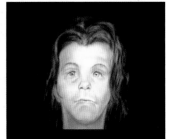

Figure 2.16   Is this the face of a Neanderthal or a modern human child? Reconstructing the skull of the Lapedo Child to gain an insight into their appearance.

on the archaeological components of this programme (although some of the evolutionary discussions have been left in for general interest). You are encouraged to watch each chapter right through, writing down a few initial notes as you go, before returning to work through each one in more detail while answering a series of structured questions, which will help you build up a picture of the archaeological investigations of the Lapedo Child.

As you watch the programme, you should pay particular attention to:

- the immediate relevance of the discovery in terms of its age and the finds
- how a biological age was assigned to the skeletal remains
- why the size and shape of different skeletal fragments were problematic in terms of the origin of the child
- the debate for and against the skeleton being a 'chunky modern human' or a typical stocky Neanderthal child
- the technique used to reconstruct the child's skull

 Now go to the DVD, click on 'Topics', find Topic 2 and work through Part 2 Activity 2.11.

2.3.2   Dating: determining the archaeological age of human remains

As well as determining the biological age at the time of death, archaeologists are also interested in the archaeological age of human remains (i.e. the time period the remains can be dated to).

■ List some of the ways the archaeological age of human remains can be determined.

☐ The archaeological age can be determined by: (a) dating the bones or teeth isotopically; (b) dating artefacts buried with the remains by typology or chemical analyses; (c) using stratigraphic evidence from the deposit in which the remains were buried; (d) radiocarbon dating of pollen collected from the surrounding sediment or found on the remains.

You might have thought of other ways in which an absolute or a relative date for human remains can be established. The actual dating method(s) used will differ depending on: the composition of the surrounding materials (e.g. the geological composition of the surrounding sediments or rocks); the composition of the objects of interest; the expected age of these materials; and the level of accuracy required (see *Greene* Figures 4.14 and 4.15, p. 160).

 Now read 'Radiocarbon samples' in *Greene* Chapter 5 (pp. 167–8 only), Section 5.5 (pp. 169–70), Section 5.8 (p. 173) and Section 6 'Derivative techniques' (p. 174 only) before answering the following questions.

Question 2.7

(a) What are the four main scientific dating techniques used to date teeth and bones? (*Hint: refer to* Greene *Figure 4.15, p. 160.*)

(b) Different scientific dating techniques produce *absolute* or *relative* dates. Match these two terms with the correct definition below:

Definition 1: any age that is based on measurable physical or chemical quantities and refers to a specific timescale (e.g. years BP) or is based on verifiable historical associations (e.g. dated coins).

Definition 2: any age that is obtained by examining the relationship of the material or object of interest with surrounding materials, allowing its age to be put into context (e.g. if layer A lies above layer B, layer A and any objects found in it must be younger than layer B and the objects in it).

(c) Referring back to your answer for (a), which (if any) of these are *absolute dating techniques* and which are *relative dating techniques*?

The term 'derivative dating' in *Greene* means the same as 'relative dating' used in this book.

Question 2.8

(a) What physical factors can alter the measured D/L ratio obtained from archaeological remains?

(b) How can the accuracy of the calculated amino acid racemisation (AAR) age be confirmed?

2.4   Health and diseases: understanding past medical histories

Health is a measure of an organism's ability to function efficiently within its physical environment (at both the cellular and the whole organism level), and to cope with any stresses that cause the normal living conditions to change. Health is directly linked to nutrition, which is concerned with how diet affects an individual's ability to maintain an effective metabolism and physiology. Poor nutrition will lead to a poor state of health and the onset of deficiency diseases (e.g. diseases caused by the lack of specific nutrients). It can also lower the immune system, making the individual more susceptible to communicable and infectious diseases, which are caused by the transference of a parasite or virus (collectively referred to as the pathogen) into the host's body (i.e. the organism infected by the disease). Diseases that are non-transferable may be congenital (e.g. caused by genetic inheritance), and be the result of genetic mutations or caused by different environmental or nutritional stresses.

In this section you will discover how archaeologists can gain an insight into the diet, state of health and range of diseases that affected individuals and communities in the archaeological past, by studying human remains.

2.4.1   Health and nutrition

Start by reading 'Diet' in *Greene* Chapter 5 (pp. 207–8), then read Box 2.7 below.

Box 2.7 Getting to grips with chemical terminology

In the section on diet in *Greene*, there are three terms in the first sentence that may not be familiar to you, namely: isotopes, trace elements and strontium.

Isotopes

Isotopes are different forms of the same element, each having a different mass number. They can be subdivided into two main types:

(a) *stable isotopes*, for example, the most common stable isotopes used in archaeology include (i) carbon: ^{13}C (pronounced carbon-thirteen) and ^{12}C (^{14}C is a radiogenic isotope); (ii) oxygen: ^{18}O, ^{17}O and ^{16}O; and (iii) nitrogen: ^{15}N and ^{14}N; and

(b) *radiogenic isotopes*, for example: the uranium–thorium (U–Th) series; rubidium–strontium (Rb–Sr) series; and potassium–argon (^{40}K–^{40}Ar), among many others.

Stable isotopes exist naturally, with each different type present in varying amounts that can be measured, allowing an isotopic ratio to be calculated. Archaeologists (geochemists, geologists and any one else interested in these isotopes) can use changes in these ratios to make inferences about climate changes, the type of plants eaten by individuals, the environments they lived in, etc. Oxygen isotopes can also be used to calculate the *absolute age* of some materials, although this is more commonly used in geology and environmental science than in archaeology.

In contrast, radiogenic isotopes break down or decay over time, with the 'parent' isotope changing into the 'daughter' isotope by the ejection or capture of one or more subatomic particles – alpha α (helium nucleus), beta β, and gamma γ particles – to produce what is called a 'decay series' (e.g. ^{234}U decays to ^{230}U by emitting an alpha particle; ^{87}Rb decays to ^{87}Sr by emitting a beta particle; ^{40}K decays to ^{40}Ar by capturing a beta particle). As radiogenic isotopes decay at a fixed rate (called the half-life, which is the amount of time needed for 50% of any remaining parent isotope to decay to its daughter product), radiogenic isotopic ratios can be used to calculate the *absolute age* of a material, as well as link it to a specific environment or source area. Different radiogenic isotopes have different half-lives operating from millions or billions of years down to seconds. In archaeology, isotopes with half-lives of hundreds, thousands or a million years are the most useful. One of the most common radiogenic isotopes used to date organic archaeological materials is radiogenic carbon, also known as carbon-14 (^{14}C). It has a half-life of 5730 years and can be used to date materials up to ~60 000 years BP.

Now read *Greene* Chapter 4, Section 5.2 (pp. 161–3) and review 'Radiocarbon samples' (pp. 167–8).

You will be glad to know that you do not need to understand the chemical or physical properties of isotopes in this course. All you need to know is that variations in isotopic ratios can be used to recognise: climatic changes; the likely source region of materials; the movement of an individual or a population to new geographical areas; and the type of environment they lived in.

Trace elements

Trace elements are any chemical element that is present in minute concentrations. In geological substances, this is defined as any element present at levels of <0.1% (1000 parts per million or ppm); in analytical chemistry, trace elements are present at levels of <100 ppm; while in biological substances, trace elements are often called *micronutrients*, and relate to elements needed in minute quantities to allow growth and development and to maintain physiological function.

If you are unfamiliar with trace element analysis, you should read 'Analysis and characterisation' in Greene *Chapter 5 (pp. 212–5). You will also find it useful to review the processes of XRF and ICP-AES analyses, in the 'Techniques' section on the DVD.*

Strontium

Strontium is a trace element commonly found in teeth and bones (as well as other natural substances). Changes in its concentration can be used to obtain information about the diet of an individual, while changes in its isotopic abundance can provide useful information about the environment a person lived in and what they ate.

There are several ways archaeologists can investigate the short- and long-term diet of an individual, including: examination of the stomach contents of intact or partially intact human remains; chemical and isotopic analyses of teeth and bones; examination of animal bones found in settlements; and macroscopic and microscopic examination and chemical analysis of human excrement (called *coprolites* in archaeology and geology).

The last meal: examining stomach contents

Studying the stomach contents of intact or partially intact human remains allows the immediate short-term diet of the individual to be determined (i.e. the last meal the person had).

■ How reliable will the stomach contents of mummies and bog bodies be in relation to discerning the normal diet of this individual (and their community)?

☐ It will depend on how the individual died. If they were the victims of sacrifice or execution, their last meal may be very different from their normal diet. In contrast, if they died of natural causes, their last meal may be representative of their normal diet.

Question 2.9

Detailed studies have been carried out on the stomach contents of the three Iron Age bog men (Clonycavan, Old Croghan and Lindow Man) and the Llullaillaco mountain children from the 16th century AD.

(a) Referring back to each study, list the range of foodstuffs recovered from each stomach.

(b) Besides giving an insight into their diet, what other inferences can be made about the type of food found in each stomach?

Dietary evidence from teeth and bones

Teeth and bones are an excellent way of studying the long-term diet and nutritional health of an individual. Within teeth, the location and type of wear can be studied by optical and scanning electron microscopy (SEM); this technique has been used in particular to determine the diets of early prehistoric humans, where the presence of vertical striations on the sides of teeth indicate a high intake of meat in the diet, whereas individuals who followed a more strongly vegetarian diet have more obvious horizontal striations on the sides of their teeth.

Isotopic analyses of teeth give an insight into changes in the source of food in the diet. For example, carbon isotopes (and, to a lesser extent, nitrogen isotopes) can be used to recognise a shift in the source of protein from a seafood diet to one that relied on land-based animals. Shifts in carbon isotope ratios in teeth can also be used to identify changes in agricultural practices moving from marine to land-based plants, and between certain types of land-based plants (e.g. wheat and corn). Variations in the isotope ratios of oxygen and strontium in teeth have been used to identify changes in the environmental conditions in which the individual lived (along with a change in the type of vegetation that formed the staple part of the diet), and to map the migration and mixing of populations from distinct areas. Isotope studies have also been made of bone collagen, using nitrogen and carbon isotopes to identify changes in the relative importance of land-based and marine plants and animals.

Evidence for malnutrition (or prolonged periods of illness) can be obtained by X-raying bones. The presence of microscopic lines of a calcified substance (called Harris lines) indicates periods when growth was temporally stopped or suspended. Interrupted growth lines caused by malnutrition (or disease) can also be found on finger and toe nails, forming fine grooves called Beau lines. The more frequently these lines occur, the more often the individual either had to survive on an inadequate diet or was unable to absorb the required nutrients for sustained growth through ill-health.

Now check that you understand the archaeological methods of investigation and the implications of health and nutrition by completing the following activity.

Part 2 Activity 2.12   Nesperennub – health matters

(The estimated time needed to complete this activity is 20 minutes.)

Main learning outcomes developed: KU1, CS2, KS2 and PS1.

In this activity, you will return to examine Nesperennub and the range of non-destructive techniques used to investigate his state of health during life and at the time of his death.

Now go to the course website, click on 'Activities' and complete Part 2 Activity 2.12.

2.4.2   Disease and deformities

■ List the different types of disease, parasites and deformities that you have encountered in the case studies so far. Which scientific techniques were used to study these ailments?

☐ So far, you have encountered parasites and tapeworms in Lindow Man's stomach identified by analysing his stomach contents; in Nesperennub, you encountered osteoarthritis detected by the build-up of calcified growths along his spine, evidence for periods of malnutrition or extended illness, from the Harris lines on his leg bones, and the presence of tooth decay or a possible abscess around one of his molars, all detected on CT scans. Reconstruction of the skull of the Iron Age woman from Wetwang (Figure 2.15c) indicates she may have had some facial deformation (identified from misalignments between skull fragments), while the skull of the youngest Llullaillaco mountain child ('Lightning Girl') had been reshaped into a more conical form by binding the head when an infant. (The deformities of the bog men's skulls do not count in this instance because they are the result of post-mortem deformation caused by the weight of the overlying bog.)

From this, it is clear that evidence for disease, infection and deformities can be obtained by studying the external and internal soft tissues and the skeletal remains (bones and teeth), using a mixture of analytical techniques, including direct observations, X-rays and CT scans.

Soft tissue samples

Where more detailed studies are required, small tissue samples can be removed from intact human remains, by inserting a fine endoscope into the body and doing a standard biopsy. If the tissue sample has been dried out (artificially or naturally), it can be rehydrated in a mixture of ethanol and sodium carbonate, before being analysed by optical microscopy or higher powered SEM. Optical microscopy can be used to study histological samples (e.g. the internal structure of tissue cells, to look for disease or infection); meanwhile, high-powered SEM images can reveal the presence of skin parasites or fungal infections.

Part 2 Activity 2.13 Analysing skin and tissue samples

(The estimated time needed to complete this activity is 15 minutes.)

Main learning outcomes developed: KU1, CS1, KS2 and KS3.

An interesting account of the preparatory techniques and types of histological investigations carried out on Egyptian mummies is given in Katie Currie's article published in 2006 in *The Biomedical Scientist*, in which *Comfort* fabric softener is used as an alternative to the usual rehydration solutions!

 Go to the course website and retrieve this article from the 'Documents' section. As you skim-read the article, pay particular attention to the discussion of the following issues, and make notes on:

- early methods of extracting tissue samples

- the range of interdisciplinary approaches used to study mummies

- why the scientists decided to do an autopsy on one mummy to help develop non-destructive techniques to study all others

- the need to rehydrate tissues (and why fabric softener is not a good rehydration solution!)

- the range of diseases that were identified.

(Note: you are not expected to understand all of the detailed scientific discussions in the article, just use it to illustrate the type of studies carried out on ancient tissue samples to investigate past diseases and infections.)

Bones

Examining the surface and the internal structures of bones by imaging (e.g. optical microscopy, SEM, X-rays, CT scans) shows the presence of different genetic and infectious diseases and disorders (e.g. Harris lines caused by malnutrition or ill health; calcified growths from osteoarthritis). Evidence of accidental and intentional trauma can also be identified by looking for broken and deformed bones, noting: the location of fractures or deformation; the size and shape of the fracture or deformity; and whether the trauma is a one-off, repeated or continuous event (see Figure 5.12 and 'Pathology' both in *Greene*, pp. 205–7). Care must be taken when examining physical damage to bones to determine whether it happened while the person was alive, contributed to their death, or was the result of burial (or excavation) during the archaeological process (e.g. when determining the taphonomic history of the bone).

Part 2 Activity 2.14 How iconic was Wetwang Woman?

(The estimated time needed to complete this activity is 25 minutes.)

Main learning outcomes developed: KU2, CS1, CS2 and PS1.

In this final activity, you will consider some of the evidence used to support the theory that the Wetwang Woman (Figure 2.17) had an iconic status in her society and was different in terms of her physical size and age compared with the population norm, as a means of explaining why she was given a special cart burial. You will then examine various sides of the argument about whether her physical appearance also played a role in singling her out from the average woman of her time.

Now go to the DVD, click on 'Topics', find Topic 2 and complete Part 2 Activity 2.14.

Figure 2.17   An impressive sight: the influential Wetwang Woman on her ceremonial cart (reconstructed outside the British Museum, London).

2.5   Summary of Topic 2

By completing this topic you should now be able to:

1   State why the physical and the chemical state of human remains can differ depending on the environment of preservation, using examples to illustrate your explanation (CS1).

2   Use a variety of learning strategies (e.g. scanning, skim-reading and summarising) to enhance your active reading skills (KS4).

3   Describe, with examples, how human remains can be preserved and conserved by natural and artificial processes (KU4, CS1).

4   List some of the key ethical issues that must be considered when working with human remains, and refer to the advisory regulations set up in the UK to help standardise these processes (CS3, PS1).

5   Compare and contrast the different social, cultural, biological and demographic information that can be obtained from one-off versus multiple burial sites (KU3, CS2).

6 Describe how the biological age, sex, stature and state of health of individuals can be determined from bones and other human remains, and how this can then be used to gain an insight into population dynamics (CS3, KS1).

7 List and describe the main non-destructive and non-invasive scientific techniques that are commonly used to analyse human remains (KU1).

8 List and describe examples of destructive (invasive) scientific techniques commonly used to analyse human remains, and the ethical considerations that are needed before carrying out such studies (KU1, PS1).

9 Explain what regression analysis is and how this approach is used to determine the height and weight of individuals from bone measurements (KS1, KS2).

10 State how remains can be dated by absolute and relative dating techniques, citing examples (KU1, CS3).

11 Briefly explain why the taphonomic history of remains is important when investigating the potential cause of death of an individual or a group of individuals (CS1, KS2).

12 Explain, using examples, how the state of health (and cause of death) of an individual can be determined by examining different types of remains, and how this can then be used to make inferences about the environment and social conditions during their life (CS1, CS2).

Remember, only the most important one or two learning outcomes are listed after each summary statement above to emphasise the ones they are specifically addressing. Each summary statement does however, relate to several of the learning outcomes developed in this course, and you should bear this in mind when reviewing the topic and working towards your End of Course Assessment (ECA).

Topic 3
Making sense of materials

3.1   Introduction

In addition to the more spectacular testaments to the past, such as the pyramids of Egypt or the Great Wall of China, an archaeologist usually deals with more mundane items: the debris from people's everyday lives such as broken pottery or the remains of stone tools. These 'leftovers', which are generally made up of a variety of materials that were originally formed into objects and had a specific function, are called *artefacts*. These can be further classified as inorganic (e.g. stone axes, glass, pottery, metal objects) or organic artefacts and materials (e.g. wooden objects, textiles, paper). The materials used to produce an artefact have to be modified by humans to varying degrees or manufactured from scratch. This may involve chipping away at a stone to produce a tool, or more elaborate work, such as converting a raw material into a completely new substance that can then be worked in some way to produce a usable item. Human societies are uniquely dependent on technology, and deliberately manufactured objects and materials, for their survival.

The Danish scholar C. J. Thomsen (1788–1865) linked the use of certain types of materials by humans to periods of prehistoric time, and devised a Three Age system consisting of successive Stone, Bronze and Iron Ages. Aside from asking how old it is, simply looking at or touching an artefact and knowing where it was found, can reveal much about the people who produced and used it, as well as their culture. You may however, want to know more: for example, what raw materials were used to make the artefact and where did they come from? Answers to these questions might lead to information about how it was made, the technologies available at a particular time and methods of trade and communication between different groups of people.

This topic covers some of the most important categories of materials recovered from archaeological sites, which have been subjected to scientific examination. You will look at their history, how they were produced and/or worked, and why certain materials were chosen for specific purposes. As you progress through this topic, you will also discover how materials decay or change over time. When an archaeologist makes a find, the object in question may have been buried for many thousands of years, and the fact that today's museums are filled with stone, pots and glass fragments, bronze axe heads and corroded metals, does not necessarily represent a complete description of the past. Instead, it is more a reflection of what has survived the burial and site formation processes.

In some cases, the act of removing an object from the ground puts it at more risk than if it was left undisturbed. This is a particular problem for materials found in exceptional conditions after being buried or stored in favourable surroundings; these include bodies naturally refrigerated in ice (e.g. Ötzi, the Neolithic 'Ice Man' found in the Italian Alps), and the perfectly preserved artefacts found in the dry atmosphere of ancient tombs (e.g. the tomb of Tutankhamun). Once removed, a strategy must be employed to ensure the object does not deteriorate when stored or put on public display (see Box 3.1). If an object has decayed significantly or been damaged, a highly skilled conservator will intervene to stabilise and preserve it (Figure 3.1).

Figure 3.1   A conservator at the British Museum, London, working on the reconstruction of the Portland Vase (see Box 3.8).

Now complete Part 2 Activity 3.1 where you will learn about the work of the conservator.

Part 2 Activity 3.1   The work of the conservator

(The estimated time needed to complete this activity is 40 minutes.)

Main learning outcomes developed: KU1, KU4, CS3 and PS1.

You will find a full list of learning outcomes and their abbreviations in the back of this Study Book and in the Study Guide.

(a) Start by reading *Greene* Chapter 5, Section 7 (pp. 219–21) to find out more about the key role of conservation in archaeology.

(b) Now go to the DVD, click on 'Topics', find Topic 3 and complete Part 2 Activity 3.1, which starts with a short film called 'The work of the conservator'.

In this film, you will meet one of the British Museum's conservators, Fleur Shearman, who takes you behind the scenes and shows you some recent examples of the essential work being done on various artefacts. As you watch, make notes on the following:

- the techniques used to first stabilise (if necessary) and clean an artefact
- the idea that many artefacts are made from composite materials, which decay to different extents on burial (this is developed further in Section 3.7.5)
- how the conservator's work can inform the understanding of an artefact by a curator (in this case, Jody Joy discusses the iron mirror from the Wetwang burial).

■ If an object is recovered partially concealed in a block of soil, how can its original form be identified?

☐ Assuming it cannot be recognised by the unaided eye or under an optical microscope then X-radiography can provide images of internal details which often reveal its true structure.

Box 3.1 Restoring the Mold gold cape

A fine example of the results of the conservator's skills is the Mold gold cape (Figure 3.2a). It was originally found in 1833 in a burial mound at Bryn yr Ellyllon (which is Welsh for 'Hill of the Elves'), near Mold in North Wales. This artefact looked nothing like Figure 3.2a when it was found, as only squashed and broken fragments of gold remained. Painstaking reconstruction was required to restore it to its original form, involving reassembling the pieces rather like a jigsaw puzzle. For the British Museum conservators who tackled this task, much was learned (and relearned) about the skills of the goldsmith during this project.

During the reconstruction work, the pieces were arranged on a plastic support and stuck together with polyvinyl acetate (PVA) adhesive. Figure 3.2b shows this work in progress – note the need for additional clamps to prevent the unwieldy structure from collapsing. Once all the pieces had been joined, a large gap still however remained in the back; this was filled with a specially produced gilded copper plate.

The story does not end there, though. When restored, experiments looking at how the cape would have been worn, showed that the wearer had narrow shoulders and was therefore more likely to be a woman than a man. The cape itself was thought to be used for ceremonial purposes and dates from about 1900–1600 BC. It started out as a single ingot and illustrates how gold can be shaped to form ornate objects. You will discover more about gold and working with metals in Section 3.2.

(a)

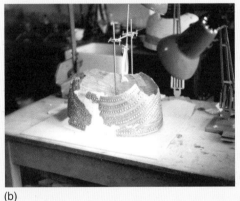

(b)

Figure 3.2 The Mold gold cape, dating from about 1900–1600 BC: (a) as it looks today; (b) during the restoration process.

Some manufacturing methods do not require a source of heat (e.g. carving wood or stone, and weaving), but many do. Originally this would have been in the form of fire caused by natural events such as lightning and volcanoes – clearly not available 'at the flick of a switch'! The point in time when humans learned to create and then control fire, set in motion a technological revolution based on the production and widespread use of materials manufactured using heat. Aside from cooking food, humans first used fire for working flint and hardening wooden tools. Later people used it to convert natural resources around them into useful materials, giving them a new-found power over their environment. This led to a less precarious lifestyle, and eventually a settled urban or rural existence. Although they did not know it at the time, these people were dabbling in the science of chemistry, which saw clay being turned into pottery, ores into metals, and sand into glass.

New and improved materials were produced as methods were developed to generate increasingly high temperatures. During the Bronze Age, it was found that if wood was partly burned in a limited supply of air, instead of being burned directly on a fire, it formed charcoal. Charcoal, which is mainly carbon, proved to be a much better and hotter fuel than wood. The temperature could be boosted further by blowing air onto the base of a charcoal fire.

Clay can be converted to pottery (see Section 3.4) by firing at about 500–600 °C but, as you will find out later, specialist pottery may need to be heated to in excess of 1200 °C. Glass was produced much later than pottery, as particular raw materials as well as a high temperature are required to make it (see Section 3.5). Enclosed chambers known as hearths, kilns and furnaces were developed (Figure 3.3a) that not only generated these high temperatures, but also enabled the atmosphere surrounding the raw materials to be controlled. This can be crucial; although some processes such as firing clay proceed effectively in high or low oxygen conditions, others such as the production of iron from iron ore, require an atmosphere depleted in oxygen to bring about the reaction.

A specialised form of kiln is shown in Figure 3.3b. This was used to produce lime, which has been used as a building material since Roman times. The remains of lime kilns such as this are scattered over chalky and limestone-rich areas of the British Isles. Figure 3.3b shows the brick pit that contained alternate layers of chalk and burning coke. This formed 'quicklime' (calcium oxide), to which water was added to make the final product 'slaked lime' (calcium hydroxide).

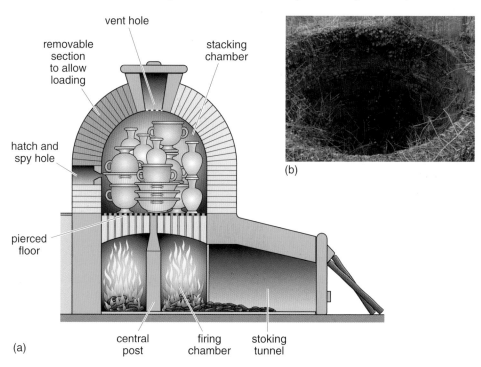

Figure 3.3   (a) Schematic diagram of an ancient pottery kiln (adapted from Williams, 1985)[3]. (b) The remains of a lime kiln.

[3]Williams, D. (1985) *Greek Vases*, British Museum Press, London.

Now complete Part 2 Activity 3.2.

Part 2 Activity 3.2   Analysis of materials: the tools of the trade

(The estimated time needed to complete this activity is 1 hour.)

Main learning outcomes developed: KU1, CS2, KS3 and KS4.

This activity refers to several analytical techniques and how they have been used to unravel some of the mysteries surrounding archaeological artefacts. Each technique provides a specific type of information, and largely can be applied to a number of types of material. *Note that in this topic, techniques are usually referred to in their abbreviated form (e.g. scanning electron microscopy = SEM); these are the commonly used acronyms, although you might find variations in other books or journals. To study the rest of this topic effectively, you need to develop an understanding about each of the analytical techniques you will encounter.*

(a) Go to the DVD, click on 'Topics', find Topic 3 and complete Part 2 Activity 3.2.

(b) As you read about the different analytical techniques commonly used when studying archaeological materials, complete Table 3.1. *(Some of the boxes are completed for you, to indicate the level of detail to record. You will find a blank version of this table in the Study Guide.)*

Note: in this section of the DVD you will also find several techniques that are not in Table 3.1. They are linked to other topics in this course.

Table 3.1 A selection of techniques used for materials analysis.

Technique	Abbreviation	Information obtained	Links to activity or box
radiography	–	internal details of an object	
optical microscopy	–		
scanning electron microscopy	SEM		Box 3.2
energy dispersive X-ray analysis (an attachment to a scanning electron microscope)	EDX		
X-ray fluorescence		identification of the elements in a sample	
X-ray diffraction			
infrared spectroscopy			
Raman spectroscopy	–		
gas-chromatography mass spectrometry			
inductively coupled plasma-atomic emission spectrometry			
wet chemical methods	–		

3.2 Metals

Metals have been used for almost 10 000 years. They have a shiny appearance and are malleable, i.e. can be hammered and shaped without breaking. As a consequence, metals have been formed into ornaments, jewellery, tools and weapons. It is believed that most of the earliest metal objects were used for personal adornment or ritual, as early finds in the shape of tools or weapons show very little sign of having been used.

Metals must be extracted from their ores, which are minerals (usually oxides, carbonates or sulfides) containing the metal. (It should also be mentioned that gold and copper exist as native mineral deposits, i.e. pure metal in its natural form.) For example, the Great Orme – a limestone headland at Llandudno, North Wales – is the site of the most extensive Bronze Age copper mines in Europe (Figure 3.4). About 4000 years ago local inhabitants used hammers made from stone and tools of animal bone to chip away at the rich veins of copper containing the minerals chalcopyrite (copper-iron sulfide) and malachite (copper carbonate).

Figure 3.4 The remains of copper mines on the Great Orme, Llandudno, North Wales. (The walkway across the mine gives an idea of scale.)

Metals are extracted from their ores by a process called *smelting*, where the mineral is heated with carbon (usually in the form of charcoal) and oxygen. In the case of the Great Orme, evidence suggests that the wood which was burned to make charcoal, was obtained from the nearby Conwy Valley. Smelting releases the metal along with carbon dioxide gas and a waste product called slag, which to an archaeologist is an important by-product, as slag heaps may be the only evidence of smelting at a particular site.

Although different metals have many properties in common, they also have their own individual characteristics, which determine their most appropriate use. For example, gold, silver and lead are rather soft, so are no good for making tools or weapons. They deform easily, cannot retain a sharp edge, and are not as good as the flint tools used throughout the Stone Age (Section 3.3). Copper and tin are also soft metals, but from about 3000 BC a harder metal with a lower melting temperature was produced by heating mixed ores of copper and tin with charcoal, to form the alloy bronze. While the relative amounts of copper and tin can vary in practice from 0 to 100% by mass, in the ancient world, bronze rarely contained more than about 20% tin. At the atomic level, copper atoms are mixed with tin atoms, a situation which increases the hardness of the material, even at very low tin levels.

Bronze was widely used as blades in daggers, the tips of spears or the heads of axes, where copper alone would have been too soft to use. At around 2000 BC however, an even harder metal began to emerge, probably originating from Anatolia or the Caucasus – this was iron. Isolated examples of iron have been found from even earlier contexts, including a mysterious four-sided piece of smelted iron found in a grave from c.5000 BC at Samarra, Iraq. Some of the earliest iron used may have been meteoric, which can be identified by the structure and presence of more than 5% nickel. Elsewhere, the Inuit people are known to have worked for centuries with iron from a large meteorite that landed in the Arctic.

Iron is normally obtained by smelting minerals such as hematite (iron oxide) or goethite (iron hydroxide) both of which are widely available from certain types of rock. The temperature required to melt iron is beyond that achievable from a charcoal fire, even when air is blown into the furnace. Instead, the slag becomes molten and can be removed, leaving a spongy mass of impure iron called the *bloom*. This is consolidated by repeated heating and hammering cycles, and most of the slag and other extraneous material is removed to leave *wrought* iron. This metal was often reasonably pure, but invariably contained minute particles of slag or iron oxide. Examination of blooms shows they often had mixed compositions: some areas might contain dissolved carbon ('steely' iron) or phosphorus (phosphoric iron), both being harder than wrought iron.

The adoption of iron was a gradual process, as it required the recognition that iron did not behave like copper and bronze, and that not all iron had the same properties. The carbon-rich parts of blooms could be identified as harder and were selected to make tools and weapons. Furthermore, whereas copper and bronze could be *cast* (see p. 122) into a shape from the earliest times, iron casting came much later (except in China) and so metal-smiths had to learn how to join pieces of iron by forge-welding them together while very hot.

Another important development was the discovery that a type of iron called steel became extremely hard when cooled rapidly by plunging it into water or oil (this is called *quenching*). This was useful for making tools that had to be sharp, such as chisels. There was a drawback however: although quenching makes steel hard, it also introduces stresses, making the metal brittle and likely to shatter when it hits anything. Not surprisingly, it was well into the Iron Age before quenching was used for swords on a regular basis, and only after the discovery that reheating the metal slightly (tempering) removed the brittleness. Despite these difficulties, no other metal has played a bigger role in the development of people's use of materials than iron. Its discovery ushered in a period of rapid change, the proliferation of iron tools and weapons entering everyday use; this was the Iron Age!

Whereas bronze was useful for producing tools and weapons, it did not replace stone completely. Only iron did that because there are many more sources of iron than copper and tin and, once making iron and steel tools was mastered, its use revolutionised agriculture, industry and architecture. The following extract from Rudyard Kipling's poem 'Cold Iron' sums up its importance:

> 'Gold is for the mistress – silver for the maid –
> Copper for the craftsman cunning at his trade,
> "Good!" said the Baron, sitting in his hall,
> "But Iron – Cold Iron – is master of them all." '

Part 2 Activity 3.3   Recovering the Wetwang mirror

(The estimated time needed to complete this activity is 15 minutes.)

Main learning outcomes developed: KU1, KU2 and CS2.

A remarkable example of the use of iron was found at Wetwang. The woman's body discovered in the Iron Age grave was accompanied by an iron mirror propped against her legs.

In Part 2 Activity 3.1, you heard Jody Joy discussing the importance of this object, not just from a materials point of view but at a cultural level, and raising the question of what was the mystical significance of a reflection at this time. In this activity, you will listen to Tony Spence describe how the mirror was removed from the grave by block excavation, and the processes of conservation and investigation that followed.

Now go to the DVD, click on 'Topics', find Topic 3, and work through Part 2 Activity 3.3.

Metal can be worked to shape as well as cast by heating it until it melts, and then pouring the liquid into a mould to produce a chosen shape or design (see Box 3.2). It can also be worked by hammering in the cold and the hot state, although prolonged beating and bending makes metal brittle. It was subsequently discovered however, that a combination of hammering and reheating the metal (the latter process called 'annealing') – allows the metal to be worked into thin sheets. These methods are still largely used to this day.

Box 3.2 Casting South American gold: the lost-wax process

In Central and South America around 2000 BC, goldsmiths working in isolation from the rest of the world developed a unique approach to working with gold.

Look again at the SEM images in the 'Techniques' section on the DVD.

A beautiful example of their craft is the gold alloy ring from Mexico (Figure 3.5), which was produced as a 'one-off' by the 'lost-wax process' with the intricacy of the surface decoration being revealed in more detail by SEM. First, a model of the object to be cast was made from beeswax and coated with clay to make a mould. This was then baked, which hardened the

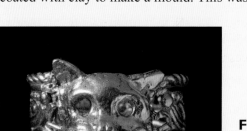

Figure 3.5   The work of early South American goldsmiths: a gold alloy ring from Mexico, dating to about 1520–1200 BC; it is 11 mm high and 20 mm wide.

clay, and caused the wax to melt and flow out. Liquid gold was then poured into the mould. After it had cooled, the finished object was removed from the clay, leaving a highly ornate and exclusive piece of jewellery. Although lost-wax casting was also used by European and Asian civilisations, decorative features on gold jewellery were usually additions that were soldered on rather than being cast into place.

You will now look at a property of metals that is of vital importance to archaeologists and conservators alike.

Question 3.1

Briefly explain why a metal object buried in soil for some time will not be in the same condition today as it was when first buried.

Corrosion is the deterioration of metals caused by chemical reactions forming new compounds; the main agents being water and oxygen. Not all metals corrode to the same extent; for example, the workmen who plundered a burial chamber at Rillaton, Cornwall in 1837 and unearthed a stunning gold cup (Figure 3.6) found it to be as bright and shiny as it was when made in the Early Bronze Age. Appearances can however, be deceptive; most 'gold' objects are not made of pure gold, but also contain some silver and copper, and unlike gold, these base metals are vulnerable to corrosion (Box 3.3). When the gold cup was analysed by XRF, it was found that there was several percent less of silver and copper at the surface than there was deeper inside the metal, this loss being due to corrosion.

Figure 3.6   The gold cup, dating to around 1700–1500 BC, found at Rillaton on Bodmin Moor, Cornwall. It is 85 mm high.

In contrast, the corrosion of iron is a reaction of iron and oxygen – forming by-products such as iron oxides. (Scientifically, this process is called 'oxidation'.) Copper and bronze also corrode, often to a rather striking green colouration, a famous example of which is the green colour on the copper surface of the Statue of Liberty in New York. Bronze can also experience 'bronze disease', which appears as light green spots on the surface of the metal forming when chlorides present in the corrosion layers are exposed to a damp environment. Corrosion can also completely change the nature of a metal artefact by converting all the metal to a mineral; for example, the only evidence for a copper or bronze object in soil may be a green stain.

One common use for metals is minting coins. Now read Box 3.3 to discover a little about the history of coin making, the analytical methods applied to coins, and some of the disreputable practices used to pass off fakes and forgeries as the real thing.

Box 3.3 What are coins really worth?

Coins made from metal were probably first exchanged as gifts or tokens, becoming used as currency around 700 BC in the Middle East. One of the earliest finds in England is shown in Figure 3.7, a coin bearing the name of Tincomarus, who was one of the kings who ruled over what is now Hampshire and Sussex in southern England, in the late first century BC, the word TINCO being clearly visible above the horse.

Figure 3.7   Coin from the late first century BC, showing the name of a ruler of southern England – Tincomarus.

■ Based on what you already know about the properties of materials, list some of the reasons why metals are traditionally used to make coins instead of other materials such as pottery, stone or wood.

☐ The strength of metals makes coins durable; pottery or stone would easily shatter and wood can easily break or be burned. The malleability of metals also means they can be fairly easily worked, allowing them to be stamped with images of royalty, a date, or anything else the maker might want to imprint. In addition, certain metals (such as gold and silver) have great value, whereas pottery, stone and wood are relatively freely available.

Early coins were typically made of gold and silver, while more plentiful later coins were made of cheaper copper alloys. In the case of China, even iron was used! The extent to which precious metals such as gold and silver are used in coins is a measure of the economic status of their country of origin. When the silver content of Roman coins declined after AD 100 as a consequence of the metal becoming scarce, the coins still appeared silvery. This is because oxidation of the copper in the alloy occurred when the coin was hot-struck with the design, while cleaning off the oxide layer with acid left a silvery surface. Recent research has shown that copper-rich coins were improved by coating them with a solution of silver in the liquid metal mercury (called an amalgam) to give a silvery surface.

It is only a small step from this type of activity into the world of the forger, and as long as coins have existed, underhand practices have been used to produce fake ones. These include using real coins to make moulds for casting counterfeits, and 'clipping' where the metal needed to make forgeries is clipped from the edges of genuine coins. The devaluing of coinage by mixing in cheaper metals meanwhile, is known as *debasement* and ultimately leads to inflation in an economy. In England, this came to a head in AD 1124 during the reign of Henry I, who, known for his brutal acts, summoned all coin makers of the realm to Winchester to assess the quality of their wares. Those found guilty of producing substandard coins were allegedly punished by the removal of their right hands and testicles.

In the past, the quality of metal was tested in several ways, including: weight; the sound it made when dropped; cutting to see if it was plated; or comparing the colour of the mark made by a good gold coin with that of a suspect coin, by streaking them on a fine-grained stone (called a touchstone). Today, modern analytical methods such as XRF or ICP-AES can be used. XRF in particular has been successfully used to distinguish between genuine and counterfeit coins by analysing the concentration of specific metals present. In addition, measurements using XRD or Raman spectroscopy can provide a definite identification of the chemical compounds formed on a coin's surface by corrosion. Analysis of ancient coins can reveal much about how they were made. Looking at the grain structure (see below) of the metal under an optical microscope or SEM reveals information about the method of minting, such as whether it included casting a globule and striking the design, or cutting a disc from a larger metal sheet.

Ancient gold coins are almost never made of pure gold so, even if they appear uncorroded, some of the copper and silver in the alloy will have been lost from the surface. One useful result of this to the archaeologist or conservator is that analysis of the surface will give an accurate indication of the metal of the coin. Corrosion products such as purplish-grey silver chloride or black silver sulfide may be formed on archaeological silver, however silver alloyed coins containing copper can be covered with the corrosion products of copper (i.e. they develop a green coating). Several factors can accelerate the decay of a coin during burial, including changes in the chemical composition of the surrounding soil. After excavation, handling by humans can cause decay as perspiration contains many chemicals that can attack metals. In a museum, coins must be stored under carefully controlled conditions, and although a metal container is preferable, mahogany tends to be the wood of choice for cabinets as other woods emit acidic vapours that promote corrosion.

Now complete Part 2 Activities 3.4 and 3.5.

Part 2 Activity 3.4   'All that glisters is not gold' (William Shakespeare, *The Merchant of Venice*, Act II, verse vii)

(The estimated time needed to complete this activity is 15 minutes.)

Main learning outcomes developed: KU3, KU4, CS3 and KS3.

In this activity you will hear Sam Moorhead (Finds Adviser for Iron Age and Roman coins at the British Museum) describe the analysis of a collection of Iron Age gold coins dating from 50 BC, to establish their true metal content.

Don't forget to make notes on the key points as you listen.

Now go to the DVD, click on 'Topics', find Topic 3, and complete Part 2 Activity 3.4.

Part 2 Activity 3.5   Cleaning coins: a cautionary tale

(The estimated time needed to complete this activity is 20 minutes.)

Main learning outcomes developed: KU3, CS1, KS2 and KS4.

Imagine you have just taken up metal detecting and, with a bit of beginner's luck, you have discovered a collection of highly corroded coins that you think may be of Roman origin. Your first instinct is to clean them to discover what lies beneath the surface.

Now go to the DVD, click on 'Topics', find Topic 3 and complete Part 2 Activity 3.5, where you will start by watching 'Cleaning coins – a demonstration' to find out why this would be a bad decision, before listening to Philippa Walton explain how to handle archaeological coins, and Sam Moorhead describe how a museum approaches coin conservation.

As the analytical methods applied to coins in general also apply to the analysis of metal artefacts, they are not considered further here, except to develop one more point. Images of polished slices of metals under an optical microscope or a scanning electron microscope (SEM) indicate their structure is composed of distinct regions or grains, the visibility of which can be enhanced by treating the metal with an etching solution. Within each grain, the atoms are arranged in regular patterns, but at the grain boundaries, the atoms do not line up, i.e. they form a *discontinuity* (Figure 3.8).

Figure 3.8 Schematic diagram showing the arrangement of atoms in the grains of a metal. Each yellow circle represents an atom of metal; the discontinuity represents the boundary of the grain.

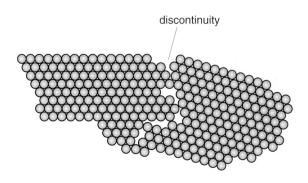

discontinuity

The shape and size of grains says a lot about how a metal artefact has been worked or cast. In general, examination under a microscope can reveal the whole history of its treatment; for example, has it been hammered, annealed, cast, or has a combination of these methods been used? At this point, turn to *Greene* Figure 5.16 (p. 212) where you will see two examples of the grain structure of metals. Note the different shape of the grains, and read the description at the bottom of the page. In addition to optical methods, radiography can also sometimes reveal porosity characteristic of cast metal and, unlike microscopy (which needs samples of the metal to be cut and polished), this is a non-destructive technique.

3.3   Stone

It was a defining moment in human development when our distant ancestors first used stone (see Box 3.4).

■   Write down what you already know about stone, and why you think it was such an attractive material for the earliest people to use.

☐   In addition to being abundant, stone is hard and resilient, and it can be shaped into useful objects such as tools and weapons, which are fundamental for survival. People also need to be sheltered from the elements, and stone was probably one of the early materials used for making crude windbreaks and later, more elaborate dwellings.

Stone is one of the most dominant materials in archaeology, and the Stone Age is usually subdivided into three periods, starting with the Palaeolithic (Old Stone Age) characterised by hunter-gatherers living on wild animals and plants, through to the Mesolithic (Old–New Stone Age transition), and the Neolithic (New Stone Age), where humans lived in communities in which farming had become established. There is no clear dividing line between these periods; humans were not hunter gatherers one day and farmers the next!

Box 3.4 Working with flint

One of the main resources of the Stone Age was flint, which is a variety of silica. Its characteristic property of fracturing into thin, sharp flakes when struck with another hard object made it ideal for making sharp tools and weapons, a process known as *knapping*. Flint has its limitations though: it is rather brittle and soon loses its sharpness through use; in addition it cannot be sharpened except by further knapping, meaning the object eventually becomes useless. It is also difficult to attach a piece of flint to a handle, limiting the size of tools that could be made (Figure 3.9). With the advent of the Bronze Age, the use of flint as a material for tools and weapons declined, although it was still deemed excellent for creating fire. Sparks caused by striking stone against stone could have been used for igniting dry material in ancient times. More recently, from the 16th to 19th centuries AD, striking flint against steel to produce sparks provided the firing mechanism in flintlock muskets.

One of the most famous flint mines in the British Isles is Grimes Graves in Norfolk (Figure 3.10), which was extensively worked during the Neolithic period, producing enough flint for many thousands of axes. The Neolithic miners used nothing more than antlers and the bones from animal shoulder-blades as picks and shovels, and worked by the light of lamps made of animal fat with wicks of moss to reach the best quality flint located some 10 m below the surface.

Figure 3.9   Flint hand axe found in Gray's Inn Lane, London in 1673, now known to be from about 350 000 years BP. The axe is 165 mm long.

Figure 3.10   Aerial view of Grimes Graves in Norfolk, England: the undulations of the ground, which looks like a 'moonscape', are tell-tale signs of the mine shafts that were sunk over 5000 years ago.

To be more precise, the term 'Palaeolithic' refers to the hunter-gatherers of the Pleistocene Epoch (about 1.6 Ma to about 10 000 years BP), a period when temperature fluctuations resulted in climatic changes called glacial and interglacial stages. The 'Mesolithic' is strictly speaking a North European phenomenon, which is applied to the time in the Early Holocene (from approximately 10 000 years BP) when hunter-gatherers used a distinctive set of tools. In the Middle East, China, India and South East Asia, farming practices began from about 10 000 years BP and as it spread, settled communities dependent on agriculture replaced the hunter-gatherer lifestyle in many, but not all areas. Where farming did spread, it brought in its wake new (i.e. 'neo') lifestyles, culminating in the 'Neolithic'. In the British Isles, this happened about 6000 years BP, which reflects how long it took for farming to spread from the Middle East through central and western Europe.

In general, stone is made up of one or more minerals. For example, granite – a widely used building material – is a mixture of mica, quartz and feldspar, all three of which are silicate minerals. If you look closely at a piece of granite, you will see hundreds of interconnected grains, each of which is a single mineral. This is where the technique of optical microscopy comes into its own. By examining thin-sections of stone, not only can the identity and arrangement of minerals be established, but it is also often possible to match the stone used in ancient artefacts to its original source (see Box 3.5). This is referred to as determining the 'provenance' of a material (you will see an example of this approach used in relation to pottery in Section 3.4). The minerals within stone can also be identified using XRD and Raman spectroscopy, while other forms of analysis can be used to detect the elements present, such as ICP-AES, and X-ray methods including SEM-EDX and XRF.

After being buried, stone artefacts are frequently recovered virtually unchanged from their original state. This allows archaeologists to look at the functional part of a tool or weapon and examine patterns of wear, which can provide information about its use. This approach has been enhanced by the use of optical and electron microscopy, and a whole research area known as *use–wear analysis* has emerged. For example, examining the cutting edge of a stone tool under a microscope may reveal patterns consistent with chopping wood as opposed to bone. Another way of identifying the use of a particular type of stone tool is to copy it. Experimental archaeologists have made replicas of stone tools and put them to use (e.g. cutting meat, plants or bone). The kind of abrasions and scuffing that develop can then be compared with the original artefact to determine what processes caused it; in fact, reference collections of known wear patterns have been compiled.

Even though stone provides one of the most durable material records of the past, some types of building stone, such as limestone and sandstone, are susceptible to decay from air pollution. The deterioration appearing on stone materials can be studied by various analytical techniques, and the effects of conservation treatments monitored. This can be done with an optical or an electron microscope, the latter having the additional capability of providing elemental analysis by EDX. Naturally occurring minerals in stone and surface encrustations have also been extensively studied by XRD and Raman spectroscopy to identify the chemical compounds present.

Box 3.5   Unravelling the secrets of Stonehenge

Situated on Salisbury Plain in Wiltshire is one of the most spectacular, and probably the most famous of all British prehistoric monuments – Stonehenge (Figure 3.11).

The reason for the construction of Stonehenge is still something of a mystery. Famously, at dawn on the midsummer solstice, the rising sun shines directly along an axis defined by the so-called Heel Stone, which lies outside the circle. Scholars have suggested this means the monument is a giant calendar to mark the changing of the seasons.

Stonehenge is not an isolated monument, but sits at the centre of a sprawling 10-km wide graveyard of prehistoric burial mounds. It was constructed between 2950 and 1600 BC, the original structure being made of wood, as the stones did not arrive until about 2550 BC, and even then, they appear to have arrived in two stages, as two different types of stone were incorporated in the structure.

As a consequence of extensive pillaging and lack of protection, what is seen today is less than half of the original monument. In fact, until 1901, visitors were allowed to chisel away the rock and take home souvenirs! Nevertheless, the basic structure is still intact and consists of:

(a) massive uprights formed from a hard type of sandstone called 'sarsen', many of which are topped by lintels to create structures called trilithons; and

(b) smaller 'bluestones' composed of the rocks dolerite and rhyolite, both of which are characterised by a bluish tinge when wet.

In 1925, the discovery of the remains of a similarly laid out wooden circle about 32 km away (not surprisingly called Woodhenge) dates to about 2500–2300 BC, and may indicate a shift from building with wood to stone, a much more durable material. The parallel with woodworking does not end there. Examination of the trilithons reveals they are held in place by mortice and tenon joints – the stock trade of a carpenter to this day, with a tenon being clearly visible on the monument's tallest stone. How the Neolithic builders moved these enormous stones into position was clearly an amazing feat; experiments have shown they must have used a sophisticated arrangement of ramps and scaffolds to do it.

Stonehenge is the keeper of many secrets, not least the origin of the stones themselves. The sarsens are thought to have originated from nearby Marlborough Downs and were transported by humans to the site; the origin of the bluestones however, is highly controversial. In 1923, H. H. Thomas (Petrographer

Figure 3.11   A classic image of Stonehenge, Wiltshire, England.

to His Majesty's Geological Survey) presented a paper to the Society of Antiquaries in which he suggested they originated in the Preseli mountains in southwest Wales (Figure 3.12), transported to Salisbury Plain by humans. One school of thought is that they were brought on rafts by sea, up the River Avon and then transported over land.

Researchers at The Open University (OU) have used analytical techniques to look into the origin of the bluestones and the possible modes of transportation, to shed more light on this mystery. The composition of the stones was determined by XRF measurements on tiny samples drilled from selected bluestones; dolerite and rhyolite samples from the Preseli area, as well as Lampeter Velfrey and Pencoed near Cardiff, were also analysed for comparison. The data

revealed that the dolerites originated from a small area around Preseli, while the rhyolite came from a much wider range of sites in northern Preseli and on the north Pembrokeshire coast. The fact that there was a spread of sources and not one carefully chosen outcrop, led to the theory that the bluestones were actually carried to Salisbury Plain by glaciers during the last Ice Age, so although 'foreign' to the local geology of the area, the stones were readily available to the builders of Stonehenge.

This is still a contentious view however, because ice sheets from the last glaciation did not cover Salisbury Plain, and there is good evidence for quarrying of the stones in the Preseli hills, which would seem to rule out this theory. So, as is often the case in science, the jury is still out on this issue!

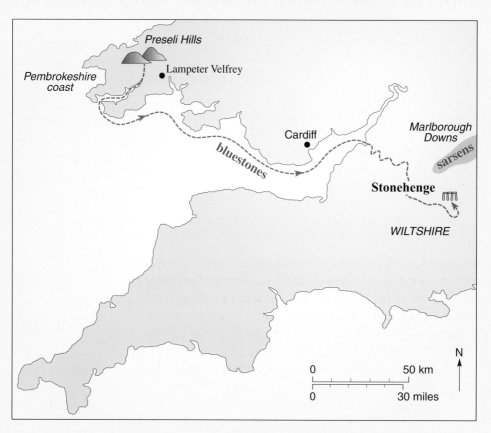

Figure 3.12   The probable route of the bluestones from southwest Wales to their present site.

3.4   Pottery

One of the most common finds at an archaeological excavation is pottery, or more frequently fragments of pottery called (pot) sherds. This is because it was (and still is) an everyday material that survives very well. Pottery has a long history: Jomon pottery from Japan was made about 12 000 years BP, and because people play a part in every aspect of its production – from locating and choosing raw materials, to forming, firing and decoration, it is an important guide to ancient cultures and traditions.

Pottery is produced from clay, an abundant natural material that can be easily shaped when wet and produces a hard material when fired in a kiln. Clays are compounds of silicon, aluminium and oxygen, in which the atoms are arranged in layers, between which are located water molecules. Many clay deposits are formed from the weathering of rocks.

Clay owes its physical and chemical properties to its structure, which comprises of tiny platelets, roughly one to two microns (i.e. thousandths of a millimetre) across (Figure 3.13). When wet, the platelets can slide over one another, allowing the clay to be easily moulded. If a clay object is then left to dry, the platelets lock together and the material becomes rigid. Firing in a kiln drives off any remaining water, and the material becomes irreversibly hardened, to eventually form pottery.

Early potters shaped clay by hand into a series of coils or slabs, to form the desired product. The true potter's wheel was introduced about 4000–5000 years BP, enabling pots to be 'thrown' in a manner familiar to this day, although slow-turning wheels (tournettes) were probably used before this to finish pots. The mud-like consistency of clay also made it an ideal early writing medium, the text being made permanent by firing. Figure 3.14 shows an example of a clay tablet from the library of the Mesopotamian king Ashurbanipal (who reigned from 668 to 631 BC) containing cuneiform ('wedge-shaped') text, which is one of the earliest forms of writing. Not all cuneiform tablets were fired.

Common clay minerals are kaolin, smectite, illite and chlorite, each with their own unique properties, most naturally occurring clays consisting of mixtures of these minerals. Even so, clays were rarely used without additional ingredients; by trial and error additives were found that produced better-quality products. A common example is *temper*, which is a filler material such as crushed shell, flint, sand or even chaff, which can give clay added strength and workability, and prevent the formation of cracks during firing. In fact, many soil clays naturally contain fragments of rocks and minerals, while one specific type of temper called grog consists of ground up discarded pottery fragments. Archaeologists call the particular combination of clay and the inclusions (e.g. particles of rocks, minerals or temper) that make up the pot its *fabric*.

The earliest pottery was made by firing common clays to little more than 500–600 °C, which is easily within the range of a garden bonfire; the terracotta mask in Figure 3.15 was fired to a temperature a few hundred degrees higher, but this is still a low temperature in the world of the potter. A general term used to describe pottery formed at these 'low' temperatures (i.e. up to about 1000 °C) is *earthenware*, which, if used straight from the kiln, has one major

0.001 mm

Figure 3.13   Clay mineral grains are too small to be seen under even the highest-power optical microscope. This image of clay was taken with an SEM and shows the flat platelets of the mineral.

Figure 3.15 Terracotta mask depicting a female character from ancient tragedy (Roman, first to second century AD). It is 21.5 cm high.

Figure 3.14 Clay tablet from the library of the Mesopotamian king Ashurbanipal expressed in cuneiform ('wedge-shaped') script.

drawback – it is porous and so tends to absorb liquids. Waterproofing by dipping the pot into a liquid clay mixture (known as *slip*), followed by firing for a second time, was found to work reasonably well, the result being a smooth, fairly non-porous surface. Slip was also added at the so-called *leather-hard* stage, which is the point in the drying process when most of the water has been lost, but the clay is still moist enough to permit some alteration of the shape of the vessel. In this case, only a single firing was required.

A better and truly waterproof coating was achieved by glazing, where a pot was covered with a suspension of finely powdered glass (see Section 3.5) or other raw ingredients in water, for example, a *lead glaze* made from a slurry of lead oxide or sulfide, and either fired for a second time or by the single firing technique described above. The secret of a good glaze is that the firing process must be at a temperature that is below the melting temperature of the clay being glazed. This has the effect of fusing the glass to the surface, and sealing the pores to give the pot a shiny smooth appearance (although this is not always true, as matt glazes have an uneven surface and may also be produced). Early pots were also often decorated by painting them with pigments such as iron ores (see Section 3.6) that were sometimes mixed with quartz or clay minerals, to fix the colour to the surface when fired. In addition, glaze was also used for decoration.

Pottery that has been fired above about 1200 °C, and is hard, highly scratch-resistant and impermeable to liquids without the need for further treatment, is known as *stoneware*. Even though it looks opaque, the superior properties of stoneware are a result of the formation of glass-like regions within the fabric (see Section 3.5), produced by a process called *vitrification*. Related to stoneware is porcelain, which is formed at an even higher temperature (around 1300 °C), and is translucent (semi-transparent) because of much greater vitrification. The high quality porcelain produced in China has proved to be the benchmark for others to emulate (Figure 3.16).

Although pottery is often easily broken, the resulting sherds can be very durable depending on the soil conditions and how well the pottery was fired; hence they may be found in excellent condition after burial and, because pot sherds are among the more common finds at a dig, some can often be given up for destructive analysis.

Archaeologists and scientists are interested in the sources of raw materials, and how pots were manufactured and used (see Box 3.6). XRD can be used to determine the chemical compound(s) (i.e. minerals) present, including the additives mentioned above, both in raw clays and after firing (i.e. when the clay has been irreversibly converted to a new material). As with stone, thin-sections of pottery can be prepared and examined under an optical microscope to identify mineral and rock components and inclusions, which may have originated from the clay itself or been deliberately added (e.g. temper). At higher magnification, SEM can reveal much greater detail, such as the development of vitreous regions on firing. If a ceramic has very fine grains, making it difficult to identify distinct mineral inclusions by microscopy, elemental analysis using SEM-EDX, XRF or ICP-AES can provide a 'chemical fingerprint', allowing the material's provenance to be determined.

Figure 3.16   Porcelain bowl from Jingdezhen, Jiangxi province, southern China, dating to about AD 1600–1620, the blue colour is a cobalt pigment (Section 3.5). It stands 17 cm high and is 34.5 cm wide.

Box 3.6 The origin of Iron Age pottery at Hengistbury Head

The composition of a thin-section of pottery can sometimes be used to pinpoint its source. One example is the study carried out by British Museum scientists of pottery from Hengistbury Head near Poole in Dorset (Figure 3.17). During the Iron Age, a large and influential trading centre emerged in the area, which controlled the River Avon and the River Stour. Excavations have produced a wide range of artefacts, but the pottery was

Look again at the petrographic image of pottery from Hengistbury Head, containing mineral inclusions, in the 'Techniques' section on the DVD.

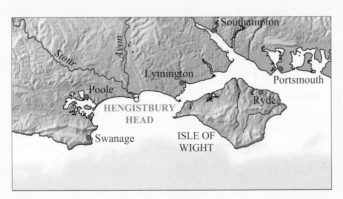

Figure 3.17 Location of the Iron Age settlement at Hengistbury Head, Dorset, England.

rather unusual for both the location and time, being unlike the majority of pot sherds found in southern England of a comparative age. This pottery was of much higher quality, wheel-thrown with a cordon (a thin raised band running horizontally around the outside surface of the pot), smooth glossy surfaces, and colours ranging from dark grey to dark brown.

Unfortunately, archaeological artefacts rarely have their place of origin marked on them! So, to shed light on the mystery of the Hengistbury Head pottery, excavated sherds were analysed by optical microscopy. This revealed that the fabric of some of the pottery contained inclusions that were not of local origin, with the minerals amphibole and plagioclase identified. These are commonly found in the rock amphibolite, which is not present in the vicinity of Hengistbury Head, the nearest location being in northern Brittany. This was taken as strong evidence for the pots being made in France and transported across the English Channel by boat, giving an important insight into trading connections across this area in the Iron Age.

Now read *Greene* Chapter 5, Section 5.1 (p. 191, right-hand column, second paragraph, as far as 'Pollen and phytoliths') where you will discover an indirect way in which pottery has provided an important source of evidence for the plants grown by early humans and their diet.

3.5   Glass

Today, glass is a material that is taken for granted. Using modern technology, it is cheap and relatively easy to manufacture on a large scale, but this was not always the case. Throughout antiquity and medieval times, glass was prized as a luxury because of the well-honed skills and high furnace temperatures required to make it. The earliest glass making may have developed before 3000 BC from the manufacture of *faience*, which originated in Egypt or Mesopotamia. This was made by coating powdered quartz with a vitreous glaze, with faience used to produce many exquisite items such as beads, pendants and amulets (Figure 3.18).

Figure 3.18   A faience eye depicting the ancient Egyptian god Horus, who was a man with the head of a hawk. The story is that Horus lost an eye in battle and it was later restored. Subsequently, the 'Eye of Horus' became a symbol of protection for the ancient Egyptians.

Before manufactured glass was available, some ancient societies used a natural form of glass, called obsidian. This is a type of volcanic rock that is cooled very quickly on eruption, which prevents any crystals from growing, forming a very glassy, black rock. As a result of its glassy nature, obsidian fractures and splinters very easily, so the craftsmanship needed to create exquisite objects such as the Aztec obsidian mirror in Figure 3.19, dating to the 14th–16th centuries AD, is to be marvelled at.

Before looking at manufactured glass in detail, read *Greene* Chapter 5, Section 6.2 (pp. 215–6), to find out more about this naturally occurring glass, noting in particular how it was exploited and traded, and how analytical techniques have been used to characterise it.

The glass that is more familiar today however, is believed to have been first produced in northern Mesopotamia before 2500 BC. One piece of evidence supporting this is that King Ashurbanipal's cuneiform tablets (Figure 3.14, Section 3.4) contain details of glass making and indicate the end product was much revered and cherished. The first glass vessels meanwhile were made in Egypt and Mesopotamia around 1500 BC, by shaping molten glass round a core of clay and dung and then rolling it out on a flat stone.

Figure 3.19   Aztec obsidian mirror, made between AD 1325 and 1521 in Mexico.

Glass has a long and rather complex history, which is beyond the scope of this course; however, a few highlights are considered here. Around 50 BC, the Romans introduced the technique of glass blowing, which involves inflating a large blob of molten glass on the end of a metal tube, or blowing it into a mould, so that particular shapes and thin-walled vessels could easily be produced. This process was revolutionary, and as the Roman Empire grew, the art of glass making spread to many countries. After the demise of the Roman Empire, glass making declined in Europe, and by the 'Middle Ages' it had all but disappeared, although Venice remained a centre for the craft for many centuries. Throughout history there have been peaks and troughs in glass production, improvements in manufacturing technologies, and the sporadic emergence of flourishing glass-producing centres. For example, large amounts of glass were used in the building of great cathedrals during the Medieval Period. It was also a main architectural feature of the homes of rich people in Tudor and Elizabethan England. For the 'average' person, however, glass was an expensive commodity, and not just for technological reasons. Throughout the British Isles, the Glass Excise Act (1745) made the cost prohibitive to many people, and windows often consisted of a hole in the wall with a pair of shutters. Those people who could afford glass took it with them when they moved house while, throughout the Georgian Period, others painted 'fake' windows on stone slabs, to make their houses look grander than they were!

The Glass Excise Act was repealed in 1845.

Glass is made by melting sand (silica) and cooling this in air. On the atomic scale, the feature that sets glass apart from the other materials covered in this topic is the irregular arrangement of its atoms. Metals and minerals are *crystalline* solids made up of atoms arranged in orderly patterns. In contrast, the atoms in glass are a random jumble, forming an *amorphous* structure, and it is this property that leads to its transparency.

In addition to sand, other ingredients are required to make glass. In the past, people discovered that mixtures of sand, limestone (calcium carbonate) and sodium carbonate fuse to form a glass. During this process, the carbonates lose carbon dioxide to form oxides, the end product being known as soda-lime-silica glass, comprising sodium oxide (soda), calcium oxide (lime) and silicon dioxide (silica). Why is it necessary for such a formulation? The temperature required to melt 'pure' sand is very high (about 1723 °C); by adding soda, this acts as a 'flux', which lowers the melting temperature. One major drawback of this, however, is that it tends to produce poor quality glass that is water soluble. This problem was solved by the simultaneous addition of lime, which stabilises the glass structure and makes it insoluble. The early source of soda is thought to be *natron* (a mineral found in some 'salt lakes', e.g. Wadi Natrun in Egypt) or ash produced by burning plants; fragments of sea shells found in sand are a possible source of lime. From about AD 1675, lead oxide was added to silica, which acts as both a flux and a stabiliser and led to the creation of lead crystal.

Question 3.2

In his accounts, Pliny the Elder (a Roman military commander and historian) relayed the following story about the origin of glass making:

> *A group of Phoenician sailors had come ashore. They were preparing to cook on the beach over a fire and, not finding suitable stones on which to put their cooking pots, used lumps of a mineral known as trona from their cargo. As the trona was heated in the fire and mingled with the sand, a strange liquid flowed. This was the origin of glass.*

Although this is probably not an accurate account of history, if you accept the statement that 'trona' contains sodium carbonate, briefly state why this version of events could be a plausible origin for glass making.

A complete spectrum of coloured glass can be made by adding metals (usually in their oxide form), to the original melt (see Box 3.7). These additives are typically from a family of elements known as the 'transition metals', which are characterised by their numerous colourful compounds. One example is cobalt glass, which is deep blue, while iron oxides give a green hue to glass. Iron is a common impurity in sand, so even supposedly clear glass (particularly if it is cheap and mass-produced) frequently has a green tint. The addition of other metal oxides can remove this tint; Roman glass makers found that adding manganese oxide to glass eliminates the green colour, although adding too much turns it pink! Other additives turn glass from transparent to opaque. These *opacifiers* include tin oxide and certain compounds of calcium and lead, which are present in glass in the form of tiny particles.

Moving on to some of the techniques used to study glass, it is important to mention one that cannot be used!

- Why would X-ray diffraction (XRD) *not* be a technique of choice for studying glass?

- ☐ XRD is used to identify *crystalline* compounds; as glass is amorphous, this technique is of little use.

Box 3.7 Seeing is believing: the extraordinary Lycurgus cup

A rather impressive example of the Roman glass maker's art is the fourth century AD Lycurgus cup. At first sight this depicts the legendary King Lycurgus being dragged into the underworld, but a closer look at the underlying glass reveals something unexpected. When the glass is held up to the light, it appears red but, when light is reflected from its surface, it appears green (Figure 3.20).

What is the origin of these colours? Studies under an electron microscope revealed tiny metal particles dispersed throughout the glass. They are typically 70 nm (nanometres) across (1 nm = one-millionth of a millimetre), and XRF showed they consist of about 70% silver and 30% gold. These particles scatter the light in much the same way that fine particles in the atmosphere cause a 'red sky at night', making the glass look red in transmitted light (i.e. light that passes through), but green in reflection. Roman glass makers frequently added scrap metals to colour their glass, and small quantities of silver and gold may have crept into the melt. So, in this case, the colour changes are probably the result of accident rather than design!

(a)   (b)

Figure 3.20   The Lycurgus cup is of Roman origin and dates from the fourth century AD: (a) the red form; (b) the green form. The cup is 165 mm high (with modern metal mounts) and 132 mm wide.

Other forms of analysis do however, produce useful information. XRF, SEM-EDX and Raman spectroscopy have proved useful in distinguishing glasses with different chemical compositions. Raman spectroscopy has also been used to identify pigments in stained glass. Meanwhile, ICP-AES has been used to determine the elemental composition of glasses, including trace elements. Although glass is a relatively durable material, throughout history it has been exposed to the worst of the natural elements, and techniques such as SEM-EDX, IR and Raman spectroscopy have also been used to study corrosion products and investigate the deterioration of glass surfaces. See Box 3.8 for an example of where analytical techniques were applied to study a well-known glass artefact from the British Museum's collection.

Box 3.8 The Portland vase

This famous cameo-glass vessel is shrouded in mystery. It is believed to have been made by a Roman glass maker in the early first century AD and preserved in a tomb. The vase has a deep blue colour overlaid with opaque white glass depicting mythological images of love and marriage (Figure 3.21). In 1845, an unfortunate incident occurred when the vase was smashed by William Lloyd, a drunken visitor to the British Museum.

Figure 3.21 The Portland vase is made from Roman glass of the early first century AD. It is 24 cm high and 17.7 cm wide.

Painstaking restoration followed, which has been improved upon in more recent times by taking advantage of developments in modern adhesives and by locating several of the missing pieces. A few, very small fragments of the blue and the white glass could not be refitted to the vase, however, and were left over. These tiny pieces were scientifically investigated to get an insight into the technology involved in the vase's manufacture, and analysed by SEM-EDX, to gain important information about its composition.

The SEM-EDX results showed the chemical composition of the blue glass was in line with typical Roman soda-lime-silica glass, with low levels of magnesia (magnesium oxide) and potash (potassium oxide). This is in contrast to glass from Islamic, Early Near Eastern or Venetian sources, which tend to have higher levels of magnesia and potash. Alumina (aluminium oxide) was also found at levels characteristic of Roman glass, and almost certainly rules out suggestions that the vase was produced much later during the Renaissance period.

The deep blue colour was shown to be due to the presence of cobalt oxide, a pigment still routinely used to produce this attractive colour today. Other oxides of iron, manganese and copper were also detected, and there has been some debate about whether these were deliberately added to fine-tune the colour of the vase or are contaminants in the ore used to produce the cobalt pigment, any modification to the colour being purely accidental.

The white glass was also shown to be of the soda-lime-silica type, and probably came from the same batch used to produce the blue glass. In addition, a high level (about 12%) of lead oxide was detected. The white colouration is thought to have been produced by adding the metal antimony (probably in its natural ore form as stibnite, which is a compound of antimony and sulfur) to the melt during production; this reacted with the lime to form the compound calcium antimonate. SEM images show tiny particles of this compound are dispersed throughout the glass, and act as an opacifier.

Finally, for many years, a disc of cameo glass had been inserted into the base of the vase; however, analysis showed this disc had no lead oxide, indicating the vase and the disc were not closely related.

Look again at the SEM images of fragments of the Portland vase in the 'Techniques' section of the DVD.

3.6   Inorganic pigments

Inorganic pigments impart colour to a range of objects, including paintings, pottery, written works and textiles. They are insoluble materials, normally used in the form of fine powders. Most early inorganic pigments were produced by grinding either natural minerals (e.g. ochres, which are coloured oxides of iron extracted from the earth) or synthetic glassy materials (e.g. Egyptian blue), or by collecting corrosion products: for example, the pigment called *lead white* is a lead carbonate-based, white corrosion crust formed on lead blocks. Later, more complex chemical processes were used to mass-produce colours such as vermilion. Pigments are often suspended in a medium called a *binder* to form paint. Various materials have been used as binders, including the white or yolk of eggs, gums and oils. Dyes (discussed in more detail below) are also often used to colour materials.

In Australia, the use of ochre to paint rock surfaces may have begun as early as 40 000 years BP. In Europe, red ochre is known from Neanderthal graves from 40 000–60 000 years BP, but it is after 35 000 years BP that paintings of animals begin to appear in the caves of western Europe, particularly in France and Spain. The oldest known examples are in Chauvet Cave in Ariège, southwestern France, which were scientifically dated to between 30 000 and 34 000 years BP. Figure 3.22 is an example from the Altamira Cave in northern Spain, which was painted using a mixture of ochre pigments for reds and yellows and manganese dioxide and charcoal for black. Large paintings like this bison were not produced with brushes (and, if used at all, brushes were used only for small details). Instead, outlines were often produced by mixing the paint with water and applying it with the fingers, by spitting or using a crayon. Large areas of colour were applied either with the palm of the hand or by dabbing it on with moss or leather pads. Although inorganic pigments do not fade on exposure to light as easily as pigments derived from organic compounds (see the next section), some can change colour as a result of chemical reactions and be destroyed by plant, fungal and bacterial infestations associated with climatic changes, in particular changes in air flow in their immediate surroundings, caused by modern activities such as tourist access.

Figure 3.22   Example of a cave painting of a bison, dating to about 14 000 years BP, from Altamira, northern Spain.

139

At first, a very simple palette of pigments were used (dependent largely on natural ochres and carbon), more colours gradually being achieved by mixing pigments. Over time, a much wider range of colours from both natural and artificial sources were developed, a selection of which include: green from the copper compounds verdigris and malachite; red from red lead (lead oxide); vermilion either from the natural mineral cinnabar (mercury sulfide) or produced by reacting mercury and sulfur together; black from charcoal; and white from chalk or the mineral gypsum (calcium sulfate). In many cases, and in particular for synthetic colours, the periods when they were used (or the date when they were first produced) are known and can help with dating artefacts.

Figure 3.23   Decorated Russian lapis lazuli carving.

Chemistry has also played a part in expanding the artist's palette; probably the first synthetic pigment was Egyptian Blue, a compound of calcium, copper and silicon. Another blue pigment with a fascinating history is ultramarine. This was originally a refined form of lapis lazuli, a rare mineral used mainly for decorative purposes (Figure 3.23). As a consequence of its expense, ultramarine was only found in the paintings and manuscripts of wealthy people until 1828, when a cheap process was discovered to produce a synthetic version from kaolin (a type of clay). The manufacture of this cheap blue pigment played an important role in the rise of the Impressionist movement of artists, who frequently used large amounts of synthetic ultramarine.

It is important to identify the pigments in artefacts to understand their history and method of production. Mineral pigments form crystalline solids, so the same techniques for characterising stone and pottery may be used. Although these techniques are not discussed further here, one is highlighted that has proved extremely useful in recent years for analysing pigments – Raman spectroscopy. The output from this technique produces a spectrum, which is a 'fingerprint' for a particular pigment. It has the added advantage of being non-destructive and, by attaching an optical microscope, measurements can be made on very small samples and individual coloured particles selected for analysis. One of the pioneers in this field is Robin Clark of University College London who, along with his colleagues, has compiled a large database of the Raman spectra of pigments that can be used in the identification of unknown samples.

Question 3.3

Describe one way in which analytical methods (such as XRD or Raman spectroscopy) could be used to date a coloured artefact.

3.7   Organic materials

'Organic materials' is a term used to describe a very wide group of substances, ranging from bulk cellular materials produced by, or derived from, plants and animals, down to individual molecules. Although some of the cellular materials are very complex mixtures of components, what links all of these organic materials is that they contain molecules with carbon atoms at their core. By including other elements such as hydrogen, nitrogen, phosphorus and oxygen, the range of organic molecules becomes almost endless, from the building blocks of life such as proteins and DNA, to manufactured substances, including synthetic polymers and drugs. This is reflected in the study of organic materials in archaeology, which also covers a wide variety of materials and compounds. Some examples of cellular organic materials (i.e. those comprised of cells) include wood, animal and vegetable fibres (adapted to make baskets or textiles), skin (often processed to produce leather), bone, ivory, horn and antler. Other organic materials can be described as being non-cellular (consisting of mixtures of individual organic molecules), including materials as diverse as amber, fats and oils, collagen and gum arabic. As you can see, this list is getting very long so, to help simplify matters, the following sections focus on a select group of these organic materials to illustrate the key issues for archaeological investigations.

While most of the analytical methods discussed in this topic so far are also applicable here (particularly for the study of cellular organic materials), some techniques are particularly useful for analysing organic molecules. At the sub-cellular level, infrared (IR) spectroscopy can provide excellent 'fingerprints', enabling classes of organic materials to be identified. However, because organic materials are often found as mixtures, chromatography may be required to separate out individual organic molecules. Chromatographic equipment is often linked to a mass spectrometer, which can then be used to identify the individual components.

One important feature of organic materials to be aware of is how they deteriorate over time. In contrast to materials such as stone or pottery, carbon-based materials are much more susceptible to decay. The processes involved are complex and can be physical, chemical and/or biological; however, the main cause of decay during burial is microscopic organisms, such as bacteria and fungi that aggressively attack and break down organic materials.

There are several ways in which the progress of decay of organic materials can be reduced. This has led to many extraordinary finds of artefacts that have been preserved naturally in remarkable condition. To delay or stop the action of harmful bacteria, the ideal atmosphere surrounding an artefact would be oxygen-free or at least oxygen-depleted (although there are certain types of destructive bacteria that do still survive in these conditions). Water is another important factor in the decay process, although at first glance this produces a slight conundrum. If water is absent from a site, destructive bacteria cannot thrive. For example, the immaculate condition of the treasures unearthed by Howard Carter and Lord Caernarvon in 1922 from the 14th century BC tomb of Tutankhamun (in Thebes, Egypt) is a testament to the extreme dryness (aridity) in which they were stored. Many of these remains were organic, including baskets, specimens of flowers, foodstuffs and mummies. On the other hand, some of the other types of exquisitely preserved organic remains come from waterlogged (wetland) sites such as lakes, marshes and peat bogs. The very fact that the object is surrounded by water effectively 'seals' the object, producing an oxygen-free environment.

A third factor controlling the decay of organic remains is temperature. For example, if you have ever experienced the putrid smells emanating from meat or fish that have been left out of the refrigerator for too long, you will know that organic materials break down faster if their temperature increases. Natural refrigeration is therefore one means of preserving organic remains. In 1991, the body of a Neolithic man (subsequently called Ötzi) was discovered by two German climbers in a glacier high in the Alps on the Italian–Austrian border. Ötzi's 5000-year-old body, which had been preserved in ice, was found to be in good condition, as were several of the items found with him. Many of these items were also made of organic materials, including leather clothing, a fur hat and a quiver (containing his arrows).

Upon excavation, the environment surrounding an artefact will change, particularly in terms of the temperature and humidity, which may have detrimental effects on the stability of the materials making up the object. For example, an organic material recovered from an arid site may swell or disintegrate as it absorbs moisture, while items from a wet site may shrink and warp, as they lose water and dry out. Organic materials may also deteriorate from exposure to light and changes in the temperature.

■ What issues did the staff at the Anatomy Department of the University of Innsbruck need to consider when Ötzi was handed over to them for safe keeping?

☐ The staff needed to ensure that his body and the organic artefacts recovered with him did not start to deteriorate because of the increased temperatures, changes in humidity and light, and possible attack from bacteria, after he was removed from the glacial ice in the Alps. (To prevent this, Ötzi is currently held under controlled conditions at −6 °C and 98% humidity, with the amount of time research scientists can work on these remains, being strictly limited.)

In certain situations, specific additions to the surroundings might assist preservation. For example, salt is an excellent preservative and, before the invention of artificial refrigeration, was widely used to prolong the freshness of meat, fish and dairy products. Copper has also been shown to promote the survival of organic remains and again, this process may not be too surprising, as copper compounds are found as 'biocides' in some modern commercial wood preservatives (see Section 3.7.1 below). Mineral-preserved organic remains are also frequently found on iron, copper alloy and even silver objects from burial contexts.

Occasionally, luck also plays a part in preserving organic remains. When the late first century AD Roman fort of Vindolanda (close to Hadrian's Wall), on the English–Scottish border was excavated, a huge collection of letters of both an official and a personal nature were found. They were written by the soldiers on thin slices of wood, and survived as a consequence of a fortuitous combination of waterlogging at the site and a favourable combination of chemicals in the soil.

3.7.1 Wood

The most ancient of our ancestors simply burned wood to keep warm, but when they realised that flint could be used to shape it, simple tools were produced and wood rapidly became one of the most useful materials used throughout time. A list of all the uses of wood since the earliest times would be extremely long, including building houses, constructing vehicles of all shapes and sizes (until the 19th century, all ships and boats were built from wood) and furniture making.

Wood is rich in the compound cellulose (a form of sugar) and a polymer called lignin, both of which are associated with the many different types of cells present in wood. When a tree is felled, the resulting strength, hardness and grain pattern of the timber depends on the characteristics and arrangement of the cells. Given that there are thousands of species of tree, woods can be selected with properties that match specific functions (see Box 3.9).

Box 3.9 How to build a coffin in ancient Egypt

Scientists at the British Museum have done extensive research on wooden coffins removed from ancient Egyptian tombs (Figure 3.24). The well-preserved state of the coffins allowed the cellular structure of the wood to be studied under an optical microscope and, by building up a picture of the different woods used, information was obtained not only about methods of woodworking, but also about the significance of imported woods to the ancient Egyptians.

The coffins were mainly constructed from several planks joined together by wooden dowels and pegs. Of the many hardwoods available, the most commonly used was a type of fig tree (*Ficus sycomorus*). This wood was available locally and it was popular with Egyptian coffin makers for making light and moderately long-lasting timber planks. Other types of local timber were all identified from optical microscopy: for example, acacia and Christ's thorn (*Ziziphus*), which was used for the dowels and pegs, along with imported woods such as the softwood known as Cedar of Lebanon, which was sometimes used for high-status individuals. Some of the coffins were found to contain a mixture of local and imported woods that had clearly been carefully selected for their specific properties, probably including surface appearance, weight, flexibility, durability and resistance to attack by insects.

Look again at optical microscopy and the image of *Ficus sycomorus* in the 'Techniques' section on the DVD.

Figure 3.24   Egyptian painted wooden coffin made of imported cedar wood, dating to around 2125–1795 BC. It was occupied by Sebekhetepi, a wealthy person. The symbolic eyes on the side were to allow the mummy to see out of the coffin.

Wood is particularly prone to deterioration and is rarely excavated from archaeological sites in good condition unless it has been desiccated, charred or waterlogged. Chemically, the sugars tend to decay faster than lignin, causing elongated cells to collapse initially, producing warping and deformation. During burial in a wet environment, wood is susceptible to bacterial attack and if oxygen levels are sufficiently high, fungi may grow and destroy the material completely. Bacterial and fungal attack are also issues during storage, but may be combated with biocides. In waterlogged wood, it may be necessary in the longer term to replace the water with a substance that, on drying, supports the cell structure. Polyethylene glycol (PEG) has been used for this purpose; for example, the preservation of the timber from the 16th century AD war ship *Mary Rose*.

3.7.2   Textiles

The term 'textile' refers to materials made (by processes such as weaving or knitting) from natural or synthetic fibres; these may be of animal origin, such as wool and silk, or derived from vegetable fibres, such as flax (linen). Textiles are rarely, if ever, preserved, as they are subject to the usual mechanisms of decay of organic materials. They can however, sometimes survive in extremely dry or waterlogged conditions.

Samples of preserved textiles are not needed to get an insight into their use by humans. Figure 3.25 shows the only direct piece of evidence for clothing in Iron Age Britain. These pieces of rusty iron date to about 300–100 BC and were excavated from an Iron Age cemetery in Burton Fleming, Yorkshire, by British Museum archaeologists. The original iron object was thought to have lain next to a piece of clothing and as the iron oxidised and the cloth perished in the damp soil, an impression of the cloth remained in the rust. The original diamond twill pattern is clearly visible, and the rectangular insets provide the earliest evidence of embroidery in Britain.

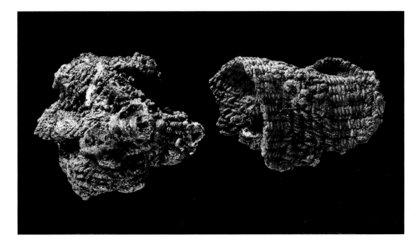

Figure 3.25   Lumps of rusty iron containing the impression of a piece of Iron Age cloth, from Burton Fleming, Yorkshire.

The study of use–wear analysis by SEM, which you met in the context of stone, has also been applied to textiles and fibres. Now turn to *Greene* Figure 5.17 (p. 213), which shows an image of fibres found at the Vindolanda excavation. Read the figure caption and note down the two pieces of information that can be obtained from such images.

3.7.3   Organic pigments and dyes

In Section 3.6 you learned about pigments based on inorganic compounds. There is also a multitude of organic pigments, mostly derived from natural sources, which were also used as sources of colour as dyestuffs and pigments.

It is useful at this point to define the differences between organic dyestuffs and pigments. A dyestuff is a *water-soluble* substance that can be used to dye or colour fibres. The colouring components penetrate and colour the fibre throughout its structure. The dyestuff may interact directly with the fibres or be bound by a water-soluble metal salt (mordant). In contrast, an organic pigment is a *non-soluble* coloured compound, often derived from a dyestuff, which can be used, when combined with a binding medium, to colour the surface of a fibre or textile.

One of the earliest known organic pigments is indigo (a deep blue colour), which was obtained from plants. A related indigo pigment is produced by certain marine animals, including the mollusc *Hexaplex trunculus*, yielding a purple colour. Although insoluble in water, indigo and the related purple pigments can be chemically converted (by dissolving them in a solution of an alkali) into a colourless, but water-soluble, form known as the *leuco* form (or 'indigo white'). In the *leuco* form, indigo can be used to penetrate and dye fibres. When exposed to the air, the *leuco* form reacts with oxygen and the insoluble blue form of indigo precipitates within the fibre, permanently colouring it. Indigo and related purple pigments are known as 'vat dyes' because of the vats that are used in producing the *leuco* form.

Some classical texts suggest that ancient Britons decorated themselves with a blue pigment which, as the Roman general Julius Caesar is reputed to have said, 'gives them a wild look in battle'. It has been speculated that they may have used an extract from the woad plant to produce this colour. From the Iron Age, indigo extracted from woad was used to dye textiles. In fact, the plant was the only source of indigo in Europe until the 17th century, when natural indigo from a related plant species grown in the tropics, flooded the market and the woad industry went into decline.

Another type of organic dye that has been used since ancient times is madder, which is a red dye extracted from the root of a herb. This is a mordant dye, which requires the addition of salts of certain metals (such as tin) to make the colour permanent. In contrast, the vibrant yellow of saffron, derived from the crocus flower, is an example of a dyestuff that can be applied directly to fabric without the need for any chemical treatment, and is known as a 'direct dye'.

3.7.4   Lipids

One class of organic compounds that may be preserved over thousands of years is lipids. 'Lipids' is an all-encompassing term covering animal fats, plant oils, waxes and resins. They have been found preserved in association with a range of finds at archaeological sites. For example, in unglazed pottery, lipids have been found in the voids within the ceramic and remain preserved and are occasionally visible on the surface. There tend to be two types of surface preservation of lipids: remnants of surface coatings, which are often waxes or resins; and carbonised food residues of which lipid components survive best. Analysis of such residues can provide important information about the vessel's use, as well as information about the people's diet at the time of use. A typical approach involves extracting the residue by dissolving it in an organic solvent, and subjecting the solution to GC-MS.

Now complete Part 2 Activity 3.6.

Part 2 Activity 3.6   Wine making in the Stone Age

(The estimated time needed to complete this activity is 30 minutes.)

Main learning outcomes developed: KU2, CS1, CS2 and KS3.

Analytical techniques have been used to provide the earliest evidence for the production of wine, some research on this being published in 1996 in the science journal *Nature* by Patrick E. McGovern and his colleagues.

(a) To help you with this activity, read *Greene* Chapter 5 (p. 201, Figure 5.8–9 caption), which briefly summarise this investigation.

(b) Now go to the 'Activities' section on the course website, find Part 2 Activity 3.6 and skim-read the article by McGovern. You are *not* expected to understand the detailed interpretations of the spectra given in the grey box; simply make brief notes on the following points:

  • how analytical techniques were used to identify the chemical composition of the residues found in the pottery

  • the origin of the tartaric acid and the function of the accompanying resin

  • why wine making can be thought of as characteristic of human behaviour, during the Neolithic.

3.7.5   Composite artefacts

So far in this topic you have encountered a range of materials that have been viewed mostly in isolation. Many artefacts however, can be classified as composite objects (i.e. composed of two or more types of material): for example, a bronze spearhead with a wooden shaft.

■ Why might all of the materials that make up a manufactured object that were originally all buried together not be present when it is recovered during an excavation?

☐ Different materials decay at different rates, so some materials may have completed or partially disintegrated, while others will be better preserved.

You will investigate examples of the different preservation potentials of artefacts in the next activity on the Wetwang excavation.

The horse harness from Wetwang is an example of a composite object, which consisted of the bronze rein rings (also called terrets), attached to a wooden yoke spanning two ponies pulling a cart. The ash wood of the yoke had decomposed in the grave, although some last remnants were found at the points where the wood was in direct contact with the metal (due to mineral preservation). In contrast, the bronze terrets were found to be in good condition, and a closer examination revealed they are inlaid with studs made of pink-red coral (calcium carbonate), which was a highly valued, decorative material. Each coral stud is fixed in position by a bronze pin and a wad of adhesive. Analysis of the adhesive by scientific staff at the British Museum revealed the presence of birch bark tar and conifer resin or tar. Resins (from which tars can be produced) are a type of lipid and are the sticky secretions that ooze out of many species of tree (particularly conifers) and were often used as an adhesive in ancient times. The chemical components of resins are organic compounds called terpenes, which can be separated and identified using GC-MS.

Look again at gas chromatography and adhesives in the 'Techniques' section on the DVD.

Now carry out Part 2 Activities 3.7, 3.8 and 3.9.

Part 2 Activity 3.7   The range of finds at Wetwang

(The estimated time needed to complete this activity is 20 minutes.)

Main learning outcomes developed: KU2, CS1, CS2 and KS2.

In this activity, you will listen to Tony Spence talk in more detail about the range of artefacts recovered from the Wetwang excavation.

Now go to the DVD, click on 'Topics', find Topic 3 and work through Part 2 Activity 3.7.

Part 2 Activity 3.8   Exploring the British Museum collection

(The estimated time needed to complete this activity is 40 minutes.)

Main learning outcomes developed: KU4, CS1 and KS2.

Go to the 'Activities' section on the course website and complete Part 2 Activity 3.8, where you will discover how the British Museum has categorised all of the materials in its vast collection.

Part 2 Activity 3.9   A Roman cosmetic: determining its chemical make-up

(The estimated time needed to complete this activity is 40 minutes.)

Main learning outcomes developed: KU1, KU3, CS2 and CS3.

In 2004, Richard Evershed of the University of Bristol (along with several collaborators) published a paper in the scientific journal, *Nature*. This describes the analysis of a Roman cosmetic found in a small tin canister in London. The material was in the form of a cream containing both organic and inorganic compounds. This study is an excellent example of how incredibly detailed information about an artefact can be obtained using a range of analytical techniques, each one providing a specific piece of information that could be pieced together to build up a complete picture of the chemical composition of the cosmetic.

Now go to the 'Activities' section on the course website and complete Part 2 Activity 3.9.

As you read through the article, make a list of each analytical technique that is used and what information it provides about this artefact. *You will find a blank table for this activity in the Study Guide, to help you summarise your notes on: wet chemical methods, IR spectroscopy, GC/MS, XRF and XRD.*

Question 3.4

What was the role of tin oxide in the cosmetic material?

3.8   Summary of Topic 3

By completing this topic you should now be able to:

1   List examples of the wide range of materials that archaeological artefacts can be comprised of, and group them into organic and inorganic categories (KU2).

2   Describe how the structure of a material at the atomic level determines its chemical and physical properties, and how this impacts on how it is used (CS4).

3   Give examples of how the introduction of certain materials (e.g. stone and metals) over prehistoric time was closely linked to key stages of human development (KU3).

4   Explain with examples, the types of scientific analyses used to investigate different artefacts and determine issues such as: what the artefact is made of; where the original materials came from; and which technologies were involved in their manufacture (KU1).

5   List examples of the types of scientific analyses that can be used to determine best how an artefact was used, who used it and how the source materials needed for its manufacture were traded (KU3).

6   Compare and contrast the variable decay rates and processes experienced by different organic and inorganic materials (CS1).

7   Explain why certain environmental conditions, such as extreme dryness, waterlogging or natural refrigeration, can lead to extraordinarily well-preserved artefacts (CS1).

8   Describe why a poorly preserved object recovered from an excavation may need to be sent to a conservator for cleaning, repair and stabilisation before being displayed (KU4).

Remember, only the most important one or two learning outcomes are listed after each summary statement above, to emphasise the ones they are specifically addressing. Each summary statement does however, relate to several of the learning outcomes developed in this course, and you should bear this in mind when reviewing the topic and working towards your End of Course Assessment (ECA).

Topic 4
Our archaeological heritage: protecting finds for the future

4.1   Introduction

At the launch of the Northern Ireland Archaeological Forum in October 2007, Tony Robinson (the presenter of the UK's Channel 4 television programme *Time Team*; Figure 4.1) commented on how archaeological features are under increasing pressure from a variety of sources. Top of this list are: climate change (e.g. increasing erosion rates affecting coastal areas and changing the physical state of soils and land areas); the construction of new roads and housing developments; changes to agricultural and forestry practices; the rising number of people interested in the natural environment (which is good, but is increasing erosion rates and introducing new land pressures); and the rising antiquities trade in archaeological artefacts. He also described how good heritage management was paramount and that this needed to be coupled with the promotion of archaeology on local, regional and global scales. He then described how archaeological research on individual finds, structures and landforms has continued to enhance our understanding of past cultures, illustrating the need to protect the archaeological landscape (in its widest context) for future generations to study. Tony ended by stating that archaeological forums (such as the one being launched) have a key role to play in advising governments on the protection, conservation and exploration of archaeological features, as well as enhancing educational outreach activities (e.g. working with schools, community groups and amateur archaeologists). Promoting a general interest in archaeology could, in turn, maximise the potential to protect, enjoy and manage our archaeological heritage for today and for generations to come.

Figure 4.1   Tony Robinson (right) and Mick Aston from UK Channel 4's *Time Team*, at the launch of the Northern Ireland Archaeology Forum in 2007.

151

Now consider the scenarios shown in Figure 4.2 and described below.

(a) After getting permission from the landowner, a metal detectorist tries his new metal detector. After an hour of field walking, the detector sound suddenly changes. He does a little exploratory digging and uncovers what looks like some old coins (28 in total), 15 of which are possibly made of silver, along with some pottery sherds. What should he do? Can he keep these finds? How can he establish whether they are of any importance or value? Should he clean them and, if so, how?

(b) While walking across heathland, something glints in the sunshine and catches a walker's eye. She goes over to see what it is and picks up what initially looks like an ordinary bit of flint. Once the loose soil is removed, it reveals a shaped arrow head. What should she do? Can she keep this find? How can she establish whether it is of any importance or value?

(a)

(b)

(c)

(d)

Figure 4.2   The four scenarios: (a) the coins and pottery sherds; (b) the flint arrow head; (c) the coin and the bead; (d) the mystery mound.

(c) Knowing that you are studying archaeology, a neighbour's child asks whether she can show you the 'treasure' she has found in the garden. In her box of broken bits of Victorian pottery, you notice a cylindrical glass bead with an interesting pattern (which looks like an Early Medieval bead you recall from a textbook), and a rather degraded bronze to dirty gold coloured coin that has a Roman-looking head on it. What do you do? Can the child keep her finds? How can you find out if the bead or coin is of any importance or value? How should these objects be cleaned and stored?

(d) After buying an old farmhouse to renovate, the new owners decide to investigate the ground at the back of their property, which is partially covered in brambles and shrubs. While scrambling over the area, they pick out a circular mound (~1.5 m high and ~65–70 m in diameter), surrounded by a deep ditch which has large boulders (50–75 cm long) around its outer edge. How do they find out whether this is a natural mound or an archaeological feature? If it is an archaeological feature, how can they establish its age and whether it is of importance? Should they clear away the vegetation from the mound or dig into it to see if it has an internal structure?

The answers to these and other questions, along with an understanding of key issues associated with archaeology and heritage management, will become apparent as you work through this final topic.

The topic is divided into two parts; in the first, you will investigate some aspects of heritage management throughout the UK and the legislative protection of archaeological finds, features and landscapes. You will then examine some of the approaches designed to improve general awareness of the need to declare and systematically record archaeological discoveries, which is helping archaeologists develop a more thorough picture of the past. In the second part of this topic, you will adopt the role of a field archaeologist, a Finds Liaison Officer and a conservator, and use your skills and knowledge from this course to carry out systematic investigations on a range of archaeological finds and features.

As an introduction to the first part of this topic, read *Greene* Chapter 6, Sections 6.1 and 6.2 (pp. 266–9), making brief notes on the different types of practical, ethical, cultural and political issues raised, as a means of recapping some of the planning controls (introduced in Topic 1), which have been devised to protect archaeological sites from development.

4.2   Protecting ancient and scheduled 'monuments'

Starting with the last of the four scenarios described above in (d), what should the new home owners do to determine whether the mound is an archaeological feature and is of historical importance?

Throughout the UK, the Ancient Monuments and Archaeological Areas Act 1979 (AMAA) covers a wide range of different types of archaeological sites, structures and physical features that lie above or below the ground and provide evidence for past human activities. These features include: caves; burial mounds and graves; any intact or ruined buildings; defensive structures (e.g. walls, earthworks (Figures 4.3a, c and d)); carved stones; wells; bridges and industrial sites (from all time periods (Figure 4.3b)); rubbish tips (middens); cultivation ridges; and visible outlines of structures now long gone (e.g. crop and soil marks). All of these features are collectively referred to as 'monuments'.

This list is only a fraction of the ~200 different classes of monuments currently recognised.

153

(a)

(b)

(c)

(d)

Figure 4.3   Comparing and contrasting different types of ancient monuments and landscapes of interest to archaeologists: (a) part of the circular mound of a rath (ring fort) near Hillsborough, Northern Ireland; (b) the results of extensive mining on Parys Mountain, Anglesey, now forming part of the protected industrial landscape of North Wales; (c) one of the many defensive structures around the coast of Guernsey, from World War Two; (d) the remains of Dun Carloway, an Iron Age broch, Isle of Lewis, Scotland.

Although many monuments have been known about for some time, and are consequently well documented, numerous others are rediscovered every year from new field surveys, aerial photography and reports by the general public. Once discovered and verified as an archaeological structure, it is categorised as either an ancient or scheduled monument. An ancient monument is any site or structure as described above, belonging to any time period (e.g. defensive structures from recent wartimes, the Iron Age or earlier; Figure 4.3c and d). A scheduled monument is any ancient monument that is not currently used or likely to be used, and that is deemed to be of national importance and so fully protected under the 1979 Act.

An ancient monument can be scheduled by a representative of the relevant government department in charge of the historical environment, with the scheduled designation depending on:

- the current state of the monument and its likelihood to remain in this state (without major restorative work)

- its importance as a whole structure, because of its location and/or the presence of a specific feature

- its relationship with other archaeological monuments

- the potential it offers to improve current knowledge and understanding of this type of monument

- any other documentation that supports the case for being of national importance either in its own right or through a role it played in the past.

In 2003 (the most recent data available at the time of writing), over 32 000 ancient monuments were at scheduled status in the UK (Table 4.1).

Assigning scheduled status protects an ancient monument from any activities that could result in detrimental changes to the structure (including the use of metal detectors without an official licence), and prohibits any land use that would cause damage or potential destruction of the monument. The AMAA legislation does not however, prevent the landowner from using the area as long as this use is not harmful to the monument, nor does it alter land ownership or rights of access. In certain circumstances, scheduling can enable the landowner to gain financial assistance to help manage and preserve the monument, ensuring it remains in good standing and is protected for future appreciation.

Now review *Greene* Chapter 2, Section 2.4 (pp. 60–1), which describes how sites and monuments information is recorded on a central database.

The Sites and Monuments Records (SMR) database described in *Greene* was replaced in 2003 by the Historic Environment Record (HER). HER addresses issues of planning, protection and education about sites, monuments and the wider archaeological landscape, and covers historic sites in England, Scotland and Wales; Northern Ireland has its own SMR database. Each database consists of a range of information, including historic photographs, archaeological and architectural reports, maps, plans and other historic information about the environment, with many beginning to incorporate free online search facilities (Figure 4.4).

Table 4.1 Number of scheduled monuments registered in the UK, 2003.

Location	Number of recognised scheduled monuments
England	19 552
Northern Ireland	1738
Scotland	7631
Wales	3558
UK total	32 479

Data from English Heritage, Environmental and Heritage Service Northern Ireland, Historic Scotland and Cadw Welsh Historic Monuments.

You first encountered this in Topic 1. Make sure you review your original notes, adding or emphasising new points, as appropriate.

Figure 4.4 Example of an online report from a Sites and Monuments Records database, showing the results: (a) a list of the scheduled sites in a specific area in Northern Ireland; (b) part of the online report for the medieval church and graveyard at Kilbroney.

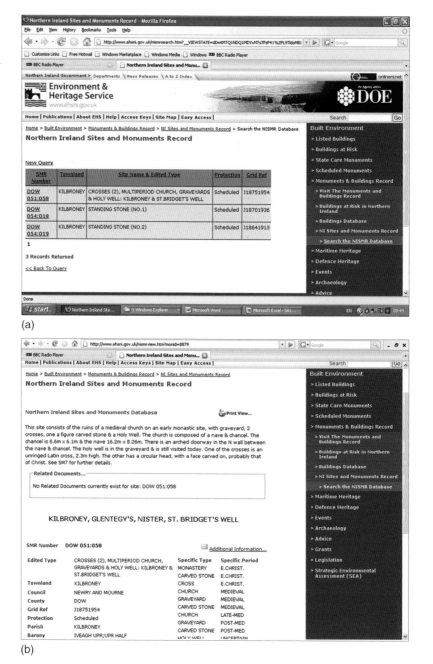

(a)

(b)

Question 4.1

Referring to Topic 1 'Reading the archaeological landscape', which other set of guidelines offers protection to ancient monuments and archaeological sites from development projects? Name one example where this has allowed archaeological objects to be rescued and preserved.

Question 4.2

Returning to the four scenarios at the beginning of this topic, what advice and guidance can you give to the farmhouse owners about the mound in their garden?

4.3   Protecting artefacts – saving portable antiquities for the nation

The level of protection offered to moveable artefacts (commonly referred to as portable antiquities) depends on where they are found, their composition, their age and in some instances, how many of them are found together.

In Scotland, all archaeological finds are protected by the ancient laws of Treasure Trove, which state '*quod nullius est fit domini regis*', which means 'that which belongs to no one, resides with the Crown'. So all archaeological finds discovered in Scotland (irrespective of where they are found or their composition) belong to the Crown State and must be officially declared; failure to do so falls under the premise of common theft. In England and Wales, archaeological finds are covered by the Treasure Act 1996, which uses the precious metal content of the find to determine whether it is 'Treasure' and so needs to be officially declared by the finder. Although the Treasure Act 1996 also covers Northern Ireland, the discovery of finds there is more complex as only qualified archaeologists are permitted to do archaeological work under licence to the Environment and Heritage Service. So, metal detecting and deliberate searching for finds is illegal in Northern Ireland, unless carried out under licence, and any archaeological object (irrespective of its age or composition) that is found unexpectedly by the public must be declared to the State; failure to do so may result in a criminal prosecution. Once a find is declared under the Treasure Act in England, Northern Ireland or Wales, it is held by the State for investigation to confirm whether it is Treasure and what should be done with it.

When written with a capital T, 'Treasure' is a legal term, with a specific meaning.

4.3.1   What is Treasure?

The next activity will enable you to answer the question 'What is Treasure?'.

Part 2 Activity 4.1   What is Treasure?

(The estimated time needed to complete this activity is 30 minutes.)

Main learning outcomes developed: KU4, CS3, PS1 and KS4.

This activity is based on the Treasure Act information leaflets (for England and Wales, and Northern Ireland), which are in the 'Documents' section on the course DVD. The activity takes you through what is meant by the term 'Treasure' and the types of archaeological objects protected by the 1996 Act, before determining the legal requirements to declare such finds.

You should record your answers in the blank version of Table 4.2 at the back of the Study Guide. (There is also a blank copy of this table in the 'Documents' section on the DVD.)

Now go to the DVD, click on 'Topics', find Topic 4 and complete Part 2 Activity 4.1.

You will find a full list of learning outcomes and their abbreviations in the back of this Study Book and in the Study Guide.

Table 4.2 Summary of the Treasure Act 1996 in Northern Ireland and in England and Wales. *(Use the blank version of Table 4.2 in the back of the Study Guide to complete your answer to Activity 4.1.)*

Question	Northern Ireland	England and Wales
1 What is Treasure?		
2 What is not Treasure?		
3 Who needs to be informed of the find? Where should the find be taken?		
4 If the find is Treasure and is bought by a museum, who is eligible for a reward?		

The official definition of 'Treasure', according to the 1996 Act, therefore covers: any object over 300 years old that contains more than 10% silver or gold; any group of coins found in one area; any object found alongside either of these first two groups; or any two or more prehistoric base-metal items, irrespective of how they originally came to be buried.

Under the pre-1996 common laws of Treasure Trove in England, Northern Ireland and Wales, discoveries of silver and gold objects had to be officially reported. If it was deemed the object had been buried *with* the intention of recovering it, but the original owner could no longer be traced, then it became 'Treasure Trove' and automatically belonged to the Crown. If the object was deemed to have been buried *without* the intention of recovery (e.g. grave goods or ritualistic – i.e. votive – offerings), then it was not Treasure Trove and so belonged to the landowner.

■   Which of the following artefacts recovered from the Saxon (AD 613) burial ship at Sutton Hoo between 1938 and 1988, were protected by the Treasure Trove law: a bronze and garnet shield; a solid gold ornate buckle; an engraved iron helmet; fragments of the ship's timbers; leather strap mounts; and a collection of gold coins?

☐   None of them, because they were buried without the intention of the original owner ever retrieving them. (So they immediately belonged to the landowner.)

In the case of Sutton Hoo, the site and artefacts (Figure 4.5) remained the private property of the landowners until 1998, when they were gifted by the Annie Tranmer Trust to The National Trust. There are however numerous other occasions when important archaeological evidence discovered before 1996 and not defined as Treasure, was sold on the open antiquities market to the highest bidder, and so was lost to research and the general public. This is the reason why the Treasure Act 1996 was passed.

Now read *Greene* Chapter 6, Section 6.5 (pp. 274–5) for an overview of the issues affecting archaeology and the antiquities trade on a global scale.

(a)

(b)

Figure 4.5   Two of the spectacular finds recovered from the Anglo-Saxon ship burial at Sutton Hoo, Suffolk, England: (a) a helmet; (b) a buckle.

■ What does this mean for the portable objects recently discovered in the scenarios at the beginning of this topic?

☐ You have probably realised that the answer to this and who owns each object depends on the country where it was found.

Question 4.3

Referring back to scenarios (a), (b) and (c) at the beginning of this topic, complete Table 4.3, showing:

(i) whether each object counts as Treasure (or Treasure Trove in Scotland)

(ii) why this is the case

(iii) what legally needs to be done with the find.

The entry for the 28 coins in scenario (a) is completed for you, as a guide to the type of information to include.

4.3.2   The value of 'non-Treasure'

Part 2 Activity 4.1 and Question 4.3 highlight some of the legal aspects of what counts as 'Treasure', but this does not mean that portable antiquities made from other materials are of no value. All archaeological objects are valuable, as they provide new opportunities to enhance our knowledge and understanding of the past and the people who made and used them.

Although there is a legal requirement to report all archaeological finds in Scotland and Northern Ireland, this is not the case in England and Wales. To address this issue, the Portable Antiquities Scheme (PAS) was established to encourage the voluntary declaration of non-Treasure finds. This scheme is supported by a series of Finds Liaison Officers located across England and Wales, who provide local support to finders to determine the legal status of all finds, and work with other specialists to identify and record all non-Treasure finds; (all Treasure is passed to the Crown Coroner).

Table 4.3 Comparison of what counts as Treasure in England, Northern Ireland and Wales and Treasure Trove in Scotland. (For use in Question 4.3.)

Object	Country	Treasure/Trove?	Why?	What next?
Scenario (a)				
28 silver and metal coins	Scotland	yes	all finds irrespective of composition or age are Treasure Trove	declare find to Crown
	England/Wales	yes	number, age and composition of coins makes them Treasure	declare find to Crown
	Northern Ireland	yes	as above	declare find to Crown (finder must have had a licence to use a metal detector)
pottery sherds	Scotland			
	England/Wales			
	Northern Ireland			
Scenario (b)				
flint arrow head	Scotland			
	England/Wales			
	Northern Ireland			
Scenario (c)				
single Roman bronze to dirty gold coloured coin	Scotland			
	England/Wales			
	Northern Ireland			
glass bead (possibly Early Medieval)	Scotland			
	England/Wales			
	Northern Ireland			

Part 2 Activity 4.2 The roles of the Portable Antiquities Scheme and Finds Liaison Officers

(The estimated time needed to complete this activity is 15 minutes.)

Main learning outcomes developed: KU3, CS1, KS3 and PS1.

In this activity, you will hear how the Portable Antiquities Scheme (PAS) is helping archaeologists with their research, and why Sam Moorhead (from the British Museum) has described the PAS as 'one of the top four or five breakthroughs in archaeology in the last 50 years'. You will then discover how the Finds Liaison Officers (FLOs) are working with the general public, metal detectorists and professional archaeologists to ensure new finds are accurately recorded and logged on the system.

Now go to the DVD, click on 'Topics', find Topic 4 and complete Part 2 Activity 4.2.

Question 4.4

(a) Referring to Topic 3, briefly describe the conservation process(es) these coins will undergo.

(b) Which analytical techniques can be used to check their metal composition and confirm whether they are Treasure?

The PAS is only applicable to England and Wales; in Scotland, the Queen and Lord Treasurer's Remembrancer (QLTR) is responsible for claiming all objects for the Crown under the Treasure Trove law, allocating finds to different museums and paying rewards to the finders. The QLTR works with three other staff in the Treasure Trove Unit and the Scottish Archaeological Finds Allocation Panel.

Part 2 Activity 4.3 Using the PAS database

(The estimated time needed to complete this activity is 30 minutes.)

Main learning outcomes developed: CS3, KS1, KS2 and PS1.

In this activity, you will use the PAS website to do different types of searches for artefacts logged on this database.

Now go to 'Activities' on the course website and complete Part 2 Activity 4.3.

This section has highlighted how the various government agencies in the UK (English Heritage, Historic Scotland, the Environment and Heritage Service Northern Ireland and Cadw Welsh Historic Monuments) have worked with the government and local authorities to devise a series of procedures to record, manage and protect the archaeological heritage of each country. The Historic Environment Records (HER) and Sites and Monuments Records (SMR), coupled with the classification of ancient and scheduled monuments, have allowed a record of different archaeological structures (above and below the surface) to be developed, with advice on their maintenance and protection offered to landowners. In addition, outreach programmes developed to enhance awareness of the legal requirement to declare finds in accordance with the laws of Treasure Trove (Scotland) and the Treasure Act (England, Northern Ireland and Wales), combined with the voluntary Portable Antiquities Scheme, have significantly increased the number of finds reported over the past decade, while also offering easily accessible help on the conservation and preservation of different types of finds.

So where does this leave you in trying to answer the questions posed in scenarios (a) to (c) at the beginning of this topic? The rights of ownership and who to inform were resolved in Question 4.3, however this still leaves the issue of how to clean the finds without damaging them.

Question 4.5

Adopt the role of a Finds Liaison Officer and decide what advice you would give to each finder on how to care for the following finds before you examine them:

(a) 28 silver and metal coins and some pottery sherds

(b) a flint arrow head

(c) a bronze-gold coloured coin and glass bead.

4.4 'CSI Archaeology': investigative science in action

Throughout this course, you have examined a wide range of topics within the realms of archaeological science in the field and the laboratory, and discovered why it is important to work systematically when collecting, recording, analysing and interpreting data. The key to effective scientific research is therefore to:

- determine the main reasons for the study (e.g. why it is of interest and what the aims and objectives are)
- select appropriate methods of analysis to ensure the right data is collected (e.g. to ensure the project aims are addressed)
- collect this data in a careful and systematic manner (to avoid errors and enable the work to be reproduced or repeated if necessary); and only then
- interpret the evidence to reach the most plausible conclusion, at that point in time.

In archaeology, there is the added ethical requirement to respect the sites and materials being investigated, bearing in mind any cultural, political and/or social considerations, as well as the fact that once destroyed, specific finds cannot be replaced or returned to their original state.

In this final section, you will draw on the archaeological skills and knowledge you have developed throughout this course to solve a series of intriguing case studies. As each activity draws on knowledge and understanding that relates to all four of the KU learning outcomes, and requires you to consider a range of ethical issues (practical and professional learning outcome, PS1), only the main cognitive and key learning outcomes are listed below. During each study, you will have to decide which method(s) of investigation to use, justify your choice, and decide what information to collect, as well as how to analyse and interpret the results. Each case study is loosely based on a real problem that archaeologists and conservators have had to resolve, so you can compare your approach with the one actually used!

4.4.1   The case studies

Read through the following brief descriptions before completing the associated DVD activities.

Part 2 Activity 4.4   The case of the square pit

(The estimated time needed to complete this activity is 30 minutes.)

Main learning outcomes developed: CS1, CS3 and KS2.

Background It is Peter Connelly's day off, and, as the assistant project director on the Hungate Dig, you have just been called over by one of the field excavators who has uncovered a rather unusual square feature, ~1 m across and consisting of stones, bricks and clay tiles (Figure 4.6). A resistivity survey of the area before excavation did not reveal any obvious structures, so you do not know the shape or exact dimensions of this feature.

Your task You need to decide how to proceed with the excavation, including the style of excavation to carry out, whether to excavate the inside or the outside first, what kind of samples (if any) to collect and analyse (e.g. soil samples, individual bricks, the coating on the tops of the bricks, the whole structure etc.) and ultimately, decide when to stop the investigation.

Links Topic 1

Now go to the DVD, click on 'Topics', find Topic 4 and work through Part 2 Activity 4.4.

Figure 4.6   The top of the mysterious square feature discovered at Hungate.

Part 2 Activity 4.5   Animal crackers: what *is* inside the mummies?

(The estimated time needed to complete this activity is 20 minutes.)

Main learning outcomes developed: CS1 and CS3.

Background While clearing out the loft of a stately home in the north of England, a box of animal mummies is discovered. As the box has been stored in a cool, dark and dry environment for ~100 years, the mummies are in remarkably good condition and do not exhibit any signs of decay or damage. The box contains six mummies of different sizes, some of which appear to depict the shape and image of the animal inside, while others are more abstract in shape and design (Figure 4.7).

Your task As one of the British Museum conservators working with mummies, your job is to create a new exhibit in the museum for this recent acquisition, saying what the mummies are, and ensuring that they do not start to deteriorate once on display.

Links Topics 2 and 3

Now go to the DVD, click on 'Topics', find Topic 4 and work through Part 2 Activity 4.5.

Figure 4.7   One of the less obvious animal mummies.

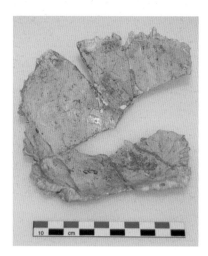

Figure 4.8 Some of the broken and marked bones recovered from the cave.

Part 2 Activity 4.6 Sticks and stones … determining the cause of the marked and broken bones

(The estimated time needed to complete this activity is 20 minutes.)

Main learning outcomes developed: CS1, CS2, KS1 and KS2.

Background The coroner contacts you at the museum to ask for help investigating some human bones found by cavers during an expedition to map a new section of cave. Analyses have been carried out on the bones and surrounding sediment, and they have been confirmed as human, dating to more than 12 000 years BP. The bones are in various states of decay and, although some are still whole, several have been broken and have what look like cut marks (Figure 4.8).

Your task You need to determine how many individuals are represented by the bones, examine the taphonomy of breaks and marks, and decide whether they were caused by depositional processes associated with the burial or excavation or were deliberately produced at the time of death. Using the evidence available, you then need to decide a possible reason for their formation.

Links Topic 2

 Now go to the DVD, click on 'Topics', find Topic 4 and work through Part 2 Activity 4.6.

Figure 4.9 Close-up view of the grand marble vase.

Part 2 Activity 4.7 The grand marble vase: a single masterpiece or a composite creation?

(The estimated time needed to complete this activity is 15 minutes.)

Main learning outcomes developed: CS1 and CS3.

Background A highly elaborate marble vase is sent to the conservators' laboratory to be checked for signs of deterioration (Figure 4.9). Although the vase has been carved in a style reminiscent of the Roman Period (in particular the Emperor Hadrian, AD 117–138), it has been classified as an 18th century replica. During your inspection, you notice parts of the vase are deteriorating at different rates and may be made of a different material from the main vase.

Your task You need to decide how you will examine the vase to determine whether it is made from one or several types of material. If it is a composite of different materials, you need to suggest what these may be and how you can distinguish them.

Links Topic 3

 Now go to the DVD, click on 'Topics', find Topic 4 and work through Part 2 Activity 4.7.

Part 2 Activity 4.8 Gold! Caring for an ancient jewel or a modern replica?

(The estimated time needed to complete this activity is 15 minutes.)

Main learning outcomes developed: CS1, KS2 and KS3.

Background Some exquisite gold jewellery is sent to the conservators' laboratory for investigation (Figure 4.10). Although the jewellery is fashioned in the Etruscan style (ninth to fourth century BC), there is reason to believe it may be a late 19th to early 20th century replica.

Your task You need to determine what the exact composition of the metal is, any issues surrounding its conservation needs, and whether it is possible to determine its age of manufacture.

Links Topic 3

Now go to the DVD, click on 'Topics', find Topic 4 and work through Part 2 Activity 4.8.

Figure 4.10 The exquisite, fine, Italian gold work.

Part 2 Activity 4.9 A hoard in a million?

(The estimated time needed to complete this activity is 20 minutes.)

Main learning outcomes developed: CS1 and KS2.

Background As the local Finds Officer, you receive a call from two metal detectorists who have found some pottery and gold jewellery in a field near Milton Keynes (Figure 4.11). They have not removed the find as it is very fragile and difficult to extract from the soil. A local professional archaeologist has confirmed that the find looks as if it may date back to the Bronze Age.

Your task You need to decide how you are going to excavate and transfer this find from the field to the museum. Once safely at the museum, you should decide what else needs to be done as regards this discovery and your role as a Finds Officer.

Links Topics 1 and 3

Now go to the DVD, click on 'Topics', find Topic 4 and work through Part 2 Activity 4.9.

Figure 4.11 The impressive gold jewellery recovered from the field in Milton Keynes, after conservation.

4.5 Summary of Topic 4

By completing this topic you should now be able to:

1 List some of the pressures that the archaeological landscape, sites and features are currently facing, and the roles government and non-governmental organisations are playing in promoting heritage management for current and future generations (KU4).

2 Name the main UK legislative act and guidelines that offer varying levels of protection to archaeological landscapes and features from damage or needless destruction (CS3).

3   Give examples of the range of features that can be described as 'monuments' under the AMAA, and describe the process involved and the potential benefits of getting a monument scheduled (CS1, CS3).

4   Briefly explain how the law of Treasure Trove in Scotland differs from the Treasure Act 1996 in England, Wales and Northern Ireland, and why the Treasure Act 1996 was passed (KU4, CS1).

5   Describe what is recognised as 'Treasure' and the legal requirements of a person finding such an object (KU4, CS3).

6   Briefly describe why the Portable Antiquities Scheme (PAS) was set up and the type of information recorded on this database (KU3, KU4).

7   Give examples of some of the different ethical issues facing archaeologists, find officers and conservators when working with archaeological features and objects (PS1).

8   Apply your knowledge and understanding of archaeological processes, to investigate unfamiliar cases and determine their authenticity (CS1, CS3).

9   Communicate information clearly, concisely and carefully, while using your own words to express course concepts in an objective and factually correct manner (CS4, KS3).

Remember, only the most important one or two learning outcomes are listed after each summary statement above, to emphasise the ones they are specifically addressing. Each summary statement does however, relate to several of the learning outcomes developed in this course, and you should bear this in mind when reviewing the topic and working towards your End of Course Assessment (ECA).

Answers to questions

PART I

Chapter 2

Question 2.1

(a) To convert 752 years BP into an AD/BC date, you need to subtract this value from the scientific baseline, i.e. 1950. So 1950 – 752 = 1198; as this is a positive number, it belongs to the AD group of dates, making AD 1198 the correct answer.

(b) To convert the AD/BC dates into years BP, you need to subtract the dates from the scientific baseline date (1950), remembering that AD dates can be considered 'positive' values while BC dates can be considered 'negative' values, i.e.:

1245 BC = 1950 – (–1245) = 3195 years BP

AD 234 = 1950 – 234 = 1716 years BP

AD 1950 = 1950 – 1950 = 0 years BP, i.e. the present

5560 BC = 1950 – (–5560) = 7510 years BP

(c) If the same dating technique is used, the pottery still dates from 2025 years BP (not 2083 years BP). This was the one and only trick question in this course, so well done if you got it right and if you didn't – don't worry because everyone falls for this at some point!

■ So, why does the pottery's age not change between the original analysis in 1950 and the repeat in 2008?

□ The scientific dating method standardises all analyses to a common baseline, which in this case is 1950. Standardising data to a known baseline value is a common approach in science.

In such cases, when an 'unknown' (e.g. the sample of interest) is analysed, it is measured alongside a known standard (a sample for which the composition or age is known and has been agreed by the international research community). The results of the unknown sample and the known standard are then compared with the expected values for the standard. By converting the difference between the measured and the expected values for the standard, a *correction factor* can be applied to calculate the final age (or composition) of the unknown sample.

Question 2.2

The two developments that allowed archaeologists to arrange artefacts according to their date of origin were:

(a) the creation of a new dating system called the Scandinavian Three-Age system, based on the progression of the use of technologies from stone to metal (i.e. the Stone, Bronze and Iron Ages)

(b) the study of the emergence of humans (i.e. our origins) by French and British scientists.

Question 2.3

The three timescales have been subdivided into different Ages and Periods because each one relates to the development of a specific culture or geographic area. The time divisions therefore represent different social, cultural and historical developments appropriate to the archaeological record for that particular area.

Question 2.4

There are several examples in *Greene*, Section 2 (p. 184) of how environmental archaeology uses a multidisciplinary approach, e.g. studying Stone Age hunter-gatherers requires an understanding of and information about:

- what the climate was like at the time, and how this affected how hunter-gatherers lived and what they could eat
- the plants and animals that were present in the area at the time and what this implies about the climate
- what the hunter-gatherers ate, the impact this diet had on their state of health, their life expectancy and evidence of changing diets due to variability in access of food (caused by over-hunting or over-gathering, or changing environmental conditions).

You could have structured your answer as a series of notes or as a flow diagram, showing how an understanding of the three main controlling factors e.g. *climate – animals and plants – stone age diets*, are interdependent (or in other words, how changes to one factor affects the others). For example, a deteriorating climate will affect the type of plants and animals that live in the area, which will cause the hunter-gatherers to either change what they eat or force them to move to new areas to find the right type and amount of food.

Question 2.5

Geological and geomorphological landform evidence increases in importance as the archaeological remains become older, e.g. understanding climatic changes caused by the last Ice Age.

Question 2.6

At Boxgrove, the archaeological materials were *in situ*, which means they were undisturbed and in the exact place where they were discarded, 40 000 years BP. *In situ* finds can be examined by careful forensic methods of investigation to gain an insight into what they were used for and why they were deposited. In contrast, the Swanscombe hand axes were removed from their original location and re-deposited in more recent sediments. Reworking of deposits makes it impossible to determine what evidence was formed at the same time as deposition. So it is not possible to establish whether the reworked hand axes all came from the same source or different sites of different ages across the whole valley. Furthermore, environmental evidence about the original use of the axes can no longer be extracted from the surrounding sediments, as these may be very different from the original environmental conditions.

Question 2.7

(a) K–Ar dating and magnetic reversal studies can be done on specific types of volcanic deposits and/or igneous rocks. K–Ar dating requires samples that are rich in minerals containing potassium; magnetic reversals depend on the sample containing iron-rich minerals, which record the Earth's magnetic field at the time of formation.

(b) Absolute dates will be obtained for the volcanic deposits (and igneous rocks), whereas the archaeological artefacts can only be assigned a relative date (e.g. older or younger than the volcanic layer).

Question 2.8

The significant development at the end of the Palaeolithic Period was the move to farming and domesticated plants and animals. This provided communities with a relatively ready supply of food, allowing them to settle in one area rather than constantly move to where food supplies were more plentiful.

PART 2

Topic 1

Question 1.1

Your completed table should resemble Table 1.6.

Table 1.6 Completed version of Table 1.1.

Description	Term
Tell es-Sa'idiyeh cemetery	site
the skeleton of a person, recovered from a grave at Tell es-Sa'idiyeh	human remains
the horse bits recovered from the Wetwang cart	artefact (or find)
the iron mirror, brooch and pig bones recovered from the Wetwang grave	finds (artefacts and animal remains)
the scooped-out hollow into which Wetwang Woman was placed	constructed feature
determining the location of the cemetery at Hungate	project
the square barrow (grave) at Wetwang	constructed feature
the Iron Age of East Yorkshire	archaeological landscape
the Hungate Dig	a project and a site!

Question 1.2

(a) As 1 ha equals 10 000 m², 13 ha is $13 \times 10\,000$ m² $= 130\,000$ m².

(b) To convert 130 000 m² into km², the value needs to be divided by 1000 000, (as 1 km² equals 1000 m $\times 1000$ m $= 1000\,000$ m²) i.e. 130 000 m² ÷ 1000 000 = 0.13 km².

Question 1.3

Your completed table should resemble Table 1.7.

Table 1.7

Field site	Length	Breadth	Area
Tell es-Saʻidiyeh	500 m	260 m	13 ha
Hungate	320 m	150 m	48 000 m² or 4.8 ha
Wetwang grave	~3.5 m	2.6 m	~9 m²
individual grave, Tell es-Saʻidiyeh	1.60 m (or 160 cm)	1.25 m (or 125 cm)	~2 m² (or 20 000 cm²)

The four missing values are calculated as follows.

- **Tell es-Saʻidiyeh**: first, 13 ha must be converted into m² (see Question 1.2a), i.e. 130 000 m². This is then divided by the known length: 130 000 m² ÷ 500 m = 260 m.

- **Hungate**: both lengths are known, so the area is 320 m × 150 m = 48 000 m². To allow this to be directly compared with Tell es-Saʻidiyeh, it should be converted to ha (i.e. 48 000 m² ÷ 10 000 m² = 4.8 ha).

You can find help on calculations and significant figures in the Maths Skills ebook on the course website.

- **Wetwang grave**: using the same method of calculation as for Tell es-Saʻidiyeh, 9 m² ÷ 2.6 m = 3.46 m (which can be rounded up to 3.5 m to quote it to the same number of figures as the breadth). Converting this area into hectares – 0.0009 ha – shows how small this site is relative to Hungate and Tell es-Saʻidiyeh.

- **Individual Tell es-Saʻidiyeh grave**: the easiest way to deal with this site is to convert the length into metres (rather than converting the area in cm²). So 2 m² ÷ 1.6 m = 1.25 m (or 125 cm) for the breadth. To convert the area into cm², you need to remember that 1 m = 100 cm, so 1 m² = 100 cm × 100 cm = 10 000 cm² (so 2 m² = 20 000 cm²). (Converting the grave area into hectares gives a value of 2 m² ÷ 10 000 m² = 0.0002 ha!)

Question 1.4

Field-walking surveys require open areas in which archaeological objects will be found on the ground surface. The only site that appears to fit this profile is Tell es-Saʻidiyeh. As this is a very large site, a survey across the whole area would be time-consuming, so the site needs to be divided into subsections to make this more manageable.

It is unlikely that any archaeological remains would have been found in the car park at Hungate before the excavations, as it was covered in tarmac. As each excavated layer is removed, information from these layers will be used to identify areas for focused examination. Field walking could destroy some of this precious evidence, unless carried out very carefully.

At Wetwang, the topsoil had been removed to expose a new compacted soil surface surrounded by a ditch. Although this surface should be checked for changes in soil colour and texture, it does not require a field-walking survey, which could destroy evidence. (As you will discover later in this topic, the filled ditch would be ideal for a test pit to see what had accumulated in this artificially created feature.)

Finally, a field-walking survey across the excavated cemetery at Tell es-Sa'idiyeh would not be suitable, as this process could destroy some of the fragile remains and evidence in the site.

Question 1.5

As the photograph has been taken at an oblique angle, the shapes of features have been distorted, the apparent distances between objects getting progressively bigger the further away they are from the camera.

Question 1.6

Compare your summary notes for each of the IFA's code rules with Table 1.8. Although your exact notes probably differ, check to see whether you extracted the same type of information.

Table 1.8 Completed version of Table 1.5.

Principle	Key points	Main points from rules: *All archaeologists should …*
1	Standards of ethical and responsible behaviour	1.2: present results responsibly; avoid exaggerating results or making misleading statements 1.4: only do work they are qualified for
2	Responsible for conservation	2.1: conserve all sites and materials for present and future studies, and keep all records safely for future use 2.2: carry out destructive investigation only if it relates to the project objectives and does not destroy rare finds 2.3: be able to justify all cases of destructive investigative work
3	Reliable information and results can be collected and recorded	3.1: keep up to date with new approaches and understanding in their area 3.2: prepare beforehand for all projects 3.3: ensure that the approaches used in a project are appropriate 3.4: keep records that can be easily used by others 3.5: ensure all records and finds collected are kept in good order
4	Results will be made available to others	4.2: prepare and release results quickly 4.3: publish the results of a project or allow others to do so 4.6: inform the general public about their work
5	Safe employment conditions and the chance for ongoing development	–

Summarising information in this way can help to identify the main points in a more complex section of text. If you compare the original IFA document (accessible via the 'Documents' section on the course website) with Table 3.1 in *Greene*, you should note that *Greene* has already started this summary process, by selecting the most important rules. Table 1.8 could be summarised further (e.g. by combining the principles and rules into a series of five sentences or phrases), but in doing so, you need to ensure that the overall meaning of this information is not lost!

Question 1.7

(a) The safety precautions include: wearing hard hats, high visibility vests and steel-capped boots at all times; never walking backwards on site; not standing too close to the edge of a trench; only walking across the site on designated routes; entering and exiting trenches at designated points.

(b) The sides of the very deep trench were stabilised by lining them with corrugated steel sheets (sheet pilling) driven into the soil, to construct a *cofferdam*. As this type of construction is very expensive, it can only be done when there is a sound archaeological reason to construct such a deep trench and the financial and logistical resources to support it.

Question 1.8

(a) At a scale of 1:20, 100 mm on the drawing equals 100 mm × 20 = 2000 mm (or 2 m) in the section.

(b) (i) At a scale of 1:10, the pottery sherd would measure 8.4 mm × 1 mm (84 mm ÷ 10; 10 mm ÷ 10).

(ii) At a scale of 1:20, the pottery sherd is 4.2 mm × 0.5 mm (the original measurements divided by 20).

(iii) A scale of 1:10 is best, as it would be very difficult to accurately draw something 0.5 mm wide.

Question 1.9

The Tell es-Sa'idiyeh site was returned to its original state (e.g. agricultural grazing land) at the end of the last excavation phase, but is protected from urban and intensive agricultural developments by the Jordanian authorities to permit future archaeological investigations.

Although houses were built across the original building plot in Wetwang, the grave site near the entrance of this cul-de-sac has been returned to grass.

At the end of the Hungate Dig, the site will be converted into a commercial and residential development with underground parking, and open air plaza (constructed above the medieval cemetery).

Topic 2

Question 2.1

(a) The two documents were written for very different 'audiences'.

(b) The British Museum document is written in 'plain English', and is designed for anyone who wants to know how the Museum works with human remains. It refers to the Human Tissues Act 2004 and the UK DCMS document.

The IFA document contains many technical and scientific terms and is designed for professional archaeologists and scientists, working with human remains on an excavation and in a laboratory. It refers to a wide range of other reference documents.

Question 2.2

The style of burial and presence and type of grave goods buried with the human remains, can be used to determine the site's age and the social and cultural practices at the time of death. Environmental analyses of pollen grains or soil samples, and examination of stratigraphic relationships can be used to estimate the site's age.

Question 2.3

The main case studies can be categorised as follows.

(a) *Unique or one-off finds*: the Lapedo Child; Nesperennub (although he could be classified as a multiple find in the realms of similarly aged mummies from the same site); Wetwang Woman; Lindow Man.

(b) *Part of a multiple find*: the Krapina Neanderthal bones; graves from the Tell es-Saʿidiyeh and Hungate cemeteries; the Llullaillaco mountain children.

Question 2.4

They will all start to decompose. (This is why they need to be professionally conserved and maintained in environmentally controlled and monitored cases or storage units.)

Question 2.5

Substituting the measurements into the correct equations from Table 2.3:

(a) Caucasian male + tibia: $(42.34 \text{ cm} \times 2.42) + 81.93 \text{ cm} = 102.46 \text{ cm} + 81.93 \text{ cm} = 184.39 \text{ cm}$ or 184 cm (to the nearest cm).

(b) African male + femur: $(50.19 \text{ cm} \times 2.10) + 72.22 \text{ cm} = 105.40 \text{ cm} + 72.22 \text{ cm} = 177.62 \text{ cm}$ or 178 cm (to the nearest cm).

Question 2.6

(a) Figure 2.13 plots height against length of the tibia so, using this measurement (35.89 cm), this can be plotted (as accurately as possible e.g. 36 cm) on the x-axis and a line drawn vertically up to the regression line. At the intersection with this line, a horizontal line can be drawn across to the y-axis, which gives a height of approximately 170 cm or 1.70 m.

(b) The information provided simply states that this individual is male. Doing a calculation similar to that in Question 2.5a gives an estimated height of 169 cm (using the Caucasian equation) or 164 cm (with the African equation) to the nearest cm. These values can be averaged: $(169 \text{ cm} + 164 \text{ cm}) \div 2 = 166.5 \text{ cm}$ or 167 cm (to the nearest cm).

Question 2.7

(a) The four main scientific dating techniques used to date teeth and bones are: radiocarbon dating; uranium-series dating; electron spin resonance (ESR) dating; and amino acid racemisation (AAR).

(b) *Definition 1* = absolute dating (e.g. by radiogenic isotopes).

Definition 2 = relative dating (e.g. typography or stratigraphy).

(c) Radiocarbon, uranium-series dating, ESR and AAR dating are all absolute dating techniques.

Question 2.8

(a) The temperature and conditions of burial can affect the measured D/L ratio.

(b) The accuracy of AAR data can be confirmed by comparing it with another dating technique that can be used on teeth (e.g. radiocarbon dating).

Question 2.9

(a) The range of foodstuffs recovered from each of the stomachs was as follows.

Clonycavan Man	no specific food items, but the diet was rich in vegetables
Old Croghan Man	milk and cereals, plus evidence that his diet was rich in meat
Lindow Man	unleavened bread made from barley and wheat, a drink of some sort and mistletoe pollen (possibly inhaled?)
Llullaillaco mountain children	a large quantity of coca leaves

(b) The types of foodstuff found in the stomach can be used to determine the most likely time-of-year of death, as certain food types are more common at specific times of year.

Topic 3

Question 3.1

As described in Part 2 Activity 3.1 'The work of the conservator', metals tend to deteriorate over time through corrosion. For example, you can easily see this by looking at some rusty iron nails that have been stored outdoors.

Question 3.2

The Phoenician sailors had simply hit upon the ideal combination of chemicals to make glass. Presumably the liquid cooled to form a glassy product. (One drawback of this simple soda-silica glass however would have been that it dissolved slowly in water!)

Question 3.3

As it is known when many colouring materials were introduced, techniques such as XRD or Raman spectroscopy could be used to identify the compound and hence estimate the age of the object.

Question 3.4

Tin oxide is a white pigment and its function was to help fashionable Roman women achieve a much-desired fair complexion.

Topic 4

Question 4.1

The Planning and Policy Guidelines 16 (PPG 16, which apply in England), and the equivalent planning policy guidelines in other countries, offer some additional protection to ancient monuments from damage or destruction by development projects or, at the very least, leads to careful records being kept of any sites that are destroyed. Although the PPG 16 and equivalent guidelines are not legal requirements, most local councils and developers adhere to them, and consider issues relating to archaeology at the start of the planning process, aiming to preserve all archaeology where possible.

There are several examples in this course of how the PPG 16 (or its equivalent) has been used to check for archaeological features and protect them, but the most obvious are the location and preservation of the cemetery at Hungate, and the initial checks for archaeological remains at the start of the building development in Wetwang village, which revealed the square barrow and subsequent rescue excavation of the Iron Age woman, her cart and grave goods.

Question 4.2

First, the owners should not dig into the mound! The metal detectorist in scenario (a) should also not have carried out their exploratory dig, on discovery of their find. Only professional archaeologists should excavate a site. The owners of the mound need to contact their local council authority (e.g. county archaeologist or SMR officer) to determine whether this feature has been logged on the SMR database. If it has, they can find out what it is and how old it is. If not, they should ask the local authority for advice on getting the site assessed. If the mound is a new archaeological monument, the local authority can give advice on managing and protecting it, and depending on its importance, the owners may be eligible for a maintenance grant.

Question 4.3

Your completed table should be similar to Table 4.4.

Table 4.4 Completed version of Table 4.3. (For use in Question 4.3.)

Object	Country	Treasure/Trove?	Why?	What next?
Scenario (a)				
28 silver and metal coins	Scotland	yes	all finds irrespective of composition or age are Treasure Trove	declare find to Crown
	England/Wales	yes	number, age and composition of coins makes them Treasure	declare find to Crown
	Northern Ireland	yes	as above	declare find to Crown (finder must have had a licence to use a metal detector)
pottery sherds	Scotland	yes	all finds are Treasure Trove irrespective of composition or age	declare find to Crown
	England/Wales	yes	sherds found alongside coin, makes them Treasure	declare find to Crown
	Northern Ireland	yes	as above	declare find to Crown (finder must have had a licence to use the metal detector!)
Scenario (b)				
flint arrow head	Scotland	yes	all finds are Treasure Trove, irrespective of composition or age	declare find to Crown
	England/Wales	no	not made of metal and not found with other Treasure, so the arrow-head is not Treasure	does not need to be officially declared; but ask local FLO to enter find on the PAS database
	Northern Ireland	no	as above	all archaeological finds must be declared to the Crown
Scenario (c)				
single Roman bronze to dirty gold coloured coin	Scotland	yes	all finds are Treasure Trove irrespective of composition or age	declare find to Crown
	England/Wales	no	single coins are not Treasure	single coins do not need to be officially declared; ask local FLO to enter find on the PAS database
	Northern Ireland	no	as above	although not Treasure, all archaeological finds must be declared to the Crown
glass bead (possibly Early Medieval)	Scotland	yes	all finds are Treasure Trove, irrespective of composition or age	declare find to Crown
	England/Wales	no	not made of metal and not found with other Treasure, so the bead is not Treasure	the bead does not need to be officially declared; ask the local FLO to enter the find on the PAS database
	Northern Ireland	no	as above	although not Treasure, all archaeological finds must be declared to the Crown

Question 4.4

(a) The first stage of cleaning involves placing the coins in water to remove surface deposits, and gently wiping the surface with a cotton bud. If the coins are corroded on the surface but have a solid core, they could be placed in an alkali solution (for a few minutes) to remove more resistant surface deposits. As the exact treatment is likely to vary for each coin or batch of coins depending on their exact composition and current physical state, different solutions will be required for each type of metal. As such, this work should only be carried out by a metals conservator. For example, if the coins are heavily corroded, placing them in the alkali solution could result in them completely dissolving – which would not be a good result!

(b) A variety of methods can be used to examine the coins – optical and scanning electron microscopy may reveal enough detail to allow the cleaned coins to be identified. XRF (or EDX in the SEM) might be useful to determine the metal composition (but errors may arise because of weathering or contamination of the surface); atomic absorption spectroscopy (AAS) might also be useful but requires the removal of a sample for analysis.

Question 4.5

According to the advice and guidance on conservation and treating finds on the websites of PAS and Treasure Trove, none of the finders should attempt to clean their objects (a–c) before a specialist adviser has examined them. As none of the objects were recovered from under water, they should be allowed to dry out slowly and any loose soil carefully removed. The finder should not attempt to remove any soil or other deposits that are stuck to the object – these should be left for the specialist to remove. The objects can then be carefully wrapped in some acid-free tissue and placed in a sealable, dry container for transportation to the local museum or FLO. The metal coins and the pottery sherds should be packed separately to ensure that the coins do not damage the pottery, and rock fragments and sand grains in the pottery do not scratch the coins.

If the object is returned to the finder to keep, more detailed advice on cleaning, storing and displaying the objects can be provided in addition to that available on the PAS website (see the section 'Conservation').

Learning outcomes

In writing this course, we had a range of learning outcomes in mind. Learning outcomes are the skills and understanding that you will acquire and develop while studying the course, and will be able to demonstrate by the time you have completed it. The course as a whole provides opportunities for you to develop and demonstrate the learning outcomes listed below. You might like to assess your progress towards them at various stages during your study.

Knowledge and understanding

Demonstrate general knowledge and understanding of some of the basic facts, concepts, principles and language relating to archaeology and scientific investigation. In particular, you should be able to demonstrate a knowledge and understanding of:

KU1 the different scientific techniques commonly used in archaeology

KU2 how evidence from other case studies can be used when investigating unknown artefacts and/or sites

KU3 the importance of combining scientific, social, cultural and historical information, as part of the investigative process of an archaeological site or artefact

KU4 issues of preservation, conservation and ownership of archaeological sites and artefacts.

Cognitive (thinking) skills

CS1 Apply your knowledge and understanding of archaeological processes to familiar and unfamiliar situations.

CS2 Describe, analyse and interpret scientific information and data in the light of existing scientific, social and cultural understanding.

CS3 Use information from different sources to determine the authenticity of an archaeological site or artefact.

CS4 Express course concepts in your own words in an objective and factually correct way.

Key skills

KS1 Apply basic arithmetic and graphical methods to solve scientific problems.

KS2 Make sense of information presented in different ways including textual, numerical, graphical and digital material.

KS3 Communicate information clearly, concisely and correctly, recognising the audience for whom it is intended.

KS4 Begin to understand how to develop effective learning strategies.

Practical and/or professional skills

PS1 Develop an awareness of the relevant ethical issues faced by archaeologists.

Acknowledgements

Grateful acknowledgement is made to the following sources for permission to reproduce material in this book:

Cover: photograph and internal X-ray image of the Gayer-Anderson cat (from Saqqara, Egypt, after 600 BC). © Trustees of the British Museum.

Part 1

Figures 2.1a and 2.1d: Arlëne Hunter; Figure 2.1b: Environment and Heritage Service; Figures 2.1c and 2.5: © Trustees of the British Museum. All rights reserved.

Part 2

Figures 1.1a, b, d and e, 1.4a, 1.10, 1.11, 1.15, 2.1, 2.5, 2.7a, 2.8, 2.15a and c, 2.17, 3.1, 3.2, 3.5, 3.6, 3.7, 3.9, 3.10, 3.14, 3.15, 3.16, 3.17, 3.18, 3.19, 3.20, 3.21, 3.24, 3.25, 4.2b and c, 4.5, 4.7, 4.8, 4.9, 4.10 and 4.11: © Trustees of the British Museum. All rights reserved;

Figures 1.1c, 1.3b, 1.13b, 1.16, 1.17, 1.18 and 4.6: York Archaeological Trust;

Figures 1.6a and 1.7a: Jill Eyers, Chiltern Archaeological Services; Figures 1.9, 4.2d and 4.3: Arlëne Hunter; Figures 1.12 and 4.1: Environment and Heritage Service; Figure 1.13a: © David R. Frazier Photolibrary, Inc./Alamy; Figure 2.3b: Tortura, G. J. and Grabowski, S. R. (1993) *Physiology*, 7th edn, Harper Collins Publishers Ltd; Figure 2.3c: Gottfried, S. (1994) *Human Biology*, Elsevier; Figure 2.3d: Ed Reschke; Figure 2.4: Niall Carson/PA Archive/PA Photos; Figure 2.6: Natacha Pisarenko/AP/PA Photos; Figures 2.7b and 2.14a: SGI; Figures 2.9 and 2.10: The Croatian Natural History Museum, Zagreb; Figure 2.11: Renfrew, C. and Bahn, P. (2000) *Archaeology: Theories, Methods and Practice*, Thames & Hudson Ltd; Figure 2.12b: CNRI/Science Photo Library; Figures 2.14b and c: Dr Caroline Wilkinson, University of Manchester; Figure 2.15b Timewatch: The Bog Bodies, BBC Television Programme 20 January 2006; Figure 2.16: Zilhao, J. and Trinkaus, E. eds (2003) *Portrait of the artist as a child: The Gravettian Human Skeleton from the Abrigo do Lagar Velho and its Archaeological Context*, Instituto Portugues de Arqueologia; Figure 3.4: Peter Webb; Figure 3.11: Irene Schrüfer-Kolb; Figure 3.13: Dr Naomi Williams; Figure 3.22: Robert Frerck/ Getty Images; Figure 3.23: American Museum of Natural History; Figure 4.2a: Roger Courthold; Figure 4.4: The Environment and Heritage Service Website www.ehsni.gov.uk. Text extract on pp. 85–6 BBC News (2006) 'Iron Age "bog bodies" unveiled', 7 January 2006, from BBC News at bbc.co.uk/news. Copyright © BBC MMVI. Text extract on pp. 88–9 © Trustees of the British Museum. All rights reserved.

Crown copyright material is reproduced under Class Licence Number C01W0000065 with the permission of the Controller of HMSO and the Queen's Printer for Scotland.

Every effort has been made to contact copyright holders. If any have been inadvertently overlooked the publishers will be pleased to make the necessary arrangements at the first opportunity.

Index

Page numbers in *italics* refer to page numbers mainly, or wholly, in a figure or table